Who's Who in Theology

Who's Who
in Theology

From the First Century
to the Present

John Bowden

Crossroad • New York

1992

The Crossroad Publishing Company
370 Lexington Avenue, New York, NY 10017

Printed in the United States of America

Library of Congress Cataloging-in-Publication Data

Bowden, John.
    Who's Who in theology : from the first century to the present /
John Bowden.
        p.   cm.
    Reprint. Originally published : London : SCM Press, 1990.
    Includes bibliographical references and index.
    ISBN 0-8245-1150-6 (hard)
    1. Theologians—Dictionaries.   2. Theology—Dictionaries.
3. Abelard, Peter, 1079-1142.   4. Zwingli, Ulrich, 1484-1531.
I. Title
BR95.B65   1991
230'092'2—dc20   91-18978
[B]   CIP

Contents

For Further Information

Further information about many of the figures described in this *Who's Who*, along with details of books about them, will be found in the following dictionaries, to which I here acknowledge my debt:

A Dictionary of Philosophy, ed. Antony Flew, Pan Books ²1979

The Fontana Dictionary of Modern Thinkers, ed. Alan Bullock and R. B. Woodings, Fontana Books 1983

New Dictionary of Theology, ed. Sinclair B. Ferguson and David F. Wright, Inter-varsity Press 1988

The New International Dictionary of the Christian Church, ed. J. D. Douglas, Zondervan Publishing House 1978

The Oxford Dictionary of the Christian Church, ed. F. L. Cross, second edition edited by F. L. Cross and E. A. Livingstone, Oxford University Press 1974

The Oxford Dictionary of Popes, ed. J. N. D. Kelly, Oxford University Press 1986

The Westminster Dictionary of Church History, ed. Jerald C. Brauer, Westminster Press 1971

Introduction

This *Who's Who* is something that I have wanted to produce for a long time. It has a simple aim: to introduce to anyone who is interested the main figures relevant to Christian thought from the end of the New Testament period to the present day. Although it will be useful for students at all levels making their first acquaintance with theology, I hope above all that it will appeal to the general reader.

There is a 'cast of thousands'. Each entry provides names, dates, and a certain amount of biographical information. It is fascinating to see from what background famous thinkers originated, where they studied, and where they spent their working life; it is also possible to begin to draw connecting links between people and places and see which centres of theology were in contact with which at particular periods. There is also an indication why particular individuals are worth remembering.

The length of the entries varies and does not correspond with the importance of the individual concerned. How can length reflect the quality of, say, the poetry of William Blake or John Donne, the stature of the theology of Augustine or Luther, the philosophy of Kant or Hegel? Better not to try to convey that here. Again, the fact that some figures had more eventful lives than others, or left them better documented, does not relate to the importance of their thought; the life stories of some minor characters are too good to miss, while major intellectual figures may seldom have gone far from their studies.

In any case, what is offered here is meant to do no more than whet the appetite and stimulate interest in further exploration. Since I do not believe that a person's thinking over a lifetime, or even in a single book, can meaningfully be compressed into a paragraph or less, the comments in this direction are intended merely as pointers. The next stage is for the reader to go on from here to one of the bigger dictionaries, of which there is a list at the beginning of the book, and from there to more comprehensive and more specialist works. Best of all would be to make as near first-hand acquaintance as possible with the thought of a selection of the figures mentioned, since description is no substitute for direct contact.

Mention of other dictionaries leads me to acknowledge my debts. It will be very evident how much I owe to reference works of various kinds in producing this *Who's Who*, not least to the second edition of the *Oxford Dictionary of the Christian Church*, which for thoroughness and scholarship stands head and shoulders above all rivals in its field. Yet – dare I say it? – I increasingly find that great dictionary over-detailed, forbidding, and sometimes difficult or cryptic. Furthermore, I have grown more and more irritated by its principles of selection and the same goes for many of its rivals, particularly those which also think fit to add value judgments.

I have tried to avoid that kind of comment, for example putting terms like 'heretic' in quotation marks where it is unavoidable. Verdicts on prominent figures in church history have come to be revised (even the notorious Arius now gets a much better press!) and often particular labels say more about the approach of those attaching them than about those to whom they are attached. I have also tried to avoid technical terms as far as possible, explaining them where they are unavoidable, so that even the reader with no theological knowledge whatsoever will not be too puzzled. Asterisks before a name indicate that there is a relevant entry elsewhere in the book; in publication dates of books, ET denotes the date of the English translation.

After a great deal of thought, I have added a brief listing of the popes. Some of them would deserve a place in the main body of the text on their own merits, and that is in fact where they began. But the history of the papacy is a fascinating topic in itself and any pope is by definition an important figure. So in the end they all make an appearance. Here the debt I owe to J. N. D. Kelly's *The Oxford Dictionary of the Popes* will be obvious.

I am particularly grateful to Richard Ray, former editor of John Knox Press and a long-time friend, for his thoroughness in working through the whole book and making invaluable comments, and also to Hal Rast and Robert Carroll for their suggestions and contributions. Susan Allen has done invaluable work in tracking down elusive facts; much of the information here which is not at all readily available derives from her efforts. All the criticisms must come to me.

Of course selection has proved an impossible task, particularly as one gets closer to the present day; I have tried to include as many relevant figures as possible, at times going beyond the bounds of theology into philosophy and literary criticism where there is a reason to. My main concern has been theological *thinking*, and that is not done in an intellectual vacuum. I hope that any serious omissions can be corrected in a future edition. Knowledgeable readers will have their opinions about who has been put in and who has been left out, and are bound to find inaccuracies – I would be glad to hear from them.

The last word must be about those pictured within. What an amazing gathering all these people make! There is endless fascination in store in getting to know more about them, and I have enjoyed myself greatly and learned a lot. I hope readers feel the same.

John Bowden

Abelard, Peter (1079–1142)

French philosopher and theologian. Born in Brittany, he became a brilliant and popular teacher in Paris. There he fell in love with Héloise, the daughter of the canon of Notre Dame in whose house he lived; she had a child by him and he then married her, but to avoid further problems Héloise retired to a convent. Her father hired men who broke into Abelard's lodgings and castrated him, after which he became a monk, spending his last years at Cluny. He was primarily a philosopher, and his use of rational criticism and analysis, his stress on the importance of doubt, and his appeal to evidence left a great mark on theological method. In many respects he was a pioneer; moreover with his respect for the ancient pagan philosophers he might be said to have been a humanist before his time. With him theology moved so to speak from a monastic to a university context. His *Christian Theology* gave a new breadth to the term; his application of logic and dialectic to the doctrine of the Trinity proved highly controversial, as did his view of the atonement as primarily a moral influence. His *Know Yourself* focussed on the role of conscience and the relevance of knowledge and intention to moral guilt. This new philosophical approach won him several condemnations by the church and the opposition of *Bernard of Clairvaux. His autobiography, *The Story of My Misfortunes*, and his letters to Héloise illuminate his personal life.

Acacius of Caesarea (died 366)

Bishop and theologian. In the controversy centred on *Arius he was leader of a party named the Homoeans, so called because they claimed that Jesus Christ was like (Greek *homoios*) the Father, in contrast to what became the orthodox view that he was 'of the same substance' (*homoousios*); he is to be distinguished from

Acacius of Constantinople (died 489)

Patriarch. He was excommunicated for making too many concessions to the monophysites (those who in contrast to the orthodox believed that Christ had only one, divine, nature = Greek *physis*). This led to a schism named after him, the Acacian schism, which lasted a generation.

Acarie, Madame (1566–1618)

A French mystic who introduced *Teresa of Avila's discalced Carmelites (i.e. the strict order who did not wear sandals) into France, a friend of Pierre de *Bérulle and *Francis of Sales. When she became a widow she was professed as a lay sister under the name Marie of the Incarnation. She was an organizer, and a mystic who had visions and ecstasies, but we know no details of these.

Adam, Karl (1876–1966)

German Catholic theologian. He was born in Bavaria, and after pastoral work taught at the university of Munich before becoming professor at Tübingen. He became known above all for his influential *The Spirit of Catholicism* (1924; ET 1929). He was opposed to rationalism and liberal Protestantism, and although he believed God could be known by natural reason, his natural theology was based on a different approach from that of science. He believed that knowledge of Christ came through the church, which he regarded virtually as an extension of the incarnation; hierarchically structured by the papacy and the hierarchy, it swallowed up the individual in community.

Adam of Marsh (died c.1258)

English Franciscan theologian. He was born in Somerset and educated at Oxford, and was later the first Franciscan master in theology there. A lifelong friend of Bishop *Grosseteste, he was influential as a scholar and politician. He was given the title of 'illustrious doctor'.

Adamantius (early fourth century)

A Greek anti-Gnostic writer, at one time mistakenly identified with *Origen. He wrote a book against the 'heresies' of *Bardesanes and *Marcion.

Adamnan (c.624–704)
Irish monk and scholar. He was born and educated in Ireland and became a novice on Iona at twenty-six, being made abbot in 679. He attempted to introduce some Roman observances to Celtic Christianity, and his 'Canon', adopted by the Synod of Tara, ruled that women and children might not be prisoners of war. He wrote an important life of *Columba and an account of a pilgrimage to Palestine.

Adelard of Bath (twelfth century)
English philosopher. He studied in France and travelled widely in Europe, North Africa and Asia Minor. He translated Euclid, and defended the ancient Greek philosophers Democritus and *Aristotle. In the great mediaeval debate over universals (general words that denote particular instances of the same species), he tried to reconcile the views of *Plato and Aristotle by arguing that the difference between universal and particular lies in the view of the beholder.

Adorno, Theodor Wiesengrund
(1903–69)
German philosopher. Born in Frankfurt, he studied music under Alban Berg in Vienna, but on returning to Germany started work on a study of *Kierkegaard. He became increasingly friendly with Walter *Benjamin and was associated with the Institute for Social Research in Frankfurt ('Frankfurt School'). After the Nazi rise to power he went to Oxford and wrote a critique of *Husserl's epistemology, but in 1938 he followed the Institute into exile in the United States, returning with it to Germany after the war and becoming its director. His major work is *Negative Dialectics* (1969). It represents a critical thought which seeks to break away from the assumptions of the capitalist world, and is one of the most difficult works of modern philosophy.

Aelfric (c.953–1020)
English Benedictine abbot. He joined the order at Winchester, and was then moved to Cerne Abbas in Dorset. In 1005 he became the first abbot of Eynsham, Oxfordshire. He was leader of a great Benedictine renewal; among other things he provided rural clergy with books in their own language. His homilies became controversial at the Reformation because they seemed to exclude the eucharistic doctrine of transubstantiation and the immaculate conception of the Virgin Mary.

Aelred (1109–69)
English Cistercian abbot. Son of a Saxon priest of Hexham, Northumberland, he was at the court of King David of Scotland before becoming a Cistercian at Rievaulx Abbey, Yorkshire, at the age of twenty-four. In 1147 he became abbot. He wrote a life of Edward the Confessor and spiritual works in the tradition of *Bernard of Clairvaux, which earned him the title 'the English St Bernard'.

Aeneas of Gaza (died 518)
Christian philosopher. He studied at Alexandria, where he was influenced by *Platonism and Neoplatonism. His *Theophrastus* defended immortality and resurrection.

Aerius (fourth century)
Presbyter of Pontus. According to *Epiphanius he denied that there was a difference between priests and bishops, claimed the observance of Easter was a Jewish superstition, and rejected fasting and prayer for the dead.

Aetius (died c.370)
Christian philospher. He came from Antioch and was the most extreme *Arian. He was the leader of the Anomoeans, so called because they claimed that the Son was quite unlike (Greek *anomoios*) the Father.

Agnellus of Pisa (1195–1236)
Founder of the English Franciscan province. *Francis sent him to found a convent in Paris, after which he returned to Italy. In 1224 he was sent to England, where he established friaries in Canterbury and Oxford, employing *Grosseteste to teach in Oxford.

Agricola, Johann (c.1494–1566)
German Reformer. Born in Eisleben, he studied under *Luther at Wittenberg and worked in Frankfurt and Eisleben before returning to Wittenberg. He was involved in a dispute with *Melanchthon on the relationship between repentance and faith, holding – in opposition to the other Reformers – that the moral law was not involved in repentance and has no place in Christian experience. Luther termed this view 'antinomian', refuted Agricola's arguments and led him to recant. However, Agricola remained alienated. He finally became court preacher to Joachim II, Elector of Brandenburg. He was the first to make a collection of German proverbs.

Agrippa of Nettesheim, Heinrich Cornelius (1486–1535)
Scholar and adventurer. After study at Cologne and Paris, and a period fighting for the King of Spain, he taught briefly at Dole, but was accused of heresy. He fled to England, then to Lombardy. In Metz he became interested in the Reformation, with which he sympathized. His two major works, *On the Uncertainty and Vanity of the Sciences and the Arts* (1530), an attack on Scholasticism and the practices of the church, and *On the Occult Philosophy* (1531), on belief as a true magic, written towards the end of his life, earned him imprisonment.

Akiba ben Joseph (c.50–132)
Jewish rabbi. One of the most influential Jewish teachers of his time, he probably influenced the Mishnah. He supported Bar Kokhba's revolt and as a result was burned alive.

Alacoque, Marguérite Marie (1647–90)
French nun and founder of the devotion to the Sacred Heart of Jesus. After an unhappy childhood, at twenty-four she entered the convent of Paray-le-Monial, France, of which she eventually became assistant superior. There she had revelations of the Sacred Heart of Jesus and instructions about devotion to it. Though the cult was not new, after initial opposition she popularized it and it became established after her death.

Alain of Lille (c.1128–1203)
Theologian and philosopher. He studied in Paris and eventually entered the monastery at Cîteaux. Otherwise little is known of him. Basically influenced by Neoplatonism, he believed that religious truths can be discovered by reason and in his mystical theology saw nature as a mediator between God and material beings. He also wrote an epic, *Anticlaudianos* (1182–3), which inspired *Dante and Chaucer. He became known as the 'universal' doctor.

Albertus Magnus (1193–1280)
German theologian and scientist. Born near Ulm, he became a Dominican at Padua and taught in Hildesheim, Ratisbon, Cologne (where *Thomas Aquinas was his pupil) and Paris before returning to Cologne. There he organized the university, becoming provincial of the German province and bishop of Ratisbon. He is famous for establishing the study of nature as a respectable discipline

for Christian thinkers. He wrote commentaries on all *Aristotle's work and was concerned to reconcile Aristotle's philosophy with Christianity. Here he was an important predecessor of Aquinas, on whom his conceptuality made an impact.

Albright, William Foxwell (1891–1971)
American Near Eastern scholar and archaeologist. Born in Chile, the son of missionary parents, he studied at Johns Hopkins University, after the First World War becoming Director of the American School of Oriental Research in Jerusalem. In 1929 he returned to Johns Hopkins as professor, remaining for almost thirty years. An active archaeologist, he aimed to restore confidence in the historical reliability of the Old Testament, stressing the positive significance of new archaeological discoveries in the face of radical German literary criticism. As a result his books influenced many evangelical theologians. Major works include *From the Stone Age to Christianity* (1940), *The Archaeology of Palestine* (1949), *The Biblical Period from Abraham to Ezra* (1963) and *Yahweh and the Gods of Canaan* (1968).

Alcuin (c.735–804)
English scholar. He was educated at the cathedral school of York, of which he became master. In 781 he met Charlemagne at Parma and became his advisor on religion and education. He became abbot of Tours in 796, and established a famous school and library there. He was an important figure in the revival of learning in Charlemagne's empire, particularly through setting up schools; he was also involved in developing a new script which ultimately led to Roman type, and in revision of the Vulgate and the liturgy. He wrote educational books, poetry and letters.

Aleander, Girolamo (1480–1542)
Catholic humanist scholar. He introduced Greek studies to France, became rector of the university of Paris, and was ultimately cardinal abbot of Brindisi. Though he himself was well aware of the need for reform in the church, he was Pope *Leo X's emissary to the emperor to call for the imperial condemnation of *Luther.

Alesius, Alexander (1500–65)
Scottish divine. Born in Edinburgh, he studied in St Andrews, where he became a canon. He was chosen to confute Patrick *Hamilton, who had become a Lutheran, but

was won over by Hamilton's arguments and martyrdom (1528) and soon after was imprisoned for his own attack on the morals of the clergy. In 1532 he escaped to Germany and met *Luther and *Melanchthon. He was excommunicated, but warmly welcomed by *Cranmer on a visit to England and made a lecturer at Cambridge. When that did not work out he returned to Germany to become professor at Frankfurt on the Oder. He was active in many Reformation causes.

Alexander of Alexandria (died 328)
Bishop of Alexandria. He was the immediate predecessor of the famous theologian *Athanasius, and from an early stage opposed the views of *Arius, which he believed heretical. Rejecting the pleas of Arius' supporters, he excommunicated Arius in 321 and later played a leading role in the Council of Nicaea, which upheld his own views. As opposed to Arius and his view that the Son had a beginning, Alexander argued vigorously what became the orthodox line, that the Son is eternally the Son of the Father.

Alexander of Hales (c.1186–1245)
Philosopher and theologian. Born in Gloucestershire, he studied in Oxford and in Paris, where he later was a brilliant teacher. He caused a sensation by becoming a Franciscan, but kept his chair, thus establishing an important link between the order and academic theology. He introduced the *Sentences* of *Peter Lombard to the curriculum and wrote a commentary on it; he was also a pioneer in exploring the significance of the newly-discovered works of *Aristotle for theology.

Alexander, Cecil Frances (1823–95)
Irish hymnwriter, wife of a country clergyman who later became archbishop of Armagh. She wrote 'All things bright and beautiful', 'Once in royal David's city', 'There is a green hill', and many other hymns, often for her Sunday school class.

Alexander, Samuel (1859–1938)
Philosopher. Born in Australia, he studied at Oxford and was professor at Manchester. He presented an evolutionary philosophy in which God is either the whole of space-time as it evolves to its next stage or the transcendence of that next stage over its predecessor. God is part of the process, but since he is also its goal, this philosophy is more than pantheistic. Alexander's best-known book is *Space, Time and Deity* (two vols, 1920).

Alphonsus Liguori (1696–1787)
Italian Roman Catholic moral theologian. Born of a noble family near Naples, he became a barrister, but retired after making a bad mistake in a case involving much money, and was ordained priest. He engaged in mission preaching and founded two Redemptorist congregations, one for men and one for women. He became bishop of a small diocese near Naples. His preaching was simple and gentle, and his *Moral Theology*, published in two volumes in 1753 and 1755, differed markedly from current *Jansenist rigour. He also wrote many devotional works.

Alt, Albrecht (1883–1956)
German Old Testament historian. Son of a pastor in Franconia, he is said to have built a model of Palestine in the garden of his home. He went to Palestine after studying at Erlangen and Leipzig, and kept returning there. He became professor in Greifswald, Basle and Leipzig, after the war travelling from East to West Germany to teach during vacations in Tübingen, Göttingen and Heidelberg. A vigorous anti-Nazi during the Hitler period, he was also a generous and encouraging teacher. His approach to Israelite history was to build up information about a cultural area or period rather than seeking to verify the historical value of particular historical narratives; he had deep knowledge of Egypt and Palestine. This led him to question the Old Testament account of history at a number of points, particularly the biblical account of the 'conquest' of Palestine. He had an illuminating theory about the religion of the Israelite patriarchs ('God of the fathers') and was a pioneer in the study of Old Testament law, distinguishing case law from apodictic law ('Thou shalt [not]'), again with consequences for historical conclusions. His major work is in the form of articles, some in English as *Essays on Old Testament History and Religion* (1966). An influence on *Noth and other German OT scholars, his more sophisticated method and radical views set him apart from *Albright and Albright's pupil John Bright.

Althaus, Paul (1886–1966)
German Lutheran theologian. Born in Obershagen, he taught in Göttingen, Rostock and Erlangen and was active both

in New Testament studies and systematic theology. His studies of *Luther's views of ethics, the eucharist, justification and the last things marked a new departure, by moving from an essentially historical interest in Luther to using Luther as a stimulus for further thinking. His major works were a dogmatics, *The Christian Truth* ([8]1969), and *The Last Things* ([9]1964), both of which went through many editions and were still being read when he died at an advanced age.

Altizer, Thomas Jonathan Jackson (1927–   )
American theologian. Born in Cambridge, Mass., he studied at the University of Chicago and after teaching at Wabash College and Emory University, in 1968 became professor at the State University of New York at Stony Brook. In the 1960s he was associated with a 'death of God' school, which in various differing ways argued that God, or the idea of God, was not, or no longer, alive. His view was that God literally died on the cross and has been dead ever since. He has written a number of books, but is best known for his *The Gospel of Christian Atheism* (1966).

Ambrose (c.339–97)
Bishop of Milan. He was born in Trier, the son of a prefect of Gaul (now Germany). After practising law, in 374 he became governor of Aemilia-Liguria, with his seat in Milan. On the death of the bishop, the laity asked for Ambrose to succeed him, though Ambrose was not even baptized. He was then baptized, ordained and studied theology, becoming a famous preacher and defender of orthodoxy. A vigorous opponent of *Arianism, both theologically and politically, he was one of the few Western churchmen to be able to read Greek. He was much concerned with the practical duties of being a bishop, including confrontation with the state (he disciplined the emperor *Theodosius). He was also a major influence on *Augustine because of the other-worldly, spiritual character of his faith and his defence of the Old Testament against the Manichaeans. His main work was a book on Christian ethics for the clergy, *On the Duties of Ministers*. He gave his name to the Ambrosian rite, is said to have introduced antiphonal singing, and introduced a new form of hymn (of which 'O splendour of God's glory bright' is an example).

Ambrosiaster (fourth century)
The pseudonym for the author of a set of Latin commentaries on Paul's letters, attributed to Ambrose; roughly contemporary with him.

Ames, William (1576–1633)
English theologian. Educated at Cambridge, he was suspended for refusing to wear a surplice and preaching against card-playing, and prevented from exercising a ministry. He moved to Holland as a chaplain and after being an observer at the Synod of Dort became professor of theology at Franeker, where he attracted students from all over Europe. He wrote a pioneering work on *Conscience* (1632), but was most active as a controversialist, principally against *Arminianism. His *Medulla Theologiae* ('The marrow of theology', 1627), an account of *Calvinist principles, was to prove particularly influential.

Ammonius Saccas (175–242)
Philosopher and teacher. Thought once to have been a porter, he taught rhetoric and a form of *Platonism in Alexandria and is one of the founders of Neoplatonism. He is important because his pupils included *Plotinus and perhaps *Origen. However, he is said to have left no writings.

Andrew of St Victor (died 1175)
Biblical scholar. Of uncertain nationality, he studied at the famous abbey of St Victor in Paris under *Hugh, and became a canon. He was then made abbot of a monastery in Hereford, England, but when it proved that he was more a scholar than an administrator he returned to France. However, about six years later he was recalled to Hereford, where he died. Inspired by Hugh and the example of *Jerome, he approached scripture critically and literally and not only made use of Jewish sources but discussed biblical interpretation with Jews. His commentaries on the Bible thus differ strikingly from others of the time.

Andrewes, Lancelot (1555–1626)
English churchman. Born in what is now East London, he studied and taught at Cambridge, becoming Master of Pembroke Hall. In 1589 he was also made vicar of the London church of St Giles, Cripplegate, where he came to the attention of Elizabeth I. At first he declined bishoprics, and was made dean of Westminster instead, but he went on to become bishop of Chichester,

Ely and then Winchester. Often involved in politics, he was a leading figure in forming a distinctive Anglican theology, reasonable and catholic, based on sound learning and with a high doctrine of the eucharist. He was most famous as a preacher; he also translated the first part of the Old Testament for the King James (Authorized) Version and wrote a classic set of daily devotions, *Private Prayers*, published posthumously (1648), full of quotations from the Greek fathers, scripture and liturgies.

Andrews, Charles Freer (1871–1940)
Anglican missionary. Born in Newcastle, he studied and taught at Cambridge before joining the Cambridge Broiherhood in Delhi. In 1913 he joined Rabindranath Tagore's Institute in Bengal, of which he became vice-president. He was active in India and a champion of the oppressed; in 1913 he spent a year in South Africa helping in the Smuts–Gandhi Agreement, and soon afterwards paid two visits to Fiji with the aim of abolishing indentured Indian labour there. He was subsequently involved in much diplomatic work in this area. He wrote many books, on India and on Christianity; perhaps the best known are *The Renaissance in India* (1914), *Christ and Labour* (1923) and *Christ in the Silence* (1933).

Angela of Foligno (c.1248–1309)
Daughter of a wealthy family, she spent most of her life at Foligno. When her husband died, she turned to a life of prayer and austerity. Associated with the Franciscans, she had many visions which were taken down by her confessor, Brother Arnold, and circulated as *A Book of Visions and Instructions*.

Angelus Silesius see **Scheffler, Johann**

Anselm (1033–1109)
Philosopher and theologian. Son of a landowner in Aosta, Italy, he studied under *Lanfranc at the abbey of Bec in Normandy, where he became a monk and succeeded Lanfranc as prior, later also following him as archbishop of Canterbury. He was a pioneer in using linguistic analysis to solve philosophical problems, but his fame rests on his proofs of the existence of God. His arguments can be found in his *Monologion* (Soliloquy, 1078), which seeks to establish the existence of God on the basis of the ideas of truth and goodness, and *Proslogion* (Discourse, with the famous phrase 'faith seek-

ing understanding', 1079), which contains his ontological argument, proof of God's existence from the concept of God (God is that than which nothing greater can be conceived; what exists in reality must be greater than what exists in the mind, therefore God exists). His other great book, *Cur Deus Homo?* (Why did God become man?, 1098) was on the atonement. In contrast to the view held since *Origen that Christ died to pay a ransom to the devil, he argued that Christ offered himself willingly as the only one who could satisfy the outrage of sin to God's majesty. However, despite all Anselm's intellectual gifts it was for his prayers and meditations that he was most known and revered during the Middle Ages. He also wrote many letters.

Antoninus (1389–1459)
Moral theologian and economist. Becoming a Dominican novice along with Fra Angelico at the age of sixteen, he later supervised many religious houses, at which he introduced reforms. He established the convent of San Marco at Florence and became archbishop of Florence in 1436. A counsellor of popes and statesmen, he wrote a moral theology; he was also the first Christian theologian to argue that it was right to receive interest on money invested in business, since this was capital.

Antony of Egypt (c.251–356)
Monk. The pioneer of solitary monasticism, around the age of twenty he gave away his possessions and about fifteen years later retired completely into the Egyptian desert. He was made famous in a *Life* by *Athanasius which depicts him as austere, always at prayer, and constantly fighting with demons. He attracted disciples who followed his way of life. He influenced not only them but the supporters of orthodoxy against *Arianism at the council of Nicaea.

Antony of Padua (1195–1231)
Portuguese hermit. Born in Lisbon, he became a Franciscan and settled in Italy after illness cut short his missionary work in Morocco. He subsequently taught in Italy and France and was a fierce opponent of the Cathari and Albigensians (he was known as 'Hammer of the Heretics'). He was a particularly famous preacher (later fable has him preaching to the fishes). He became patron saint of the poor and was invoked for the return of lost property.

Aphraates (Aphrahat, early fourth century)
First of the Syrian church fathers. Little is known of his life except that he was an ascetic and held high office. He wrote a collection of *Homilies*, composed on the plan of an acrostic; they provide information about Persian Christianity.

Apollinarius of Laodicea (c.310–90)
Christian theologian. Son of a Beirut grammarian, and a friend of *Athanasius, whose hostility to *Arianism he shared, he became bishop of Laodicea. He seceded from the church because he could not accept what was to become the orthodox view that Christ had a human spirit. He believed that the only active principle in Christ was the divine Logos, so that Christ had perfect Godhead but was not human as other human beings are. Little of his writings remain since he was condemned as a heretic.

Apollonius of Tyana (died c.98)
Neopythagorean philosopher. Founder of a school in Ephesus, he was said to have been so virtuous that his life was presented as a pagan counterpart to Christ – doing good, performing miracles and suffering trial for his actions. Unlike Christ he was said to have been delivered and to have gone to heaven.

Aquila (second century)
Supposedly a relative of the emperor Hadrian, he lived at Sinope in Pontus. He is said to have become a Jew after being excommunicated; after a rabbinical education which taught him Hebrew, he made a new, very literalistic Greek translation of the Hebrew Bible into Greek, intended to replace the Septuagint which was used by the Christians.

Aristides (early second century)
Christian philosopher. Active in Athens, he was one of the earliest apologists, defending Christianity to the pagans. His *Apology*, addressed to the emperor, argues that Christians have a fuller understanding of God than pagans or Jews, and that they alone love God as he wills.

Aristotle (384–322 BCE)
Greek philosopher. He was born at Stagira on the Chalcidice peninsula, the son of a court physician. At the age of seventeen he went to Athens and spent twenty years at *Plato's academy as pupil and teacher. After twelve years away, for three of which he was tutor to Alexander the Great, he returned to Athens to found his own school, the Lyceum, where he taught for twelve years until forced out by hostile sentiment following Alexander's death. Most of his surviving works are lecture notes and memoranda. He created the discipline of logic and was a pioneer in ethics and physics. He differed from his teacher by his stress on empiricism and natural science; rather than beginning with 'ideas', he started from individual objects and reflected on the cause of their existence, which he analysed in some detail; among other things, this analysis led him to postulate a 'first cause', God, the unmoved prime mover. While his thought was by no means unknown during the first Christian millennium, being used by e.g. *Porphyry and *Boethius (who translated his *Categories* into Latin), its real impact on Christian theology came in the eleventh and twelfth centuries, when knowledge of his writings spread through Latin versions of Arabic translations of his works and commentaries on them, and particularly via *Averroes and *Avicenna. Initially, with their materialism and description of an eternal universe, these works came as a shock and were either banned or assigned to a separate area from Christianity; there was considerable controversy over this issue at the university of Paris in the thirteenth century. However, they were harmonized with Christian thinking by *Albertus Magnus and Thomas *Aquinas, leading to Scholasticism. It is ultimately from Aristotle that many traditional theological concepts derive, particularly contrasting concepts like substance/accident, genus/species, potency/act, matter/form. The introduction of his thought into theology also underlies contrasts like those between philosophy and theology, faith and reason, and nature and supernature.

Arius (c.250–336)
Christian theologian. Probably born in Libya, he was a popular preacher in charge of one of the main churches in Alexandria, Egypt, enjoying a reputation for asceticism. When *Alexander became bishop, Arius came under criticism for his view that the Son had a beginning and was subordinate to the Father. There was a long and bitter controversy, in which Arius was not without his supporters, but as a result of the efforts of Alexander and later *Athanasius he was excommunicated. Arianism in its various forms was regarded as the main heresy of

the fourth century, and the Council of Nicaea (325) was summoned in order to refute it; after the Council Arius was banished, and eventually died in Constantinople. Nowadays he is being reassessed, and from his own perspective has more to be said for him than has been acknowledged in the past.

Arminius, Jacobus (Jakob Hermandszoon, 1560–1609)
Dutch theologian. Born in Oudewater, son of a cutler, he studied at many European centres including Marburg, Geneva and Rome. He returned to Holland, first as a minister and then as professor at Leiden. He challenged *Calvinistic views about predestination and later sought to revise the two main Calvinistic confessional documents of the Dutch church; at the same time he was drawn into political disputes. Since he gained many followers (Arminians, or Remonstrants, after a Remonstrance, a statement of belief, issued in 1610), he caused a major split in the Reformed Church in Holland. He was also influential abroad, e.g. on John *Wesley.

Arnauld, Antoine (1612–94)
French theologian and philosopher. Born in Paris the twentieth child of a middle-class family, he was influenced by his sister Angélique (see below), was later ordained priest and joined the *Jansenist centre of Port-Royal. His first book *On Frequent Communion* (1643) was highly controversial, and it and later works, widely read, led to his condemnation in 1656. He was restored to favour by Louis XIV in 1669 and continued to write until the end of his life. He was the major influence in spreading Jansenist principles.

Arnauld, Jacqueline Marie Angélique (1591–1661)
Abbess. Sister of Antoine, she became abbess of Port-Royal in 1602 and introduced disciplinary reforms, which led to its later success. Influenced by *Saint-Cyran, she became a vigorous supporter of *Jansenism.

Arndt, Johann (1555–1621)
Lutheran mystical theologian. A follower of *Melanchthon, after studies at Wittenberg, Strasbourg and Basle he held several pastorates, finally becoming general superintendent of Celle. His main work, *Four Books on True Christianity* (1606–9), which stressed the presence of Christ in the human heart, was a great influence on Pietism. Arndt claimed that orthodox belief was not enough, and that moral purification through righteous living and communion with God was also needed.

Arnobius
1. (active c.304–10) Christian apologist. A teacher of rhetoric from Numidia, he was converted to Christianity and wrote *Adversus Nationes*, exposing the errors of pagan worship; the work is valuable because of the detail about this worship that it contains.
2. (fifth century) An African monk who attacked *Augustine's teaching on divine grace and argued that immortality is not something given but has to be won.

Arnold of Brescia (1100–55)
Radical reformer. He studied in Paris, probably as a pupil of *Abelard. On returning to Italy he attacked the church, arguing that clergy should not possess material goods or have secular authority, and that personal sinfulness in priests affected the validity of the sacraments. He also rejected the secular rule of the pope, and took part in a revolutionary commune in Rome. Condemned, along with *Abelard, on the instigation of *Bernard of Clairvaux, he was excommunicated and eventually executed.

Arnold, Gottfried (1666–1714)
German Protestant theologian. Born in Saxony, he studied in Wittenberg and came under the influence of *Spener. Finding a professorship at Giessen too distracting, he spent the rest of his life in writing and pastoral work. He wrote and translated devotional literature and mystical works, in the pietistic and quietist tradition; his own theological speculations were bizarre, e.g. that Adam before the Fall was androgynous and Christ restored androgynous nature to human beings. He was opposed by official Lutheranism.

Arnold, Matthew (1822–88)
English poet and critic. He was the oldest son of Thomas Arnold, the famous educational reformer and headmaster of Rugby School who transformed the education of the sons of middle-class parents. Born at Laleham on Thames, after studying at Oxford he became a private secretary, government inspector of schools and Oxford Professor of Poetry. In addition to poetry, he wrote a series of books which attacked many

of the formal religious attitudes of his time and stressed the moral, personal and cultural aspects of Christianity. In addition to his famous *Culture and Anarchy* (1869), these include *St Paul and Protestantism* (1870) and *Literature and Dogma* (1873). He made the famous comment about religion that 'Men cannot do without it; they cannot do with it as it is', and his view of Christianity reduced it to a non-dogmatic, non-supernatural faith. He was a major influence on Victorian England.

Asbury, Francis (1745–1816)
Born in Birmingham, England, he went to America following an appeal by John *Wesley, stayed through the Revolutionary War and identified himself with the new nation. In 1784 Wesley appointed him and Thomas *Coke joint superintendents, and Asbury subsequently took the title of bishop. He was a key figure in shaping American Methodism.

Astruc, Jean (1684–1766)
French Roman Catholic physician. The son of a Protestant pastor, converted to Catholicism, he became professor of anatomy at Toulouse, Montpellier and Paris. He is seen as one of the founders of modern Pentateuchal criticism, since in his *Conjectures on the Original Memoranda which Moses seems to have used to compose the Book of Genesis* (1753) he argued that Moses made use of earlier documents in writing Genesis, using the divine names Elohim and Jehovah as criteria.

Athanasius (c.296–377)
Theologian and bishop. Probably educated in Alexandria, he became secretary to *Alexander, with whom he went to the Council of Nicaea, and on his death succeeded him as bishop. He was the main opponent of *Arius, and because of the latter's popularity was attacked and much exiled. He wrote against paganism (*Contra Gentes*) and the Arians (*Contra Arianos*) and defended the incarnation (*De Incarnatione*); he also wrote a life of *Antony. In his theology he stressed the role of the Logos and the *homoousion* (the Son 'of the same substance' as the Father).

Athenagoras (second century)
Athenian grammarian and Christian apologist. He wrote a defence of Christianity addressed to the emperor Marcus Aurelius, rejecting false accusations of immorality, and was the first to develop a philosophical defence of the Christian doctrine as God as Trinity. His thought was influenced by popular Platonism.

Auerbach, Erich (1892–1957)
German literary historian. Born in Berlin, he became professor in Marburg and Istanbul and then moved to the United States to teach at Yale. He is particularly important for his literary-critical study *Mimesis* (1946, ET 1953), which examines changing conceptions of reality from Homer to Proust as expressed in literary texts.

Augustine (354–430)
Christian theologian. Born of a middle-class family at Tagaste, North Africa, with a pagan father and a Christian mother, Monica, he studied law at Carthage. Reading the Latin author Cicero aroused his interest in philosophy; he was then attracted by dualistic Manichaeanism, and moved to Rome. Here he became disillusioned and left to become professor of rhetoric in Milan. Influenced there by the preaching of *Ambrose, he became a Christian; after his famous experience in a garden, where he heard a voice telling him to study the Bible ('Take and read'), he was baptized in 387. Returning to North Africa he established a kind of monastery, but on a visit to Hippo, by popular acclaim he was first urged to become priest there; he subsequently became bishop, never to leave Africa again. He was a great controversialist, and it was in controversies that his influential views were expressed. Against the Manichaeans, he stressed that creation was good and that God is its sole creator; against the Donatists, with their stress on the character of the clergy, he argued that the church contained good and evil and that its sacraments cannot be affected by its ministers; against the Pelagians, with their view that human beings can take the first basic steps towards salvation, he stressed his view that original sin arises from the Fall, with disastrous consequences which can be countered only by divine grace. His most famous works are his autobiography, the *Confessions*, and *The City of God*, prompted by the sack of Rome in 410, which became an account of history in terms of two different 'cities'. In this vast work he contrasts the city of man as the rise and fall of empires with the city of God, made up of those who serve God. Refusing to see the hand of God at work in the history of his time, he argued that God's activity could not

readily be identified. He was subsequently immensely influential in the Christian church through his views of the relationship between faith and reason, the love of God and renunciation, grace and free will, the corruption of human nature, the idea of the heart (which is restless until it finds rest in God) and his mediation of *Platonism. He is sometimes said to have been the first modern man.

Augustine of Canterbury (died c.604)
Missionary. A Roman prior, he was sent by Pope *Gregory the Great to refound the English church. In this work he clashed with other existing missions, notably that of the Celtic church, and was unable to reconcile the differences which arose between it and Rome. He became first Archbishop of Canterbury.

Aulén, Gustav (1879–1978)
Swedish Lutheran theologian. After study at Uppsala, he taught there, and was then made professor at Lund, subsequently becoming Bishop of Strängnäs. His approach was to seek the essential truth behind the form in which a Christian doctrine is expressed. He wrote a much-used textbook, *The Faith of the Christian Church* (1923), but his best-known work is *Christus Victor* (1931), a restatement of the 'classic' view of the atonement as a victory. His theology generally proved to be critical of mediaeval scholasticism and Lutheran orthodoxy, contrasting them with the early church and *Luther himself. He was also a musician and composer.

Averroes (Ibn Rushd, 1126–98)
Islamic lawyer and philosopher. He was born in Cordova, Spain, and after ranging from medicine and mathematics to law and theology became *cadi* (magistrate) there and in Seville, subsequently becoming physician to the caliph. He wrote commentaries on *Aristotle, whom he understood in Neoplatonic terms, and through them Aristotle's thought entered the mediaeval Western world. Since they were not properly understood, even by *Albertus Magnus and Roger *Bacon, these commentaries (which in fact ruled out providence and personal immortality) were even accepted as texts in the thirteenth-century university of Paris, where they were particularly championed by *Siger of Brabant. *Thomas Aquinas was one theologian who wrote against them, attacking what he saw as their view of a 'double truth' (religious and scientific), and eventually they were banned. In the Arab world, Averroes himself had been accused of heresy and exiled, though he was recalled just before his death.

Avicenna (Abu 'Ali al Hosain ibn 'Abdallah ibn Sina, 980–1037)
Persian Muslim physician and philosopher. He wrote commentaries on *Aristotle in a Neoplatonic vein, and a standard medical textbook (*Canon of Medicine*). Like *Averroes after him, he was particularly important in mediating Aristotle to the Middle Ages.

Azariah, Vednayakam Samuel (1874–1945)
Ecumenical leader. The son of an Anglican minister, he was first involved in the YMCA and indigenous missionary societies. He was ordained priest in 1909 and went to Dornakal, near Madras; as the church there expanded he was consecrated bishop, the first native Indian to hold this office. He became a major Indian church leader and was host of the 1938 World Missionary Conference at Tambaram.

Baal Shem Tob (R. Israel ben Eliezer: the Hebrew title means 'The Good Master of God's Name', 1700–60)
The founder of Hasidism, a mystical movement within Judaism. He was an orphan, born in Podolia, and lived a humble country life, engaged in various types of basic manual work. A holy man, he taught and healed, outside the synagogue system, gaining a wide following. He introduced a new form of holiness and mystical prayer to Judaism; believing that the Talmudists followed the law so literally that they lost sight of God, he saw God in everyday life and in nature: for

him the decisive thing was not that God is, but that God is in all that is.

Bacon, Francis (1561–1626)
English philosopher. Of a distinguished family, he studied at Cambridge and then became a lawyer and member of Parliament, rising to the post of Lord Chancellor under James I, though in 1621 he was charged with corruption and banished from court. The first of the British empiricist philosophers, he believed that it was possible to discover basic principles by arguing from experience. His thinking was particularly forward-looking, as is evident from his frequent use of the word 'new', e.g. *Novum Organum* (1620) and *New Atlantis* (published posthumously in 1660). Seeing knowledge as power, he sought the separation of reason from revelation and was optimistic about the beneficial consequences science would have. He was also a pioneer in drawing attention to psychological motivations for philosophical positions.

Bacon, Roger (1214–94)
British philosopher and scientist. He was born in Somerset and studied in Oxford and Paris, before returning to England, where he worked under *Grosseteste. After becoming a Franciscan he returned to Paris, where he was one of the first to lecture on *Aristotle. A polymath, he was interested in science (he may well have invented a telescope and gunpowder) and also stressed the importance of knowing Greek and Hebrew in studying the scriptures. However, he did not leave behind any systematic body of thought. He is known in the Roman Catholic church as Doctor Mirabilis.

Baeck, Leo (1873–1956)
German Jewish theologian. Born in Prussia, he became famous through his book *The Essence of Judaism* (1905, ET 1948), which presented a modern rational view of Judaism combining idealistic philosophy with old rabbinic thought-patterns and saw faith as a human response to divine imperatives. Later work contributed towards his rediscovery of a sense of mystery in Judaism; here he was involved in a variety of different areas: mysticism, New Testament studies and interfaith dialogue. In 1933 he was made head of the German Jewish community and was later imprisoned in Terezin (Theresienstadt) concentration camp, offering a noted spiritual resistance to Nazism. His last book, *The People of Israel: The Meaning of Jewish Resistance* (1955, ET 1966), was written in Terezin. He survived to be a postwar leader concerned for reconciliation and dialogue.

Baillie, Donald Macpherson (1887–1954)
Scottish theologian. Raised in a strict *Calvinist tradition, he studied in Edinburgh and then in Marburg (under *Hermann, whose *The Communion of the Christian with God* was a major influence on him). After serving in Scottish parishes for many years he wrote his first major work, *Faith in God and its Christian Consummation* (1927), which led in 1934 to his appointment as professor at St Andrews, where he spent the rest of his life. His only other book was *God Was in Christ* (1948), exploring the paradox of grace ('not I, but the grace of God in me'), which he applied to incarnational theology. He was deeply committed to Christian unity and involved in the ecumenical movement.

Baillie, John (1886–1960)
Scottish theologian, brother of Donald. He studied at Edinburgh, Jena and Marburg and taught in Canada and the USA as well as in Edinburgh, where he was professor for twenty years. An influential churchman, he was also the author of the devotional classic *A Diary of Private Prayer* (1936). The most significant element in his theology was his moral approach to the knowledge of God: the relationship of that knowledge to spiritual and moral experience. This can be seen in *Our Knowledge of God* (1939). Other important books were *And the Life Everlasting* (1934) and *The Sense of the Presence of God* (1962).

Baius, Michel (Michel de Bay, 1513–89)
Flemish theologian. He was educated at Louvain, where he later taught, being condemned and censured on several occasions. His theology was an anticipation of *Jansenism: original sin is corrupt desire transmitted genetically, and redemption is the recovery of original innocence which makes it possible to live a moral life.

Baker, Augustine (1575–1641)
Benedictine monk. He worked at Cambrai and Douai in Belgium and as a chaplain in England. He wrote much on spirituality, but his teaching was distilled after his death into a single work, *Holy Wisdom* (1657), by which he is best known.

Balthasar, Hans Urs von (1905–87)
Swiss Roman Catholic theologian. Born in Lucerne, he studied in Vienna, Berlin and Zurich, and became a Jesuit; after post-doctoral studies he turned to free-lance writing, becoming director of his own publishing house. He wrote an early, sympathetic study of *Barth; subsequently his work was influenced by his visionary colleague Adrienne von Speyr. His theology was ascetic, contemplative and eclectic, and deliberately elitist. His major, multi-volume work *The Glory of the Lord* (1961ff., ET 1982ff.), which he called a theological aesthetics, brings together philosophy, literature and theology in a study of the beautiful, the good and true; it seeks to show how the biblical vision of divine glory revealed in the crucified and risen Christ fulfils and transcends the perception of Being in Western metaphysics.

Barclay, Robert (1648–90)
Scottish theologian and apologist. Born in Scotland, the son of a soldier, and part-educated in Paris as a Roman Catholic, he became a Quaker. He led a much-travelled life, with many ups and downs, ranging from friendship with royalty to imprisonment; in 1683 he was appointed governor of East New Jersey. One of the most substantial of apologists for Quaker principles, he wrote many books, the best-known being his *Apology for the True Christian Divinity. Being an Explanation and Vindication of the People Called Quakers* (1678). This is a classic account defending the doctrine of the 'inner light'.

Barclay, William (1907–78)
Scottish biblical scholar. Born in Wick, he studied in Glasgow and Marburg and from 1933 to 1947 served as minister of an industrial Clydeside parish. He then became lecturer and professor in the university of Glasgow. A gifted journalist and popular writer, he was noted for the way in which he could communicate the insights of modern New Testament study in a readable and understandable way. Though well aware of the complications of modern criticism, he chose to offer his readers what they would understand and benefit from. His multi-volume *Daily Study Bible* (on the New Testament) is still very widely used.

Bardenhewer, Otto (1851–1935)
German patristic scholar. Born in München-Gladbach, he studied at Bonn and Würzburg and was professor of Old Testament at Münster and New Testament at Munich. However, it is for his work on the early church that he is best known; his *History of the Literature of the Early Church* (1902) is still an important work.

Bardesanes (Bar-Daisan, 154–222)
A native of Edessa in Syria, he was converted to Christianity, but later excommunicated, so that he had to flee to Armenia. He seems to have taught a kind of astrological belief, and held that Christ's body was a phantom and that there was no resurrection.

Barr, James (1924–)
Old Testament scholar and philologist. He has been professor in Montreal, Edinburgh, Princeton, Manchester, Oxford and Vanderbilt. He became prominent for his iconoclastic views, first expressed in a philological study *The Semantics of Biblical Language* (1961), which devastatingly challenged much of the etymological approach then used in biblical interpretation and the fashionable school of biblical theology. In addition to philological work, he has been keenly interested in the phenomenon of fundamentalism and the interpretation of the Bible in the modern world. Other major books are *Comparative Philology and the Text of the Old Testament* (1968) and *Fundamentalism* (1981).

Barrett, Charles Kingsley (1917–)
English New Testament scholar. Son of a minister, he studied at Cambridge (where he was influenced by *Hoskyns) and after a brief period as theological college teacher and Methodist minister went to teach at Durham university. He spent the rest of his life there, becoming professor. In addition to commentaries on the letters of Paul, he is best known for his work on the Fourth Gospel. Major books include *The Gospel according to St John* (1955, ²1978), *Jesus and the Gospel Tradition* (1967) and *The Fourth Gospel and Judaism* (1985).

Barrow, Henry (c.1550–93)
Church reformer. While studying at Cambridge, he was converted from a dissolute life as a courtier by a gospel preacher. In 1590 he was imprisoned for circulating seditious books (printed in Holland) expressing his belief that any form of church order was utterly corrupt, and later hanged. He is sometimes considered to be one of the founders of the Congregationalist church.

Barth, Karl (1886–1968)
Swiss Reformed theologian. He was born in Basle and after studying at German universities became assistant pastor in Geneva and pastor in the Swiss village of Safenwil. There, disillusioned with liberal theology at the outbreak of the First World War, he rediscovered the power of the Bible (commenting repeatedly on its 'strange, new world'; his views of this period are expressed in *The Word of God and the Word of Man*, ET 1928), and in due course wrote a revolutionary commentary on *The Epistle to the Romans* (1918, ²1921, ET by *Hoskyns, 1933) which brought him widespread attention. His approach at the time was dominated by the idea of the Word of God breaking in vertically from above, making contact without any help from human beings as a tangent touches a circle. His fame led to an invitation to a special theological chair at Göttingen, from where he moved to Münster then to Bonn, being dismissed for refusing to take an oath of allegiance to Hitler. His theology, termed 'dialectical' because of its characteristics, dominated the inter-war period in Germany, and he was also a leading light in the Confessing Church, playing a major part in the drafting of the famous Barmen Declaration of 1934. Having been forced to return to Switzerland, he became professor in Basle, devoting the rest of his life to writing a multi-volume *Church Dogmatics* (1936ff.), which he never finished. Massively centred on Christ, and more scholastic than that of his first period, it represented a systematic account of Christian theology freed from the influence of philosophy and focussed on the Bible and the theologians of the early church and the Reformation. Here as in all his later works Barth stressed the 'Godness' of God and the impossibility of human religion attaining to him, though as time went on his views about the role of humanity mellowed. However, 'Barthian' thought has long had a strong negative impact on inter-faith dialogue and on understanding the significance of culture on religious belief.

Barthes, Roland (1915–80)
French literary critic. Born in Cherbourg, he became director of studies at the École Pratique des Hautes Études in Paris and later professor at the Collège de France; he died in an accident. After studying classics and working in the theatre, he was struck by the barrenness of academic criticism. Reading Marx and French existentialist philosophers led him to the idea of a kind of neutral ('white') writing; this critical approach focussed only on the text and not on the conditions under which it was produced. This view is presented in his *Writing Degree Zero* (1953, ET 1972), which was followed by *Mythologies* (1957, ET 1972), a critique of the myths in everyday life by which society presents what it has produced as being of the natural order. This brought him near to *Saussure's structuralism. Often seen as the beginning of 'the new criticism', his work moves from a distinction between the author and a work to the relationship between a work and its reader; it has been very influential on literary criticism and critical thought.

Basil of Caesarea
('The Great', c.330–79)
Church father. He was trained in Athens, taught rhetoric and then became a hermit before being ordained and then consecrated bishop. One of the 'Cappadocian Fathers' (the others were *Gregory of Nyssa and *Gregory of Nazianzus), he stood up for Nicene orthodoxy at a time when the emperor was an *Arian. He was particularly important as a church leader, organizing monasteries, and establishing charitable institutions, hospitals and schools. He stressed the deity of the Spirit, which was not sufficiently emphasized at the time; his two main works are *Against *Eunomius*, and *On the Holy Spirit*.

Basilides (early second century)
Gnostic theologian. All that is known of him is that he taught in Alexandria around 132–5. He was very influential, but only fragments of his work survive in quotations from his orthodox critics. He is one of the earliest known authors of a biblical commentary, adopted Christian ethics to Stoic categories and wrote poetry and songs; he also produced his own Gospel.

Batiffol, Pierre (1861–1929)
Catholic church historian. He spent his life in Paris, except for a period at Toulouse. His writings encouraged critical study of liturgy and church history in France, but because of his association with the Modernists a book of his on the eucharist was condemned. In later years he concentrated on a history of the early church and the growth of papal power.

Bauer, Bruno (1809–82)
German biblical critic. At first conservative and *Hegelian, he taught in Berlin, but on

moving to Bonn he became an extremist and eventually had his licence to teach removed, after which he was known as 'the hermit of Rixdorf'. A vigorous antisemitist, he had very negative views of early Christianity, believing that there never was a historical Jesus, that the Gospels were individual artistic works and that the New Testament was produced in the second century.

Bauer, Walter (1877–1960)
German New Testament scholar. He specialized in the history of primitive Christianity and the early church; his *Orthodoxy and Heresy in Earliest Christianity* (1933) stressed the great variety in early Christianity and the blurred lines between orthodoxy and heresy; he was also a distinguished Greek lexicographer (his *Lexicon of NT Greek* in the edition by Arndt and Gingrich is still a standard work, ²1979).

Baur, Ferdinand Christian (1792–1860)
German church historian and dogmatician. Born in Württemberg, he studied at Tübingen, where he spent most of his teaching life. He is widely seen as one of the first to apply the historical method consistently to Christian theology. Thus in *Paul, The Apostle of Jesus Christ* (ET 1873–5), he denied the authenticity of many Pauline letters and argued that in the early church there was opposition between Peter and Paul and that Acts glosses over the split; he also stressed the historical value of the Synoptic Gospels as over against the then preferred Gospel of John. However, his views were dominated by the *philosophy of Hegel, which led him to interpret his findings regularly in terms of a pattern of thesis-antithesis-synthesis. His major works include a five-volume *History of the Christian Church* (1852ff.) and a four-volume set of *Lectures on the History of Christian Dogma* (1865–7).

Bautain, Louis Eugène Marie (1796–1867)
French Roman Catholic theologian and philosopher. He accepted *Kant's view that it is impossible to prove the existence of God by rational argument. His answer was the theory of fideism: faith depends on feeling, not reason, and can arrive at superior truths inaccessible to reason. This view was condemned by Pope *Gregory XVI, and Bautain recanted.

Bavinck, Herman (1854–1921)
Dutch Reformed theologian, he was professor at Kampen Reformed Seminary and then became successor to *Kuyper at the Free University of Amsterdam when the latter became Prime Minister of the Netherlands. Going back to *Calvin, he wrote an influential *Reformed Dogmatics* (⁴1928–30), which is still a standard work.

Bavinck, Johan Herman (1859–1964)
Dutch missiologist, nephew of Herman. He worked for twenty years in Java before becoming professor of missions in Kampen; during the war he was involved in the Dutch underground. After the war he specialized in religious psychology and founded a mission centre in Baarn. His theology, which is strongly Calvinist, stresses the uniqueness of the gospel. His major work is *An Introduction to the Science of Missions* (1960).

Baxter, Richard (1615–91)
English Puritan divine. He was born in Shropshire and self-educated. Acquaintance with Nonconformists aroused his sympathy for dissent, but he remained in the Church of England, working as a curate in Kidderminster. He served as a Parliamentarian chaplain in the Civil War and worked for the return of King Charles II, but his objections to episcopacy led to his being debarred from holding church office and later suffering persecution. His many writings show his liberal and catholic sympathies, and his personal generosity and tolerance are evident in his two best known books, *The Saints' Everlasting Rest* (1650) and *The Reformed Pastor* (1656).

Bayle, Pierre (1647–1706)
French philosopher. Son of a Protestant minister, he became professor of philosophy at Rotterdam, but was dismissed because of his views on religious toleration. He championed freedom in religion, denied that Christianity has any distinctive contribution to make to morality, and in his criticism of popular understanding of the Bible anticipated some of the insights of later biblical criticism. His most influential books were his *Thoughts on the Comet* (1682) and a *Historical and Critical Dictionary* (1695–7).

Beck, Johann Tobias (1804–78)
German systematic theologian. After teaching in Basle he became professor in Tübingen, where he developed the biblicism of *Bengel in a *Hegelian climate. Though

in the Lutheran pietist tradition, he had many distinctive views of his own, seeing the Bible as the work of the Spirit progressing towards human salvation. He offended Lutherans by claiming that in justification human beings were made righteous as well as being reckoned righteous.

Becker, Carl Lotus (1873–1945)
American historian. Born in Blackhawk County, Iowa, he spent most of his life as professor at Cornell. He is important for his opposition to the view that history is about 'facts'; he stressed the role of the historian in creating facts and projecting views on to the past: each period has its own climate of opinion. His *Everyman his own Historian* (1935) has been eclipsed by his classic *The Heavenly City of the Eighteenth-Century Philosophers*, which examined the relationship between Christianity and the secular views of the Enlightenment.

Becon, Thomas (c.1511–67)
English Reformer. Born in Norfolk, he studied in Cambridge and, after having charge of two parishes, became chaplain to Cranmer. Imprisoned in the Tower of London under Queen Mary, he was released and fled to the continent until the accession of Queen Elizabeth I, when he became a canon of Canterbury cathedral. His writings were popular and circulated widely, but became more strident as time went on.

Bede, The Venerable (672–735)
English monk, theologian and historian. He was born in Northumbria, sent to the monastery at Wearmouth and then to Jarrow; he spent his life there. His writings on chronology (related to the calculation of Easter) and history were instrumental in introducing the practice of dating events from the birth of Jesus. His *Ecclesiastical History of the English People* (731), the best-known of his works, is important for its identification of source material and its attempt to distinguish historical information from tradition and legend. He also wrote a scientific work *On the Nature of Things* (c.725) and a number of biblical commentaries.

Beecher, Henry Ward (1813–87)
American Presbyterian / Congregational minister. He was born in Connecticut, son of Lyman *Beecher, and studied at Amherst and in Cincinnati in his father's seminary there. After two frontier pastorates, he was chiefly active in Brooklyn, becoming famous as a witty and dramatic preacher. He moved away from *Calvinism towards a moral interpretation of the Bible; he was open to modern thinking, not believing in hell and accepting evolution. Politically active, he reflected national feelings of optimism and development, though scandal overshadowed his later life.

Beecher, Lyman (1775–1863)
American Congregational minister. Father of Henry Ward *Beecher (and also of Harriet Beecher *Stowe), he was born in New Haven, studied at Yale, held a parish on Long Island, and after a further parish in Litchfield, Connecticut, became president of Lane Seminary, Cincinnati. He clashed with the conservatives there over their refusal to allow discussion of the abolition of slavery in the seminary. He was liberal in his religious and political beliefs but also a revivalist; he was arraigned for heresy (but acquitted) because of his work in more conservative Ohio. He then resigned and lived with his son.

Bell, George Kennedy Allen (1883–1958)
Bishop and ecumenist. From a clergy family, he studied at Oxford and, after ordination and parish work, taught there. He became secretary to the archbishop of Canterbury, and was involved in the 1920 Lambeth Conference. In 1924 he became dean of Canterbury and in 1929 bishop of Chichester. Further international involvement in Life and Work, and later in the World Council of Churches, gave his life an ecumenical dimension. He was one of the first to recognize the threat of Nazism through his friendship with Dietrich *Bonhoeffer and was hostile to Allied policies of unconditional surrender and saturation bombing during the Second World War.

Bellah, Robert Neely (1927–   )
American sociologist. He was born in Altus, Oklahoma and after studying at Harvard became research associate in the Institute of Islamic Studies at McGill University, Montreal. He then became professor first at Harvard and subsequently at the University of California, Berkeley. His major works are *Beyond Belief* (1970) and, with colleagues, *The New Religious Consciousness* (1976), *Varieties of Civil Religion* (1980) and *Habits of the Heart* (1985). He is widely recognized for his contributions to a survey of the mix of traits essential to the American character.

Bellarmine, Robert (1542–1621)

Italian Roman Catholic theologian. He was born in Montepulciano, became a Jesuit, and after being ordained priest was made professor at Louvain, where he encountered non-Roman Catholic thought. For health reasons, in 1576 he returned to Rome, where he became professor at the new-founded Roman College, cardinal, and then archbishop of Capua. A fair-minded controversialist with Protestantism, he was seen as one of the best exponents of post-Tridentine doctrine. He had a sympathetic interest in *Galileo.

Belloc, Joseph Hilaire Pierre (1870–1953)

Roman Catholic writer. Half-French, he was born near Versailles and went to the Birmingham Oratory school under *Newman. Before studying at Oxford he served in the French artillery. After one term as a member of Parliament he spent the rest of his life as a journalist. He was closely associated with G. K. *Chesterton. A staunch champion of Catholic liberalism and European civilization he wrote much; perhaps *Europe and the Faith* (1912) is his best-known book, though its popularity hardly bears comparison with that of his light verse.

Benedict of Nursia (c.480–547)

Italian monk. Little is known of his life. After living as a hermit and establishing a number of monasteries, he eventually founded his best-known community on Monte Cassino, south of Rome, the beginning of the Benedictine order. Its basis was his famous *Rule*, which proved an important force by providing a disciplined focus for Christian life and thought throughout Europe. He is often called the father of Western monasticism, and became the patron saint of Europe.

Bengel, Johann Albrecht (1687–1752)

German New Testament scholar. Born in Württemberg, after becoming a Lutheran minister he served first as a seminary professor and then as a general superintendent. His fame rests on his New Testament commentary *Gnomon*, on which *Wesley based his *Explanatory Notes on the NT*. He also produced an edition of the Greek New Testament and was the first to recognize 'families' of manuscripts. He wrote on biblical eschatology and indeed expected the millennium in 1837.

Benjamin, Walter (1892–1940)

Born in Berlin to a middle-class family, as a student he was influenced by Jewish kabbalistic and messianic ideas. A brilliant thesis on German drama failed to get him an academic post, so he had to turn to freelance journalism. Under the influence of Ernst *Bloch he became a Marxist, and was also a friend of Bertholt Brecht. He fled to Paris on the rise of Hitler and when the Nazis invaded France tried to leave for Spain but was denied entry. He then committed suicide. His influence has been extended through his friendship with Gershom *Scholem. His thought combines Jewish messianic quasi-mysticism with artistic modernism and a somewhat unorthodox brand of Marxism. His most influential writings are collected in *Illuminations* (1968) and *One-Way Street* (1979).

Bentley, Richard (1662–1742)

English classical scholar and literary critic. An infant prodigy, he went to Cambridge at the age of fourteen and later became Master of Trinity College. Particularly distinguished as a classical textual scholar, he pioneered developments leading to nineteenth-century critical scholarship. But he was also an able apologist, using *Newton to prove the existence of an intelligent creator in controversy with the deists.

Bentzen, Aage (1894–1953)

Danish Old Testament scholar. A pupil of Johannes *Pedersen, he became professor in the university of Copenhagen. He helped to communicate the biblical researches of the Uppsala circle of scholars, from the perspective of the history of religions, to a wider European audience. A prolific author, he is best remembered for his commentary on Daniel (1937), a two-volume *Introduction to the New Testament* (1941, ET 1948), and a study on royal ideology in Israel, *King and Messiah* (1955).

Berdyaev, Nicolai Aleksandrovich (1874–1948)

Russian religious philosopher. Born in Kiev and educated in Moscow, he was originally a sceptic but joined the Orthodox church after the 1905 Revolution. He later established a philosophical school in Berlin and then from 1922 lived in Paris. His theology is an ethical type of Christian existentialism which also affirms the primacy of a transcendent world of spirit, known by a near-mystical act of intuition, over the mere world of things. This does away with the need for formal worship, and doctrinal and moral definitions. Two important works are *The Destiny of Man* (1937) and his autobiography *Dream and Reality* (1951).

Berengarius (c.999–1088)
Scholastic theologian. His family was associated with St Martin's, Tours, where he became a canon, returning as director of the school there after service in Angers with the Count of Anjou. He was an opponent of the eucharistic doctrine of transubstantiation put forward by *Paschasius Radbertus, though his objections were regularly withdrawn in the form of recantations. The controversy was instrumental in leading to a reformulation of the doctrine.

Berger, Peter Ludwig (1929–   )
American sociologist. He was born in Austria, but emigrated to the United States, where he studied at Wagner College. After military service he went on to hold a variety of teaching posts before becoming professor, first at Rutgers and then at Boston. His books on sociology have had some influence on modern theology. His early works criticized the church for doing no more than reflect the beliefs and attitudes of secular society. *A Rumor of Angels* (1969) marked a shift to rediscovering the supernatural inside and outside the churches, and *The Heretical Imperative* (1979) indicated limits to secularization.

Bergson, Henri Louis (1859–1941)
French philosopher. He was born in Paris of Jewish descent, and for most of his life taught at the Collège de France. Criticizing all forms of intellectualism, he argued for intuition and creativity. Central to his thinking was 'creative evolution', in which the *élan vital* or life force drives matter on to take its various forms and is also at work in human beings. His thought proved congenial to many religious contemporaries. Two important books are *Time and Free Will* (1889) and *Creative Evolution* (1907).

Berkeley, George (1685–1753)
Irish philosopher. He was educated at Trinity College, Dublin, where he then taught, becoming dean of Derry and later bishop of Cloyne; he also travelled abroad. He is particularly known for his 'immaterialism'. He argued that material objects do not exist unless someone perceives them, and since no one doubts that objects exist when we do not perceive them, there must be another mind aware of them – God. Only spirits have a primary existence. His best-known book is *Principles of Human Knowledge* (1710).

Berkhof, Hendrikus (1914–   )
Dutch systematic theologian. In the Reformed tradition, he was professor of theology in Leiden and has been influential on the World Council of Churches. His *Christ the Meaning of History* (1962, ET 1966) sought to present an approach mediating between existentialism and salvation history; his major work is *Christian Faith* (1986), which combines an appreciation of classical Reformed dogmatics with a sensitivity to developments in contemporary theology and philosophy.

Berkhof, Louis (1873–1957)
American Calvinist theologian. Born in the Netherlands, he emigrated to the United States at the age of fifteen and studied at the Calvin Seminary of the Dutch-speaking Christian Reformed church, where he later taught for thirty years, becoming its president. His *Systematic Theology* (1941), influenced by *Bavinck, was the medium through which most Christian Reformed preachers learned the subject.

Berkouwer, Gerrit Cornelis (1903–   )
Dutch Reformed theologian. He taught in the Free University of Amsterdam, rising to be professor. He had a critical interest in both *Barth and Roman Catholicism, and was invited to be an official observer at the Second Vatican Council. He is best known for his eighteen volumes of *Studies in Dogmatics*, which with their stress on faith and revelation are anti-speculative and firmly based on scripture.

Bernadette of Lourdes (Marie Bernarde Soubirous, 1844–79)
Visionary. She was the daughter of a miller in Lourdes and experienced visions of the Virgin Mary which made Lourdes a place of international pilgrimage. She spent the latter part of her life in a religious order.

Bernanos, Georges (1888–1948)
French novelist. Born in Paris, he studied at the Institut Catholique and the Sorbonne; he then served in the cavalry in the First World War, was wounded and decorated. Firmly right-wing, an ardent supporter of the monarchy and a committed Catholic, he wrote a number of novels, psychological studies of

the conflict between the soul and evil; most famous of them is *The Diary of a Country Priest* (1936), which won him international recognition. He left France in the late 1930s and returned after the war as a supporter of Charles de Gaulle, whom he had known from college days.

Bernard of Clairvaux (1090–1153)
Cistercian abbot. Born of noble parents near Dijon, he entered the monastery of Cîteaux, but three years later was asked by the abbot to establish a new monastery. His choice, Clairvaux, became one of the main Cistercian centres and Bernard as abbot a very powerful man in church politics. He was bitterly hostile to the 'heretics' in Languedoc and supported the Second Crusade. However, he was above all an austere and saintly monk and is sometimes called the 'last of the Fathers', since he stood at the end of a long tradition in seeing reason and faith as belonging closely together in the love of God. This made him an opponent of *Abelard, whom he condemned. He wrote many books on spirituality, the best known of which is *On Loving God*.

Bérulle, Pierre de (1575–1629)
French cardinal and reformer. Born in Champagne, after ordination he became a spiritual director. He was also a skilled diplomat. In his university days he had been influenced by Mme *Acarie. In 1611 he founded the French Oratory on the model of the Oratory of *Philip Neri, and its members played a major role in reforming the French clergy. This trend became known as the French school of spirituality.

Besant, Annie (1847–1933)
British theosophist and educator. Born in London, she married an Anglican clergyman but their marriage broke up. She became a radical and a socialist and in 1893 went to India. There she founded many educational institutions and became president of the National Congress, the first woman to hold this post. She travelled widely, giving a vast number of lectures. She became a theosophist in 1899 and on the death of Helena *Blavatsky became president of the Theosophical Society.

Beyschlag, Willibald (1823–1900)
German Protestant theologian. He was court preacher in Karlsruhe and then professor of pastoral theology in Halle. Though he rejected orthodox christology as it had been defined at the council of Chalcedon, he was equally hostile to radical scholars like *Renan and *Strauss, advocating what was known as a 'mediating theology'. He also supported the Old Catholic Church and was involved in drawing up the new constitution of the Prussian church after 1870.

Beza, Theodore (1519–1605)
French Reformer. Born to a noble Catholic family in Burgundy, he studied law in Orleans and went on to practise it in Paris. Severe illness in 1548 led to a conversion to Protestantism, after which he went to Switzerland and became a professor of Greek in Lausanne. Ten years later he moved to Geneva at *Calvin's invitation, soon becoming rector of the academy there. He succeeded Calvin as Reformed leader on the latter's death in 1563; the next year he wrote a eulogistic biography of Calvin. A man of wide interests, he produced the first critical edition of the Greek New Testament, and his textual criticism influenced the King James Version. He discovered an early codex manuscript, which bears his name. He was active in defending and supporting French Protestantism, and wrote a history of the Reformed movement in France; a strict Calvinist, through his theological writings he did much to make the movement more rigid and doctrinaire.

Biddle, John (1615–62)
English Unitarian. After studying at Oxford he taught in Gloucester, where he wrote a controversial *Twelve Arguments against the Holy Ghost* (1647), which was publicly burned, following it with two pamphlets against the Trinity. As a result of these and other works he was imprisoned several times and narrowly escaped execution. He also helped to edit an edition of the Greek Old Testament. He is seen as a founder of the English Unitarian movement.

Billerbeck, Paul (1853–1932)
Biblical commentator. A German pastor of Jewish descent from Brandenburg, he is known for his four-volume commentary on the New Testament which provides parallels to it from the Talmud and the Midrash. To secure publication he had to accept the fiction of co-authorship with the scholar H. L. Strack, now virtually forgotten.

Blake, William (1757–1827)
English visionary poet. He lived in London, and when apprenticed to an engraver, spent

much time in Westminster Abbey, falling under the influence of its Gothic style. Most of his poetry was engraved by hand and illustrated by coloured drawings. His best known works are his collections of poems, *Songs of Innocence* (1789), *Songs of Experience* (1794), *Jerusalem* (1818) and his set of engravings, *Illustrations of the Book of Job* (1825). Stressing the reality of the spiritual world, and using imagination to the full, his work made a deep impression precisely because of the religious depths of its art, which is not limited to any particular category.

Blavatsky, Helena Petrovna (1831–91)
Russian spiritual figure. With Henry Steel Olcott she founded the Theosophical Society. After a wandering life, which included visits to Tibet and India, while in the United States she became interested in spiritualism; she claimed to reveal truths shown to her by certain 'trans-Himalayan masters of wisdom'.

Bloch, Ernst (1885–1977)
German philosopher. He was born in Ludwigshafen, son of a railway manager, and taught in Leipzig. On the rise of Hitler, in 1933 he moved to the USA; he became professor in Leipzig in 1948, but after falling foul of the authorities moved to a chair in Tübingen. His work is characterized by a sense of the 'not yet', perhaps arising out of the conflict between his own vision and the industrial surroundings in which he grew up. His first book was on *The Spirit of Utopia* (1918), covering poetry, art and myth; he then wrote a book on *Münzer (1921). However, he is best known for *The Principle of Hope* (1954–9, ET 1986), a massive and complex work which sees history as a development towards greater humanity. As well as influencing many Marxists, Bloch's thought has also made a mark on Christian theology, especially through *Moltmann.

Blondel, Maurice (1861–1941)
French Roman Catholic lay philosopher. He was born in Dijon, and taught at Montauban, Lille and Aix-en-Provence. Though associated with the Modernist movement he remained loyal to the church. His book *L'action* (1893) was the basis of the French school of philosophy of action: human beings cannot avoid action; dissatisfaction with their actions leads them to further action and this process presses towards the supernatural.

Blumhardt, Johann Christoph (1805–80)
Protestant pietist. He was born in Stuttgart and studied in Tübingen, after which he worked with the Basle Mission, founded by his uncle. In 1838 he became pastor of Möttlingen, which experienced a revival accompanied by healings. This led him to resign and open up a healing centre at Bad Boll, which attracted much attention. His motto was 'Jesus is victor!'

Blumhardt, Christian (1842–1919)
Son of Johann Christoph *Blumhardt, he took over the leadership of Bad Boll on his father's death. Moving out of pietism, he was more positive than his father about the benefits of the contributions of the sciences and came to be involved in socialism, becoming a Württemberg representative of the Social Democrats.

Boehme, Jakob (1575–1624)
German mystic. The son of a farmer, he became a shoemaker. He had mystical experiences on the basis of which he wrote obscure but influential works, much influenced by *Paracelsus and drawing on Neoplatonism and the Jewish Kabbalah. He saw God as the primal abyss containing the possibilities of both good and evil. His works were banned in his lifetime, and became underground literative; he proved to be an influence on the Quakers, William *Law, the Romantics and Idealists, *Berdyaev and *Bulgakov.

Boesak, Allan (1946–   )
South African liberation theologian. Educated in the Netherlands, he was a university chaplain and church minister in the Western Cape, and has been particularly involved in the fight against apartheid and in political action. He became president of the World Alliance of Reformed Churches. Sadly his career was blighted by sexual scandal. His books include *Farewell to Innocence* (1977), *The Finger of God* (1979) and *Black and Reformed* (1985).

Boethius, Anicius Manlius Torquatus Severinus (480–524)
Christian philosopher and statesman. Son of a consul, he was educated in Athens and Alexandria and himself became a consul and imperial adviser. Accused of treason when he attempted to prevent a forced requisition of grain, he was imprisoned in Italy, where he wrote his most famous book,

The Consolation of Philosophy, to show how philosophy can lead the soul to the vision of God. Though not specifically Christian, it was extremely popular and was translated into Anglo-Saxon by King Alfred. He himself translated two works of *Aristotle, including his *Categories*, into English, thus preserving them through the dark ages. He was ultimately executed. He is a transitional figure between the ancient and modern world and laid the foundations for the later study of theology.

Boff, Clodovis (1944–   )
Brazilian Roman Catholic theologian. He was born in Concordia, Brazil, is a member of the Servite order and professor of theology at the Catholic University of São Paulo. As a liberation theologian he works with the poor in basic Christian communities; his theology is particularly concerned with methodological reflection, as is evident from his main book *Theology and Praxis* (1978, ET 1987). He is brother of

Boff, Leonardo (1938–   )
Brazilian Franciscan theologian. After studying under Karl Rahner in Germany, he became professor of theology in Petropolis, Brazil, and adviser to the Brazilian conference of bishops. His liberation theology gained prominence when as a result of his *Church: Charism and Power* (1981) he was summoned to Rome for censure, but accompanied by his bishops for support. Opposed to a hierarchical church, he stresses the church as the community of the people of God, especially for the dispossessed.

Bonald, Louis Gabriel Ambrose de (1754–1840)
Conservative French fideist and traditionalist. He saw Christianity as a means of holding society together and in 1796 wrote a *Theory of Political and Religious Power in Civil Society*, attacking revolutionary principles and defending the divine right of kings and the ultimate authority of the pope.

Bonaventura (Giovanni di Fidanza, 1221–74)
Scholastic theologian and mystic. Born in Italy, he was educated in Paris and then became a Franciscan, studying under *Alexander of Hales and writing a commentary on the *Sentences* of *Peter Lombard. He became minister-general of the order and played a major part in settling internal disputes. Subsequently he was made cardinal

archbishop of Albano. Basically a conservative, in his theology he subordinated knowledge to faith; he believed that all human wisdom was folly compared to mystical illumination from God. His mystical account of the soul's journey to God (*Itinerarium Mentis in Deum*) was particularly influential. He is known in the Roman Catholic church as the 'seraphic doctor'.

Bonhoeffer, Dietrich (1906–45)
German Protestant theologian. Son of a Berlin professor of psychiatry, he studied in Tübingen and Berlin and then went to Barcelona and New York before returning to Berlin as lecturer and chaplain. Opposed to Nazism from the start, he became a leading member of the Confessing Church. When the preachers' seminary of which he was head was shut down, he joined the political resistance against Hitler, was imprisoned and ultimately executed. His main books reflect his life's work: *The Cost of Discipleship* (1937, ET 1959) the demands on a Christian in an oppressive political situation; *Life Together* life in the seminary (1938, ET 1954); *Ethics* (1949, ET 1955) the moral problems for Christians in the modern world. His posthumous *Letters and Papers from Prison* (ET 1953, ²1971), smuggled out, are not only a moving human document but also contain pioneering radical thought, expressed in terms of the 'world come of age', 'religionless Christianity' and Jesus as 'the man for others'. It was widely discussed in the religious controversies of the 1960s.

Bonino, José Miguez (1924–   )
Argentinian Protestant theologian. Dean of studies at Union Theological Seminary, Buenos Aires, and one of the presidents of the World Council of Churches, he is a leading figure in political theology. His writings focus on a political ethics centred on commitment to the poor; his most important books are *Revolutionary Theology Comes of Age* (1975) and *Toward a Christian Political Ethics* (1983).

Booth, William (1829–1912)
English evangelist. Born in Nottingham, he was at first apprenticed to a pawnbroker. He was converted to Methodism but resigned because of its restrictions, becoming a freelance evangelist in London's East End. He was fond of using military terminology, and the organization which was eventually founded in 1878 under his leadership, the Salvation Army, was run on military lines. It

began to engage in social work from 1887, following a programme laid out in his *Darkest England – and the Way Out* (1890).

Bornkamm, Günther (1905–90)
German New Testament scholar. Born in Görlitz, he taught in Königsberg, but was dismissed by the Nazis in 1936 because of his involvement in the Confessing Church. He became professor at Göttingen and then at Heidelberg. A pupil of *Bultmann, he differed from him in being more positive about the possibility of knowing about the historical Jesus. He did pioneering work in redaction criticism (study of the distinctive contribution of the authors of the Gospels to their writings) with particular reference to Matthew; his *Jesus of Nazareth* (1956, ET 1960) was the main work in the 'new quest for the historical Jesus', and he followed it with an influential book on *Paul* (1969, ET 1975), both popularizing the results of German critical scholarship.

Borromeo, Charles see **Charles Borromeo**

Bosanquet, Bernard (1848–1923)
English philosopher. He studied at Oxford and taught there until 1881, after which he lived privately in London, though he spent a brief period as professor in St Andrews. In the Hegelian tradition, he was an idealist; his religious views were pantheistic and he saw religion itself as a stage towards metaphysics.

Bossuet, Jacques-Bénigne
(1627–1704)
French Catholic preacher. Son of a judge in Dijon and an infant prodigy, he went to a Jesuit school and trained for the ministry in Paris, to which he returned after a period in Metz. He became bishop, first of Condom and then of Meaux, and was also a tutor to the Dauphin. A precocious sermon preached when he was sixteen revealed his most outstanding gift. He was also a skilled apologist, arguing for what was best in the religion of his time, and seeking to commend Catholicism to those who differed from it. His *Discourse on Universal History* (1681) was a classic account of the workings of providence and his *Meditations on the Gospel*, which appeared after his death, became a French devotional classic.

Boston, Thomas (1676–1732)
Scottish theologian. Born in Duns, he studied at Edinburgh and became a presby-

terian minister. He was influenced by a banned *Arminian work, Edwin Fisher's *The Marrow of Modern Divinity*, and popularized its doctrines, preaching especially against legalism. His best known book is *Human Nature in its Fourfold Estate* (1720), at one time as popular in Scotland as *Pilgrim's Progress*.

Bousset, Wilhelm (1865–1920)
German New Testament scholar. Born in Lübeck, after teaching at Göttingen he became professor at Giessen. One of the founders of the history of religions school, he was concerned to illustrate the New Testament from comparative religion. In *The Religion of Judaism in the New Testament Age* (1903) he showed how Judaism was influenced by Hellenistic features; his best known book, *Kyrios Christos* (1913, ET 1970), extends this approach to Christian thought about Jesus from the New Testament to *Irenaeus.

Boyle, Robert (1627–91)
Irish philosopher. Son of the Earl of Cork, he was converted to Christianity as a boy during a storm in Geneva. A gifted scientist, and known as the 'father of chemistry', with *Newton he founded the Royal Society. He saw science and religion as being in harmony and in addition to scientific studies also wrote many religious works.

Bradley, Francis Herbert (1846–1924)
British philosopher. Born in London, he studied in Oxford and then taught there until his death. In the idealist tradition, he was concerned to know reality, that which goes beyond contradiction, rather than mere appearance, hence the name of his major book *Appearance and Reality* (1893).

Bradwardine, Thomas (1290–1349)
English theologian. Born in Chichester, he taught at Oxford and became chancellor of St Paul's Cathedral and royal confessor. He died of the plague in 1349, the year he was made archbishop of Canterbury. A gifted mathematician as well as a learned theologian, he defended the tradition of *Augustine (especially the importance of grace) and *Anselm (including the ontological argument) in the context of a revival of the ideas of *Pelagius.

Bremond, Henri (1865–1933)
French Christian humanist. He became a Jesuit, but left the order for more freedom

to write. However, his sympathy for the Modernists caused him trouble, and one of his works was banned. His main work was a sympathetic eleven-volume *Literary History of Religious Sentiment in France* (1915–1932). He was concerned for an intelligent and human understanding of Christianity.

Brentano, Franz (1838–1917)
Austrian philosopher. He was ordained to the Catholic priesthood and taught in Würzburg, but in 1873 left the church because of difficulties over the Trinity, though he continued to believe in God. Critical of idealism, he adopted an empirical approach and was especially influential on the phenomenology of *Husserl. His most important books are *Psychology from an Empirical Standpoint* (1874) and *The Origin of Moral Knowledge* (1889).

Bretschneider, Karl Gottlieb (1776–1848)
German Protestant theologian. He became general superintendent in Gotha. He did pioneering work in the New Testament, distinguishing John from the Synoptists, but he is best known as the founder of the *Corpus Reformatorum*, a major edition of the works of the Reformers.

Bridges, Robert Seymour (1844–1930)
English poet. Educated at Eton and Oxford he became a physician, but in 1882 gave up medicine to devote himself to literature and music, living in Yattendon, Berkshire, and Oxford. In 1913 he became Poet Laureate. Though he rejected dogma, he was sympathetic to Christianity and sought to reconcile it with science, and was also very interested in church music. His *The Testament of Beauty* (1929) is his major work. He supervised the posthumous publication of the poems of Gerard Manley *Hopkins.

Briggs, Charles Augustus (1841–1913)
American biblical scholar. He was a Presbyterian minister and professor at Union Theological Seminary, New York. In the latter post he championed historical criticism to such a degree that he was arraigned for heresy and ultimately condemned, after which he became an Episcopalian, advocating Christian union. He was one of the editors of the standard Hebrew–English lexicon and of the International Critical Commentary.

Brooks, Phillips (1835–93)
American Episcopalian preacher. Born in Boston, he had a ministry in Philadelphia before returning to Boston of which he was ultimately consecrated bishop. He was particularly concerned to interpret contemporary religious movements and was also the author of 'O Little Town of Bethlehem'.

Brown, Raymond Edward (1928–   )
American Roman Catholic New Testament scholar. For many years he has been professor at Union Theological Seminary, New York. Author of a number of distinguished biblical studies, he is best known for his commentaries on the *Gospel according to John* (1970) and *The Epistles of John* (1982), and his studies on the narratives of Jesus' infancy in Matthew and Luke (*The Birth of the Messiah*, 1977) and *The Community of the Beloved Disciple* (1979).

Brown, Robert McAfee (1920–   )
American theologian. Born in Carthage, Illinois, he studied at Amherst College, Union Theological Seminary, New York, and Columbia University, and then in Oxford. After teaching at Manchester College, St Paul, he joined the faculty of Union; in 1962 he became professor at Stanford, returning to Union as professor in 1976. He has distinguished himself as an advocate of issues relating to peace, justice and liberation, drawing upon and interpreting theologians of the Third World for those who live in the First World.

Browne, Robert (c.1550–1633)
English Puritan. A relative of Lord Burleigh, he was born in Rutland and studied in Cambridge, where he came under Presbyterian influence. As a result he organized independent churches in East Anglia, was imprisoned, and then emigrated to Holland. After disputes there, he returned via Scotland to England and was formally reconciled with the Church of England, being ordained and given a parish in Northamptonshire. He died in prison after being arrested for attacking a policeman. He was an influence on the first Congregationalists (known as 'Brownists'). He believed that the civil powers had no spiritual jurisdiction over the church and that church membership was contractual rather than residential.

Browne, Thomas (1605–82)
Physician and writer. He studied medicine at Oxford, Montpellier and Padua, and then

settled in Norwich, where he practised as a physician. He is famed for two remarkable books, *Religio Medici* (1642), a combination of scepticism and faith, and *Hydrotaphia or Urn Burial* (1658), a study of burial customs.

Bruce, Alexander Balmain (1831–99)
Scottish theologian. After studying in Edinburgh he became a Free Church minister and then professor in Glasgow. Open-minded, he used contemporary biblical criticism in his interpretation of the Gospels, but escaped censure; his *The Humiliation of Christ* (1876) is an important study of the kenotic theory, the view that in Christ God 'emptied' himself.

Bruce, Frederick Fyvie (1910–   )
Scottish New Testament scholar. Born in Elgin, he studied at Aberdeen, Cambridge and Vienna; he then taught in Edinburgh and Leeds, becoming professor in Sheffield and Manchester. Author of many books and commentaries, he is a leading evangelical scholar, tending to conservative solutions presented in a readable form. His best-known books include two commentaries on Acts (on the Greek text in 1951 and on the content in 1954) and *Paul – Apostle of the Free Spirit* (1977).

Brunner, Heinrich Emil (1889–1966)
Swiss Protestant theologian. Born in Winterthur, he was a pastor before becoming professor of theology in Zurich in 1922; on his retirement in 1953 he taught for three years at the International Christian University in Tokyo. Though often paired with Karl *Barth because of his opposition to liberalism and his acceptance of dialectical theology and stress on the priority of revelation, Brunner's thought was independent; he was more influenced by *Kierkegaard and *Buber and by the Christian socialism of *Kutter and *Ragaz. He parted company with Karl Barth in accepting the possibility of the revelation of God in history and the principle of analogy as a basis for knowledge of God. For him, there was a point of contact between the gospel and non-Christians. Of his many books, *The Mediator* (1927, ET 1934) and *The Divine Imperative* (1932) are perhaps the best known.

Bruno, Giordano (1548–1600)
Italian Renaissance philosopher. He became a Dominican in Naples in 1562, but was censured for unorthodoxy and had to flee, thenceforward leading an itinerant life until he was captured in Venice in 1592, imprisoned in Rome, and burnt as a heretic. He was a champion of *Copernicus' new astronomy, but coupled this with a form of pantheism, an approach which led to his condemnation.

Buber, Martin (1878–1965)
Austrian Jewish philosopher and theologian. Born in Vienna, he studied art and philosophy there and in Berlin and then became an active Zionist. In 1906 he turned to religious studies, which led him to discover Hasidism, a major influence on his subsequent thought. He was professor of Jewish religion in Frankfurt university until forced to leave by the rise of Hitler. In 1938 he settled in Palestine and spent the rest of his life there as professor of sociology at the Hebrew University of Jerusalem. He wrote on many subjects, and particularly on Hasidism, but the book which most influenced Christian theology was *I and Thou* (1923, ET 1937). Human beings have two kinds of relationship: that in which they enter into dialogue or communion (I-Thou: subject-subject) and that in which they are observers (I-it: subject-object); God is the eternal Thou, the only I-Thou situation which human beings can sustain.

Bucer, Martin (1491–1551)
German Reformer. Born in Alsace, he became a Dominican in 1506 but in 1518 came to know *Luther, and three years later got dispensation from his monastic vows, marrying the next year (one of the first German Reformers to do so). He was excommunicated for preaching reform and became leader of the Reformation in Strasbourg, where he had a formative influence on *Calvin. He remained there for more than twenty years, but problems in the city meant he was more effective outside it. Because of his skill in statesmanship he was involved in diplomacy all over Europe, and was also instrumental in providing constitutions for many Reformed churches. He tried to overcome the division between *Luther and *Zwingli over eucharistic doctrine, but was less than successful. His opposition to the Augsburg interim settlement with the Catholics in Germany led to exile in 1548 and at *Cranmer's invitation he went to England, where he became professor in Cambridge and influenced the production of the 1549 Book of Common Prayer. He was also the author of many biblical commentaries.

Buchman, Frank (1878–1960)
Founder of 'Moral Rearmament'. An American Lutheran minister from Pennsylvania, he was 'converted' in Keswick, England, believing that his previous work had been useless, and went on to work as an evangelist in the United States, India and China. He then returned to England, where a new plan began to take distinctive shape. In 1929 he founded the Oxford Group (which in 1938 became Moral Rearmament). Its main emphasis was a stress on national and social morale and the importance of personal ethical change.

Budde, Karl (1850–1935)
German Old Testament scholar. He was professor first in Strasbourg and then in Marburg. Following in the steps of *Wellhausen, he was particularly interested in demonstrating that the Pentateuchal sources extended more deeply into the Bible than Wellhausen supposed.

Bulgakov, Sergei Nikolaevich (1871–1944)
Russian religious philosopher. The son of a Russian priest, as a result of his acquaintance with *Hegel's philosophy he became a sceptic. However, disillusioned by the 1905 revolution he began to return to the church. He was expelled from Russia in 1922, after which he lived in Paris and taught at the Orthodox Theological Seminary, which he helped to found and of which he became dean. His theology focussed on divine wisdom or Sophia; this wisdom was the mediator between God and the world. His main works are *The Orthodox Church* (1935) and *The Wisdom of God* (1937).

Bullinger, Johann Heinrich (1504–75)
Swiss Reformer. He was attracted to the Reformation after reading the works of *Luther and *Melanchthon and hearing *Zwingli preach, and became chief pastor in Zurich after Zwingli. He played a part in the composition of the First and Second Helvetic Confessions and wrote much theology of a mediating kind. He had a particular interest in England and provided theological support for English monarchs.

Bultmann, Rudolf (1884–1976)
German New Testament scholar. Born in Oldenburg, after studying in Marburg, Tübingen and Berlin he spent most of his life as professor at Marburg. He was deeply involved in historical research along the lines of the history of religions school and a pioneer of form criticism, analysing the pre-literary units of which the Synoptic Gospels are made up (*The History of the Synoptic Tradition* (1921, ET 1963), and wrote a classic *Theology of the New Testament* (1948–53, ET 1952, 1955). He was associated with the dialectical theology of Karl *Barth, but parted company with Barth when he saw *Heidegger's existentialist philosophy as crucial to interpreting the New Testament. In an attempt to help German army chaplains in their work he was led by this to propose the 'demythologization' of the New Testament, i.e. the reinterpretation of its mythology in terms of existentialist conceptuality (*Jesus Christ and Mythology*, 1958, ET 1960).

Bunyan, John (1628–88)
English Baptist minister. Brought up to be a tinker, after army service he joined a Baptist church in Bedford. He was imprisoned for twelve years after 1660 for belonging to what was then an illegal organization, and wrote a great deal in prison. Though his early spiritual autobiography *Grace abounding to the Chief of Sinners* (1666) aroused much attention, he is best known as author of *The Pilgrim's Progress* (1682).

Burkitt, Francis Crawford (1864–1935)
English biblical and patristic scholar. He studied at Cambridge, becoming professor there in 1905 and never leaving it. A man of many interests, he worked on the Syriac text of the New Testament and other textual questions, but his concern with the historical Jesus is demonstrated in his best-known work, *The Gospel History and Its Transmission* (1906).

Burney, Charles Fox (1868–1925)
English biblical scholar. He spent his academic life teaching in Oxford, in 1914 becoming professor there. After work on the period of the judges, including a classic commentary (1918), his interest turned to the Aramaic background to the New Testament: he sought to demonstrate the Aramaic origin of the Fourth Gospel and get back to original Aramaic sayings of Jesus (*The Poetry of Our Lord*, 1925).

Bushnell, Horace (1802–76)
American Congregationalist theologian. Born in Connecticut, he graduated at Yale and after teaching and journalistic work returned there to study law. However, a revival

renewed his faith and he became a pastor in Hartford, Connecticut, where he had a long ministry. His first book, *Christian Nurture* (1847), was opposed to the Puritan tradition and its new expression in revivalism, and with its stress on infant baptism and the family went back to an earlier tradition, looking to an audience on which revivalism made no mark. *God in Christ* (1849), on the social nature of language, atonement and the divinity of Christ, stands at the heart of his theology. The titles given him, the 'American *Schleiermacher' and 'father of American religious liberalism', are not inappropriate. However, his thought always maintained a tension between the liberal and the conservative, which is particularly evident in his *Nature and the Supernatural* (1858).

Butler, Joseph (1659–1752)
Christian apologist. Born in Wantage, Berkshire, of Presbyterian parents, he abandoned his parents' beliefs and, after study at Oxford, became an Anglican priest. After attracting attention for his brilliant preaching, he was marked out for preferment and eventually became bishop of Bristol, then of Durham. He is particularly known for his *Analogy of Religion* (1736), a refutation of deism and a defence of natural theology. It was one of the most influential books of his time, arguing that probability must be the guide to understanding, and points to the existence of God.

Butler, Josephine Elizabeth
(1828–1920)
Social reformer. Wife of a canon of Winchester, she was first concerned with women's education, but then turned to the rescue of prostitutes and the abolition of white slavery. Objecting to the dual sexual morality for men and women, she achieved much legal reform in this area. A deeply spiritual person, her inspiration was *Catherine of Siena. She wrote about her experiences in *Personal Reminiscences of a Great Crusade* (1896).

Cadbury, Henry Joel (1883–1974)
American New Testament scholar. A Quaker and Nobel peace prizewinner, for many years he was professor at Bryn Mawr and Harvard. In the biblical sphere, his most important work was on the Acts of the Apostles (*The Making of Luke-Acts*, 1928), and questioned the current views that Luke-Acts was written by an eyewitness and that the author could be shown to have been a doctor. He also wrote a distinctive study on *The Peril of Modernizing Jesus* (1937), challenging the idea that there was a plan in Jesus' life. He was sceptical about both the possibility of historical knowledge of the life of Jesus and the identity of a single form of early Christian preaching, a *kerygma*. He introduced form criticism to the English-speaking world.

Caird, Edward (1835–1908)
Scottish philosopher and theologian. He was professor of moral philosophy and then became Master of Balliol College, Oxford, in succession to *Jowett. An Idealistic philosopher in the *Hegelian tradition, he argued that Christianity was the absolute religion. His major work is *The Evolution of Religion* (1893).

Cajetan (Gaetano da Thiene, 1480–1547)
Born in Vicenza of noble family, after being ordained priest with the future pope *Paul IV he was involved in founding the austere order of Theatines, which was concerned with the care of the sick and poor.

Cajetan, Thomas de Vio ('Gaetano', 1469–1534)
Born in Gaeta (hence his name), he became a Dominican and taught in Padua, Pavia and Rome, becoming general of his order and later cardinal and bishop of Gaeta. He came to be involved in controversy, opposing *Luther and being against the planned divorce of Henry VIII of England. He wrote an important, if conservative, commentary on the *Summa Theologica* of *Thomas Aquinas and a number of works of scriptural exegesis.

Calvin, John (1509–64)
French Reformer. He was born in Noyon, Picardy, second of five sons of a public notary in the service of the bishop. His father, who had secured two ecclesiastical positions for him, was prompted to send him to study theology in Paris, but on breaking with the bishop, ordered him to Orleans to study law. He returned to Paris on his father's death, a young humanist scholar, and wrote a commentary on Seneca's *On Clemency*. Later he was converted to Protestantism, becoming active in the Reformation movement. In 1533, anti-Protestant feeling forced him to leave to avoid arrest, and he spent the next years travelling. However, this did not prevent him from writing in Latin a brief defence of Protestantism, entitled *Institution of the Christian Religion* (1536), which achieved considerable popularity. On his way to Strasbourg, where he could expect peace for study and writing, he stopped in Geneva and was invited by the Reformer Guillaume Farel to stay there to help to reform the church. So strict was their disciplinary approach, however, that they were both exiled; *Bucer invited Calvin to Strasbourg, where he became pastor to the French refugee congregation and married. He also wrote a commentary on Romans, drew up a liturgy and a metrical psalter, and laid the foundations for his later reputation. In 1541 he was urged back to Geneva, where he became the dominant figure. His aim to make it a holy city again caused conflict and indeed riots; Calvin even supervised the burning of *Servetus at the stake. Calvin's Reformation, and the strategic geographical position of Geneva, made the city a focal point for Reformed Christianity, and both Calvin and Geneva gained an international reputation. His 1536 Latin *Institution* was five times revised and rewritten in French as the *Institutes of the Christian Religion* (definitive edition 1559); as well as becoming a basic theological handbook for Protestants it influenced the development of the French language. Calvin also wrote commentaries on most of the books of the Bible. His biblical theology, much influenced by Augustine, with its famous focus on predestination, left a lasting mark on Europe.

Camara, Helder (1909–   )
Brazilian Roman Catholic archbishop. He was born in Fortaleza, Camara, and in 1964 became archbishop of Olinda and Reçife in North-east Brazil, the poorest region of the country. Though mention of his name was banned on the media, he became an international figure through his championship of the poor and of non-violent social change, inspired by Martin Luther *King and Mahatma Gandhi. He has become well-known through his spiritual writings, including *Church and Colonialism* (1969), *Spiral of Violence* (1971) and *The Desert is Fertile* (1976).

Campanella, Tommaso (Giovanni Domenico, 1568–1639)
Italian philosopher. He became a Dominican, but was suspected of heresy because of his rejection of *Aristotelian philosophy, and was sentenced to life imprisonment. Released in 1629, in due course he fled to Paris, where he spent the rest of his life. More sympathetic to *Platonism, he began from human consciousness, arguing that the existence of God could be inferred from the idea of God in human consciousness.

Campbell, Alexander (1788–1866)
Founder of the Disciples of Christ. Son of a Scottish Presbyterian, he emigrated to the United States. First becoming a Baptist, because of differences in belief he subsequently founded his own Disciples of Christ, with a strong emphasis on the rejection of creeds and the expectations of an imminent second coming of Christ.

Campbell, John McLeod (1800–72)
Scottish theologian. He became a minister after studying in Glasgow and Edinburgh but in 1831 was arraigned for heresy and deposed for preaching universal atonement and forgiveness, and that assurance is of the essence of faith. In due course his views were incorporated into a book, *The Nature of the Atonement* (1856); the climate had by then changed sufficiently for this to be recognized as a major contribution to Scottish theology. From 1833 until 1859 he served as minister of an independent church in Glasgow.

Campbell, Reginald John (1867–1956)
English Congregationalist minister. Convinced that the contemporary church was irrelevant, he wrote a book, *The New Theology* (1907), which attracted considerable attention and was rediscovered in the next wave of 'new theology' in the 1960s.

Camus, Albert (1913–60)
French writer. Born in Mondovi, Algeria, the son of an itinerant worker killed in the First

World War and an illiterate charwoman, after an impoverished childhood, and a victim of tuberculosis, he turned to writing. He came to France in 1938 and became a member of the Resistance. He made his name by *The Outsider* (1942, ET 1946) and *The Myth of Sisyphus* (1943, ET 1955), depicting a world of utter absurdity. Postwar works like *The Plague* (1948) and *The Rebel* (1951) conveyed his rejection of both Christianity and communism and led to a clash with *Sartre. He was killed in a road accident. His views have long been seen as a challenge by Christian theologians.

Canisius, Peter (1521–97)
Roman Catholic theologian. After studying at Cologne and Mainz, he became a Jesuit and founded a Jesuit college in Cologne. A particularly influential catechism made him famous, and he was put in charge of Southern Germany, founding a number of colleges. He contributed a great deal to the success of the Catholic Reformation.

Cardenal, Ernesto (1925–   )
Nicaraguan priest, poet and politician. A student activist, he was converted to Catholicism and became a Trappist novice under *Merton in Colombia. He was then co-founder of a Christian commune in Solentiname, an archipelago in Nicaragua, which attracted large numbers of peasants. Originally following a non-violent course, after *Merton's death and a visit to Cuba Cardenal turned to a more active, revolutionary approach and his commune was destroyed in 1977 after an attack on a nearby garrison. After the fall of the dictator Somoza he became minister of culture in the Sandanista government. His *The Gospel in Solentiname* (1975–77, ET 1976–80) gives the flavour of the commune; internationally he is perhaps best known as a poet.

Carey, William (1761–1834)
Baptist missionary. Born in Northamptonshire and baptized an Anglican, he became a Baptist, preaching and teaching, while earning his living as a shoemaker, and learning foreign languages. He became a missionary and translated the New Testament into Bengali. In due course he was made professor in Calcutta and distinguished himself by producing many other translations, dictionaries and grammars. He also contributed, through his protests, to the abolition of suttee.

Carlstadt (Andreas Rudolf Bodenstein, 1480–1541)
German Reformer. Named after his birthplace, he studied at Erfurt and Cologne and then taught at Wittenberg, where he was a supporter of the views of *Thomas Aquinas. However, after a spiritual crisis he went over to the Reformed side and became an extremist, coming into conflict with *Luther. He became an influence on the Radical Reformation, though he opposed its violent aspects, and eventually had to flee to Switzerland.

Carlyle, Thomas (1795–1881)
Scottish historian. He studied at Edinburgh University, where he later became rector. Though he rejected creeds and churches, he was a profound believer in an invisible religious principle and opposed to materialism. He admired the Puritans, and attached much importance to the will of the individual. In addition to his famous *History of the French Revolution* (1837), he wrote major studies of Cromwell (1845) and Frederick the Great (1858–65), his choice reflecting his conviction of the importance of hero figures as rulers. His religious views are expressed in *Sartor Resartus* (1843–4) and *Past and Present* (1843).

Carnell, Edward John (1919–67)
American evangelical theologian. He taught ethics and philosophy at Fuller Theological Seminary, of which he became president. One of the leaders in the revival of conservative evangelicalism after the Second World War, he was particularly concerned with an intelligent and articulate exposition of evangelicalism. His books include *An Introduction to Christian Apologetics* (1949) and *Christian Commitment* (1957).

Carpocrates (second century)
Gnostic teacher. He came from Alexandria, and among other things taught the transmigration of souls and that Jesus was a mere man. His followers were renowned for their licentiousness.

Cartwright, Thomas (1535–1603)
English Puritan divine. After studying at Cambridge, he had to leave when Queen Mary came to the throne and did not return until after her death, eventually becoming professor there. His criticism of the Church of England led to his dismissal, and he left for Switzerland. From then on he was a vigorous supporter of Presbyterianism and

Puritan values. He was one of the most gifted of the Puritans.

Casaubon, Isaac (1559–1614)
Classical scholar and theologian. Born in Geneva, he studied and became a professor there. He then moved to a professorship in Montpellier and to Paris, eventually settling in England. Opposed to both Roman Catholicism and Calvinism, he was sympathetic to Anglicanism. Though he worked on important editions of classical works he was particularly interested in theology and produced a translation of the New Testament.

Case, Shirley Jackson (1872–1947)
American New Testament scholar. Born in New Brunswick, Canada, he studied at Yale and for thirty years was professor at Chicago Divinity School, doing much towards the development of the Chicago school of theology. He was particularly interested in social history and a supporter of the Social Gospel movement, writing on the evolution of Christianity. His best-known book is *Jesus: A New Biography* (1927).

Cassander, Georg (1513–66)
Belgian Catholic theologian. Born near Bruges, he studied in Louvain and Ghent and then lived in Cologne. He sought to mediate between Catholics and Protestants; his main work was *On the Duty of Pious Men who love Public Tranquillity in Dissent over Religion* (1561). He argued that the abuses in the Roman Catholic Church were not so bad as to justify the Reformation but that the claims of the papacy were excessive. He also tried to interpret official Protestant statements in a Catholic way. However, he ended up by pleasing neither side, and his books were banned by Rome.

Cassian, John (c.360–435)
Monk. Born in Scythia, he went to a monastery in Bethlehem, then to Egypt and Constantinople, before settling in Marseilles. He introduced Eastern monasticism to the West. His *Institutes* influenced the Rule of *Benedict and was long regarded as a spiritual classic. His *Conferences* recount his conversations with the great leaders of Eastern monasticism.

Cassiodorus, Flavius Marcus Aurelius (475–570)
Statesman and monk. A Roman nobleman, on the collapse of Gothic rule, in which he had been involved, he withdrew to a monastery which he founded and made it a centre of secular and religious learning, helping to create the tradition which preserved classical culture through the dark ages. He was responsible for the idea that copying manuscripts was a suitable occupation for monks.

Cassirer, Ernst (1874–1945)
German philosopher of culture. Born in Breslau, he taught at Hamburg before leaving Germany on Hitler's rise to power; thereafter he taught in Oxford and Göteborg before moving to the United States. Beginning from the philosophy of physics, he argued that physics was one symbolic representation of reality among many; it is the language of symbols which is important. His major work is the three-volume *Philosophy of Symbolic Forms* (1953–57). He is particularly important for his capacity to enter into the thought of other thinkers and other periods.

Catharinus, Ambrosius (Lancelot Politi, 1484–1553)
Dominican theologian. Born in Siena, he studied law at several Italian universities and became a Dominican under the influence of *Savonarola. Used by his superiors to attack Lutheranism, he offended them by defending doctrines opposed by the Dominicans, like the Immaculate Conception. He wrote his major work, *Opuscula Magna* (1542), in exile in France; he had distinctive views on e.g. predestination and original sin (children who died unbaptized were consoled by angels), but nevertheless played a major part in the Council of Trent and was ultimately made an archbishop.

Catherine of Genoa (Caterinetta Fieschi, 1447–1510)
Born of a noble Ligurian family, she was married at sixteen for diplomatic reasons and after ten miserable years had a deep religious conversion; her husband, having fallen on hard times, was also converted and helped her in caring for the sick in a hospital in Genoa until his death in 1497. Details of her teaching and spiritual life come from an anonymous compilation *Life and Teaching*, published posthumously in 1551. Her teaching here focusses on purgatory as the continuation of a process of suffering which is necessary for souls seeking God, but this is a suffering which must inevitably end in perfect joy.

Catherine of Siena (Caterina Benincassa, 1347–80)
Italian mystic. One of the large family of a dyer, she became a Dominican lay sister, and after three years of seclusion she began to work in public, forming a family of disciples around her. A long series of letters involved her in public affairs, notably contemporary conflicts surrounding the papacy, about to be involved in schism. This prompted a great concern for church reform.

Caussade, Jean-Pierre de (1675–1751)
Spiritual writer. He became a Jesuit in Toulouse at eighteen, and was active throughout his life as a teacher and confessor in south-west France. He was important for rehabilitating mysticism at a time when it was under a shadow. He is known for a collection of notes from lectures not published until the nineteenth century when, along with some of his letters, they became a spiritual classic: *Self-Abandonment to Divine Providence*. His main emphasis was that every situation should be seen as God's purpose for the person concerned.

Celsus (second century)
Pagan philosopher. He was author of the first known critique of Christianity, entitled *The True Doctrine*, criticizing miracles and absurdities; he was particularly offended at the incarnation and crucifixion. His work is known to us only through its refutation by *Origen (*Contra Celsum*).

Chadwick, Henry (1920–   )
English church historian. Born in Kent the son of a barrister, he studied at Cambridge and subsequently taught there, becoming professor in Oxford in 1959 and then Dean of Christ Church; he returned to Cambridge as professor in 1979. He has written many books on the thought and history in the early church, not least on lesser known figures.

Chadwick, William Owen (1916–   )
English church historian, brother of Henry *Chadwick. He studied at Cambridge, and went on to teach there, becoming professor and then Master of Selwyn College. He has written many books on English and European history, particularly during the Victorian period, but his studies extend back through the Reformation and forward to the Second World War. Major works include *The Victorian Church* (two volumes, 1966, 1970)

and *The Secularization of the European Mind in the Nineteenth Century* (1976).

Challoner, Richard (1691–1781)
Roman Catholic devotional writer. Born in Lewes, Sussex, a Presbyterian, he became a Roman Catholic as a boy. He trained in Belgium at Louvain, where he later became professor, and returned to England to be consecrated bishop in 1741. Author of many books and translator of the Bible, he is best known for *The Garden of the Soul* (1740), a popular prayer book for the laity.

Chalmers, Thomas (1780–1847)
Scottish minister. A brilliant mathematician, after he was converted he became minister at the Tron church, Glasgow, where he had spectacular pastoral and evangelical success through his preaching. He left it to be professor first at St Andrews and then at Edinburgh, became Moderator of the Free Church of Scotland, and was a symbol of evangelicalism. He led the movement to have ministers elected by their parishes rather than appointed by patrons.

Channing, William Ellery (1780–1842)
American Unitarian minister. After study at Harvard he became a Congregationalist pastor in Boston. Of liberal views, he moved in the direction of Unitarianism as a result of theological controversy with conservatives. However, while he denied the doctrine of the Trinity and the divinity of Christ, total depravity and substitutionary atonement, he was not interested in developing Unitarianism as a church.

Charles Borromeo (1538–84)
Catholic reformer. Of noble family, he was born by Lake Maggiore and was given his first ecclesiastical appointment at the age of twelve. After studying law at Pavia, at the age of twenty-two he was made cardinal and archbishop of Milan. He was involved in the last stages of the council of Trent and worked to implement its reforms, creating a model seminary, encouraging the religious orders, visiting widely, preaching and helping the poor.

Charles, Robert Henry (1855–1931)
Irish biblical scholar. After studies in Belfast and Dublin, he became a parish priest in London. Research at Oxford resulted in his becoming professor, first in Dublin and then in Oxford, before ending his career at Westminster Abbey. He is best known for his

work on apocalyptic literature; he produced what for a long time has been the standard edition of *The Apocrypha and Pseudepigrapha of the Old Testament* (1913 and still in print).

Chateaubriand, François René de (1768–1848)
French Romantic writer. Born in Britanny, in his early twenties he went first to America and then to England, and was converted to Christianity in London following the deaths of his mother and sister. An aristocrat and distinguished politician, he gained lasting fame from his book *The Genius of Christianity* (1802), arguing for Christianity on aesthetic grounds.

Chemnitz, Martin (1522–86)
German Lutheran theologian. He lectured in philosophy at Wittenberg, becoming a friend of *Melanchthon, and spent the rest of his life as a pastor in Brunswick, refusing advancement. He helped to consolidate Lutheranism after *Luther and was much involved in church order. Among other works he wrote a notable four-volume critique of the Council of Trent.

Chesterton, Gilbert Keith (1874–1936)
English author and critic. A journalist all his life, first an Anglican and then converted to the Roman Catholic Church, he championed the cause of Christianity with wit and vigour, attacking agnostic indifference on the basis of his belief in meaning and common-sense realism. He wrote on many topics, and his novels include a classic series of detective stories with 'Father Brown', a Roman Catholic priest, as the main character. His religious concerns are expressed in *Heretics* (1905) and *Orthodoxy* (1908).

Cheyne, Thomas Kelly (1841–1915)
British Old Testament scholar. He studied in Oxford and Germany, and apart from a period as rector of an Essex parish, held teaching posts in Oxford. He pioneered the critical approach to the Old Testament, and became notable for his extreme and unconventional views.

Childs, Brevard Springs (1923–   )
American Old Testament scholar and Reformed Calvinist theologian. After study at the universities of Michigan, Princeton, Heidelberg and Basle, he taught at Mission House Seminary, Plymouth, Wisconsin. He is now professor at Yale Divinity School.

He is particularly known for his attempt to establish 'canonical criticism', the view that criticism of biblical books must relate to their final form and their place in the canon (*Introduction to the Old Testament as Scripture*, 1979; *Old Testament Theology in a Canonical Context*, 1985; *The New Testament as Canon: An Introduction*, 1984). His distinctive approach to the nature of biblical commentary is demonstrated in his *Exodus* (1974), which makes the history of exegesis an integral element of the process of interpretation.

Chillingworth, William (1602–44)
English apologist. Originally an Anglican, he studied and taught at Oxford, where he was converted to Roman Catholicism and went to Douai. However, when set to write against the Church of England he changed his mind and said that he was a Protestant, returning to the Church of England. He was made chancellor of Salisbury and died in captivity during the Civil War, in which he served as a Royalist chaplain. His best known work is *The Religion of Protestants a Safe Way to Salvation* (1637), arguing that the Bible alone is the religion of Protestants.

Chrysostom, John (347–407)
Bishop and preacher. Born at Antioch of noble parents, he studied law and theology before becoming a monk. When the monastic rule damaged his health he returned to Antioch where he became a famous preacher ('golden mouth'). Somewhat against his will he became patriarch of Constantinople, and proved a vigorous reformer. His measures caused hostility, leading him to be condemned for heresy and ultimately exiled. His works comprise hundreds of sermons and many letters.

Clarke, William Newton (1841–1912)
American Baptist theologian. He was pastor in Massachusetts and professor at Colgate. His thought combined an evolutionary approach with Christian theology; his *Outline of Christian Theology* (1898) enjoyed immense popularity.

Clement of Alexandria (c.150–c.215)
Christian scholar. Probably born in Athens, he became head of the famous catechetical school in Alexandria, but had to flee in the face of persecution. His trilogy, *Stromateis, Protrepticus, Paedagogus*, influenced by Gnosticism, attempted to bring Greek cul-

ture into a fruitful relationship with the truth of the faith of his time, in a concern to win over the educated classes.

Clement of Rome (c.96)
Bishop and 'apostolic father'. He is known only from a letter (I Clement) which seeks to restore order to a community upset by a rebellion. Subsequently much other literature (*Clementine Homilies* and *Recognitions*) formed around his name.

Cobb, John Boswell, Jr (1925–   )
American theologian. Born in Kobe, Japan, of missionary parents, he studied at Chicago University and Divinity School, where his original pietism was shattered, giving place to the influence of *Hartshorne's process theology. After teaching at Candler School of Theology and Emory, he became professor at Claremont, California. From process theology his interests have moved through ecological concerns to a view of Christ as 'creative transformation'. Not least as a result of his childhood background he is also interested in interfaith dialogue, particularly between Christians and Buddhists. His major publications include *Living Options in Protestant Theology* (1965) and *Christ in a Pluralistic Age* (1975).

Cocceius, Johannes (Johann Koch, 1603–69)
Dogmatic theologian. Born in Germany, he studied in Holland, becoming professor first in Franeker and then in Leiden. A knowledgeable linguist, he sought to present a biblical theology and was opposed to the Calvinist orthodoxy of his day. He interpreted relations between God and humankind in terms of a personal covenant, and his teaching was thus known as federal theology. It contributed to the rise of Pietism.

Coke, Thomas (1747–1814)
Methodist bishop. Originally an Anglican, born in Wales, he joined *Wesley, becoming his right-hand man. He was chosen by Wesley as superintendent for America and was made the first American Methodist bishop. He was vigorously opposed to slavery and was responsible for missionary work in the West Indies and Africa.

Colenso, John William (1814–83)
Missionary bishop. Born in Cornwall, he studied in Cambridge and after teaching mathematics at Harrow school, returned to Cambridge to teach and then became vicar of a Norfolk parish. In 1853 he was made missionary bishop of Natal, as a result of which he was forced to consider problems of biblical criticism. His *The Pentateuch and Book of Joshua Critically Examined* (1862–79), which brought out the absurdities of these books if taken literally, led to his excommunication. He also denied eternal punishment in hell.

Coleridge, Samuel Taylor (1772–1834)
English romantic poet. Born in Devon, the son of a vicar, he studied at Cambridge and came into contact with the Wordsworths. A brilliant lecturer, he had to earn his living by public speaking; he had an unhappy life complicated by painful rheumatism and an addiction to opium. As well as being a poet, he had a philosophical interest, influenced by Kant; he was the originator of the term 'existentialist'. Open minded in religious matters, he helped to introduce German biblical criticism to England. He was profoundly original in his views, expressing a subjective religion based on moral experience. His best-known book in this area is the posthumous *Confessions of an Inquiring Spirit* (1840).

Collins, Anthony (1676–1729)
English Deistic philosopher. Educated at Cambridge, he ultimately became deputy lieutenant of Essex. Influenced by *Locke, he wrote many works against the church and especially the clergy, which provoked retorts from churchmen. He argued against the accepted distinction between what is above and what is against human reason and for the efficacy of human reason and free enquiry. His main work is *A Discourse on Freethinking* (1713).

Columba (c.521–97)
Celtic missionary. Born into a noble Irish family, he was trained in monasteries and went on to found several in Ireland himself. Around 553 he established a community on Iona which he used as a base for successful missionary work in the area.

Comblin, José (1923–   )
Liberation theologian. A Belgian Catholic and social critic and member of the faculty of the university of Louvain, he went to live in Latin America in 1958. Expelled from Brazil in 1972 for his commitment to the poor, he was allowed to return in 1980 and since then has lived and worked in a poor

peasant community in north-east Brazil. His books include *Jesus of Nazareth* (1978) and *The Holy Spirit and Liberation* (1989).

Comenius, John Amos (1592–1670)
Bohemian Protestant educational reformer. Expelled from Bohemia as a non-Catholic during the Thirty Years' War, he settled in Leszno in Poland, where he became rector of the gymnasium. The great success of his book on teaching Latin, followed by his *magnum opus*, *Didacta Magna* (1657), on education, gave him an international reputation as an educational reformer. He travelled to England, Sweden and Hungary and ultimately settled in Amsterdam when Leszno was burnt by the Poles. His educational ideals were influenced by his own religious experience and he hoped that education and character development would lead to ecumenism.

Comte, Auguste (1798–1857)
French mathematician and philosopher. Born in Montpellier, he studied science and mathematics in Paris, losing his faith in the process. Under the influence of *Saint-Simon, he sought a philosophy which could command universal assent after the chaos of the French revolution and would replace lost religious faith, and produced positivism. His view was that the human race goes through three stages: theological, metaphysical and scientific. His fervour, which turned positivism into a substitute religion, centred on humanity, even with priests and sacraments, cost him his job, leaving him dependent on followers, including *Mill. His main work is his *Course of Positive Philosophy* (6 volumes, completed 1842, ET 1903).

Cone, James Hal (1938–   )
American Black theologian. Born in Fordyce, Arkansas, he studied at Garrett Theological Seminary and Northwestern University, Evanston, later becoming professor at Union Theological Seminary, New York. A pioneer in Black theology, he succeeded in introducing it to the lecture room, from which it had previously been absent. His books include *Black Theology and Black Power* (1969), *A Black Theology of Liberation* (1970) and *The Spirituals and the Blues* (1972).

Congar, Yves (1904–   )
French Catholic theologian. Born to a devout family in Sedan, he studied for the priesthood in Paris (under *Maritain, among others) and became a Dominican, going to the study centre of Le Saulchoir, then based in Belgium to escape church pressure. Work on *Möhler took him to Germany, where he encountered Lutheranism. On his return to France he went to lectures given by Reformed church professors. He also visited England, encountering Anglicanism in Lincoln under Michael *Ramsey. During the war he was a military chaplain and was imprisoned in Colditz; subsequently he developed a great interest in the Orthodox churches. However, there was hostility to his ecumenical concerns after the war: Le Saulchoir was condemned and his work was censured by his own order. For a while he was suspended from teaching, but the change of climate at Vatican II saved him; he played a major role in its preparation. Failing health has led to his being cared for in the great French military hospital of Les Invalides. Prophetic yet traditional, a loyal critic, and a preacher and pastor rather than an original thinker, he has written influential books, including *Lay People in the Church* (1953, ET 1957), *Diversity and Communion* (1984) and *I Believe in the Holy Spirit* (1983).

Constantine (275–337)
Roman emperor. Son of another emperor, after childhood as a hostage in a divided and troubled empire, he was proclaimed emperor at York and became absolute ruler after defeating his rival Maxentius at the Milvian Bridge north of Rome, allegedly having seen the emblem of the labarum ('In this sign you will conquer') in a vision. He decreed toleration for Christianity, thus providing a turning point in its history, made Sunday an official holiday, and convened the Council of Nicaea. However, the price of the subsequent rise of Christianity to become the official religion of the empire under *Theodosius was its involvement with imperial politics and ideology.

Conzelmann, Hans (1915–89)
German New Testament scholar. A pupil of Rudolf *Bultmann, he was professor in Zurich and Göttingen. He is particularly known for his work on the character of Luke as an author (*The Theology of St Luke*, 1956) and a commentary on Acts (1963). He was also involved in the 'new quest for the historical Jesus'.

Coornheert, Dirck Volckertzoon (1522–90)

Dutch theologian. Brought up in Spain and Portugal, after living in Amsterdam he moved to Haarlem, where he worked as an engraver and publisher. A liberal, he was opposed to the dominant Calvinist doctrines and favoured an inner religion, of the Bible and the Holy Spirit, rather than a visible church.

Copernicus, Nicolas (1473–1543)

Polish clergyman, mathematician and astronomer. Born at Torun, he studied at Cracow and in Italy and then lived in Prussia all his life. Rejecting the established view of the universe dating from *Ptolemaeus, with the earth as centre, in his book *On the Revolutions of the Heavenly Orbs* (1590) he argued that it was centred on the sun. His views were slow to spread, since their significance and truth were not at first appreciated, so he escaped the fate of *Galileo, though his book was banned after his lifetime.

Cornelius à Lapide (Cornelis Cornelissen van den Steen, 1567–1637)

Flemish biblical scholar. Born near Liège, he was trained as a Jesuit at Maastricht and Cologne, then becoming professor in Louvain and Rome. He wrote a series of commentaries on all the Bible except Psalms and Job, which were subsequently used above all by preachers because of their mystical exegesis based on the church fathers and mediaeval theologians.

Courayer, Pierre François le (1681–1776)

French theologian. A Roman Catholic professor and librarian in Paris, he entered into correspondence with the Archbishop of Canterbury on Anglican orders and in 1721 completed a book defending their validity. Censorship delayed its publication and even then it had to appear under a Brussels imprint. Five years later he was formally condemned, excommunicated and fled to England, though he never became an Anglican himself.

Couturier, Paul (1881–1953)

French ecumenist. Born in Lyons, the son of a factory owner with traditional faith, when the family business collapsed he spent his early years in Algeria. After returning to France for schooling he was ordained priest and lived in Lyons for the rest of his life. His interest in the ecumenical movement was aroused by contact with Russian Orthodox refugees and by Cardinal *Mercier's work, and he was instrumental in establishing, by stages, the Week of Prayer for Christian Unity.

Coverdale, Miles (1488–1568)

Bible translator. He was born in Yorkshire and after ordination was an Augustinian friar in Cambridge. There concern for church reform led him to leave his order and become a Lutheran. He had to flee the country because of his fervent preaching, and after helping *Tyndale in translation work he produced his own version, incorporating some of Tyndale's. This was the first English printed Bible, and Coverdale's translation of the Psalms was incorporated into the Anglican Book of Common Prayer. He eventually returned to England, becoming a Puritan leader.

Cowper, William (1731–1800)

English poet. He trained for the law and became a barrister, but suffered from increasingly severe depressions. Becoming more devout as a result of these, he worked as lay assistant to John *Newton, in the parish of Olney, and at his suggestion began to write poetry. Newton and Cowper collaborated on a famous collection, *Olney Hymns* (1779, including 'God moves in a mysterious way'). The rest of his life was dogged by his illness.

Cox, Harvey Gallagher (1929–   )

American theologian. Born in Phoenixville, Pennsylvania, he studied at Harvard and Yale Divinity School, and after holding chaplaincy posts and working for the American Baptist Home Mission Society became professor at Harvard. His best known book was *The Secular City* (1965), which analysed the consequences of urbanization in a secular world and proposed a strategy to meet its demands. Subsequent books have moved towards dialogue between Eastern and Western religions, most recently *Many Mansions* (1989), but none has quite caught the imagination to such a degree.

Cranmer, Thomas (1489–1556)

English Reformer. Born in Nottinghamshire, he studied and later taught at Cambridge. After his ordination, he was used by Henry VIII as a European ambassador in connection with his divorce of Katherine of Aragon and subsequently made archbishop of Canterbury. He was later counsellor to Edward VI, and his ideas moved in an increasingly Protestant direction, in the hope of a union of all the European Reformation churches. His great contribution was to liturgical revision, and he was the architect of the Book of Common Prayer. He was burnt as a heretic under Queen Mary.

Cremer, August Hermann (1834–1903)
German Lutheran theologian. All his life he combined a city pastorate with a professorship at Greifswald. Opposed to liberalism and the Enlightenment, in a book on Paul he affirmed traditional views about the atonement. His surviving monument is his *Biblico-Theological Lexicon of NT Greek* (ET 1878).

Cruden, Alexander (1701–70)
Scottish biblical scholar. After a mental breakdown he was a tutor, sold books and did proof-reading in London. The failure of the first edition of the *Concordance* (1737) by which he is known caused another breakdown, but the next editions were successful and brought him recognition and profit.

Crusius, Christian August (1715–75)
German philosopher and theologian. He studied in Leipzig, where he later became professor. A pietist and conservative, he opposed the deterministic philosophy of *Leibniz and *Wolff and the view that the Bible can be read like any other book. He seems to have been an influence on the ethics of *Kant.

Cudworth, Ralph (1617–88)
English philosopher. Born in Somerset of a clergy family, he studied at Cambridge, where he became, among many distinguished posts, professor of Hebrew and later Master of Christ's College. He was the most prominent of a group known as the Cambridge Platonists, opposed to both atheism and Christian dogmatism. His *magnum opus*, never finished, was *The True Intellectual System of the Universe* (1678), which argued that Christianity is the only source of true knowledge.

Cullmann, Oscar (1902–   )
French New Testament scholar. Born in Strasbourg, he studied there and in Paris. A Lutheran layman, after a time as professor in Strasbourg, for most of his life he was simultaneously professor at the Sorbonne and in Basle. He was the champion of a

biblical theology; his main works, highly influential in their time, were on *Christ and Time* (1946) and *Salvation in History* (1965); he also wrote an influential *Christology of the New Testament* (1957). He argued for a distinctive biblical view of time and an approach to the Bible in terms of salvation history; he produced the image of Christ's death and resurrection as a V-day: the victory has been won, but over the world fighting still continues. He attended the Second Vatican Council and has been active in ecumenical affairs.

Cupitt, Don (1934–   )
English philosopher. He studied at Cambridge, and after work in a Manchester parish returned there. He has taught there ever since. His philosophy has developed into a non-realistic view of religion: human beings make language, values and meaning. It is important for them to rid themselves of outdated assumptions and do this well. Despite his radicalism he still remains within the Church of England. Important among his many works are *Taking Leave of God* (1980) and *The Long-Legged Fly* (1987).

Curé d'Ars *see* **Vianney, Jean-Baptiste Marie**

Cyprian (Thascius Caecilius Cyprianus, c. 200–58)
The son of wealthy pagan parents in Carthage, he became a pagan rhetorician, but was converted to Christianity, and his skill and dedication to poverty and celibacy led him soon to be made bishop. His life was marked by persecution and controversy, and he suffered exile and ultimately martyrdom. He had a high view of the Catholic church ('outside the church there is no salvation') and was a rigorous disciplinarian; he wrote many fairly short works, chief among which is *On the Unity of the Catholic Church* (251).

Cyril (826–69)
Until he became a monk his name was Constantine. With his brother *Methodius, from a Greek senatorial family in Thessalonica, he worked as a librarian in Constantinople. Subsequently the brothers were sent to organize the Slav church in Moravia. This led Cyril to invent a new alphabet based on Greek minuscules, called Glagolitic (confusingly, not Cyrillic, as one would expect, though Cyrillic is named after him. It differs from Glagolitic in being based on Greek

uncials). He died young, on a visit to Rome.

Cyril of Alexandria (c.375–444)
Christian theologian. He became bishop of Alexandria in succession to his uncle. A ruthless controversialist, he vigorously attacked those whose views differed from his, especially *Nestorius, whom he had condemned, though in circumstances which also involved his own temporary deposition. He advocated above all a view of the person of Christ in which the divine was wholly dominant, a stress which favoured the rise of what later became the doctrine of monophysitism (the view that Christ had only one,

divine, nature). He wrote many commentaries and letters.

Cyril of Jerusalem (c.315–86)
Bishop. Little is known of his early years; he became bishop of Jerusalem at the age of forty. Jerusalem was a difficult place to be bishop of, and his inability to satisfy both his *Arian superior *Acacius and the orthodox, not to mention factions, led to much exile. Cyril is famous for his *Catechetical Lectures*, which give valuable information about the worship of the Palestinian church at the time; he also organized the church year into a series of historical anniversaries.

Daille, Jean (1609–85)
French Reformed theologian. Born in Chatellerault, after study at Poitiers and Saumur he became a private tutor and travelled much. From 1625 he was a pastor, first in Saumur and then in Charenton. He attacked the use of the church fathers in theology and believed that all Christian doctrines are either clearly stated in scripture or can be deduced from it.

D'Ailly, Pierre (1350–1420)
French theologian. Born in Compiègne, he studied and taught in Paris, eventually becoming chancellor of the university and confessor to King Charles IV. He was appointed bishop of Le Puy, which he never visited, and Cambrai; he worked hard to end the contemporary papal schism. A theologian in the nominalist tradition of *William of Ockham, among his important views were that bishops and priests receive their jurisdiction direct from Christ and not through the pope, and that popes and councils are not infallible. These views were to be acted on later by *Luther and the Reformation.

Dalman, Gustaf Hermann (1855–1941)
German biblical scholar. From a Moravian background, after teaching at the Jewish Institute in Leipzig founded by *Delitzsch, he became director of the German Archaeological Institute in Jerusalem and then professor in Greifswald. He wrote widely-read (but now dated) studies on the

background to the New Testament and on Jesus: *The Words of Jesus* (ET 1902) and *Jesus-Jeshua* (ET 1929), seeking to demonstrate that Jesus spoke Aramaic.

Dante Alighieri (1265–1321)
Italian poet and philosopher. He was born in Florence; little is known of his early life, except for his encounters with Beatrice, a woman he barely knew but who became for him the symbol of human perfection. After her death in 1290 he studied philosophy in Florence, but involvement in politics led to exile and a wandering life which took him as far as Paris. He died in Ravenna. A supporter of the emperor, in his *On Monarchy* (1310) he argued that for human happiness there was need of a universal monarchy independent of the church; this book was condemned. His *Divine Comedy* (1314) in three parts, 'Hell', 'Purgatory' and 'Paradise', belongs with the world's greatest literature. In his focus on the individual soul and its destiny, he was a forerunner of the later Christian humanists and spiritual writers.

Darby, John Nelson (1800–82)
Founder of the 'Darbyites'. From a distinguished Anglo-Irish family, he was called to the Irish bar before being ordained. Dissatisfied with the Church of Ireland, he broke away and joined a group in Dublin which was to become the Plymouth Brethren. He travelled widely, translated the Bible and

wrote hymns. A gifted teacher, he was often over-prejudiced.

Darwin, Charles (1809–82)
English scientist. Born in Shrewsbury, after study in Cambridge in 1831 he sailed as a naturalist in a naval ship, *The Beagle*, on a five-year voyage to South America. During this time he collected evidence which he used in writing his pioneering book *The Origin of Species* (1859); this was followed by *The Descent of Man* (1871). His theory of evolution, that living beings evolve by natural selection from very few simple forms as a result of the survival of the fittest, led to vigorous controversy with Christian theologians during the nineteenth century. Darwin's views still continue to be opposed by many theologians because of their implications for an understanding of reality.

Davenport, John (1597–1620)
English Puritan. After study in Oxford he became vicar of a London parish, but on clashing with Archbishop Laud in 1633 he resigned and became a pastor at the English church in Amsterdam. Four years later he sailed to Boston and founded the colony of New Haven. He finally became minister of the first church at Boston. He wrote many books, including *The Power of Congregational Churches Asserted and Vindicated* (1672).

David of Augsburg (1200–72)
German mystic. Born in Augsburg, he became a Franciscan, and gained a great reputation as a preacher. Some of his works are in Latin, but he was the first author to write spiritual works in German. He taught the need for obedience and humility, and though his spirituality was practical, it also included the goal of the mystical union of the soul with God.

Davidson, Andrew Bruce (1831–1902)
Scottish biblical scholar. After study at Aberdeen and Edinburgh, he became professor in Edinburgh, being one of the first to introduce historical criticism of the Old Testament to Scotland, though his doctrinal views always remained firmly within orthodoxy. In addition to the Hebrew grammar by which he is best known, he wrote several commentaries and a theology of the Old Testament (published posthumously).

Davies, William David (1911–   )
Welsh New Testament scholar. Born in Carmarthenshire, he studied at Cambridge and after ordination into the Congregationalist church served as a minister and became professor at Yorkshire United College. In 1950 he emigrated to the United States, becoming professor at Duke University Divinity School, Princeton, and Union Theological Seminary and Columbia University, New York. In 1966 he returned to Duke. He has specialized in the Jewish background to the New Testament. His best known books are *Paul and Rabbinic Judaism* (1958) and *The Setting of the Sermon on the Mount* (1964).

De Benneville, George (1703–93)
Universalist preacher. Born in London of a French Protestant family, after preaching in Germany and Holland he travelled to the United States, and in Pennsylvania began preaching universalism, the doctrine that all will be saved. He converted a local Baptist preacher who resigned his pulpit in Philadelphia and with him founded a universalist church, which spread to other areas.

De Foucauld, Charles Eugène (1858–1916)
French hermit. Born an aristocrat, and very rich, he developed a passion for Africa through service as a cavalry officer. After a period of spiritual unrest, he was won back to the Catholic faith by Abbé *Huvelin. He made a pilgrimage to Palestine and then was ordained and became a Trappist monk, later going to Algeria to live as a hermit, first at Beni Abbes, then at Tamanrasset, among the Tuareg Muslims. For a decade until his assassination by one of them he devoted himself to their welfare, also producing dictionaries and translations. He composed rules for communities of 'Little Brothers' and 'Little Sisters', but had no companions during his lifetime; these communities were formed later (see **Voillaume**).

Deissmann, Gustav Adolf (1866–1937)
German New Testament scholar. He was professor first at Heidelberg, then in Berlin. He is particularly important for his identification of New Testament Greek as *koine* Greek (i.e. ordinary Greek, not a special sacred language) on the basis of papyri discovered in Egypt. His best known book in this area is *Light from the Ancient East* (1908). His discoveries led him to see Christianity as a popular cult developing out of a mystical response to Jesus; drawing attention to Paul's talk of 'in Christ', he argued that Christ and Spirit were interchangeable and Paul's belief was mystical.

All this led him to play down the importance of doctrine. A popularizer as well as a scholar, he also had ecumenical concerns and edited a book of essays, *Mysterium Christi* (1930), with Bishop George *Bell.

Delitzsch, Franz Julius (1813–90)
German biblical scholar. Of Jewish descent and a pietistic Lutheran, he was born in Leipzig, and taught at Rostock and Erlangen before returning to Leipzig for the rest of his life. He wrote many commentaries and works on rabbinic studies, but was slow to grasp the significance of historical criticism. Hostile to antisemitism, he nevertheless sought to convert the Jews, founding a Jewish Institute in Leipzig which came to bear his name.

Delitzsch, Friedrich (1850–1922)
German Assyriologist. Son of Franz, he was professor at Leipzig, Breslau and Berlin. His Assyrian and Sumerian studies led him to claim that much of the Old Testament was of Babylonian origin in a controversial book, *Babel und Bibel* (Babylon and the Bible, 1902), delivered as lectures before the Emperor. In addition to major works on Assyriology, he wrote further polemic against Christianity.

De Maistre, Joseph (1753–1821)
French Roman Catholic theologian. Born in Chambéry, he was trained by the Jesuits. Originally a rationalist, he was frightened by the French Revolution and became a reactionary, looking to the church to provide stability. He was Sardinian minister in St Petersburg for seventeen years until shortly before his death. His major work, *On the Pope* (1819), took an authoritarian view of society focussed on the Pope. His views did much to strengthen Roman rather than French influence in the Catholic Church in France (Ultramontanism rather than Gallicanism).

Denifle, Heinrich Seuse (1844–1905)
Austrian church historian. Born in the Tyrol, he became a Dominican and after ordination taught in Graz before being appointed associate to the general of his order, travelling widely with him in search of material for a new edition of the works of *Thomas Aquinas. He then became a Vatican archivist, and from 1887 was editor of the records of Paris university, of which he wrote a monumental history. He also helped to found an archive for mediaeval literature

and church history, and wrote on the mystics and on *Luther.

Denney, James (1856–1917)
Scottish theologian. Trained in Glasgow, after parish ministry he became a professor in the Free Church College in Glasgow. After a commentary on Romans, he wrote his best-known book, *The Death of Christ* (1902), arguing a substitutionary view of the atonement. Becoming increasingly more evangelical in his views, he made the famous remark that he was interested only in a theology that could be preached.

De Nobili, Robert (1577–1656)
Italian missionary. From a wealthy family in Montepulciano, he became a Jesuit and went out to India, where he sought to understand the local culture, dressing as a *sannyasi* (a Hindu who renounces all he possibly can) and living in the Brahmin quarter. He was the first European to know Sanskrit and the Vedas. His methods led to opposition, but he was allowed to continue. His efforts to reconcile Christianity with local culture proved of permanent importance.

Derrida, Jacques (1930–   ).
French philosopher. Born in El Biar, Algeria, he studied at the École Normale Supérieure in Paris, to which he returned as professor after a period teaching at the Sorbonne. Seeing philosophy as a critical reading of texts, he has made critical studies of thinkers from Greek philosophy via *Hegel to phenomenology. A leading 'deconstructionist', taking up ideas from *Heidegger, *Husserl, *Nietzsche and *Saussure, he argues that it is wrong to seek an essential truth behind things, thus challenging the primacy of the word as the foundation of religion and metaphysics. The object of study should be language, which contains only differences. Hence the title of his best-known book, *Writing and Difference* (1967, ET 1978).

Descartes, René (1596–1650)
French philosopher. Born in La Haye, in the Touraine, and educated by Jesuits, he studied law in Poitiers. In 1618 he began to travel in Holland and Germany and the next year conceived of a plan to reconstruct philosophy. Yet more travel took him also to Italy, but in 1628 he settled in Holland, where he lived quietly in the country and wrote his most important books. In 1629 Queen Christina of Sweden invited him to Stockholm to tutor her in philosophy. This

proved fatal since his habit had been to spend the morning in bed meditating; rising at 5 a.m. to teach the queen, he caught pneumonia and died the next year. The new philosophical method that he adopted was based on doubt. Making no prior assumptions, in a quest for certainty he began from the one thing of which he could be certain, 'I think, therefore I am', and used the principle of radical doubt to achieve clarity and distinctness. Coupled with this was a consequential distinction between, and total separation of, mind and matter, the relationship between which his philosophy never resolved ('Cartesian dualism'). His major works are the *Discourse on Method* (1637) and the *Meditations* (1641); their influence on subsequent thought has been prodigious.

De Vaux, Roland Guérin (1903–71)
French Catholic Old Testament scholar. An archaeologist working at the École Biblique in Jerusalem, he was intimately involved in the purchase and publication of the Dead Sea Scrolls. His main works are *Ancient Israel* (1961), an account of its institutions, and an uncompleted *Early History of Israel* (1971, ET 1978).

De Wette, Wilhelm Martin Leberecht (1780–1849)
German biblical scholar. Born to a family of theologians and pastors near Weimar, he studied at Jena and taught in Heidelberg, Berlin (from where he was expelled for his rationalism) and, after a period of enforced leisure which he spent in Weimar editing *Luther, in Basle. He was much influenced by *Schleiermacher's *Speeches* (1799), which came out before he went to university; he followed Schleiermacher in seeing feeling as basis of religion. He made his mark on Old Testament scholarship by arguing persuasively that Deuteronomy was the book of the law found in the Jerusalem Temple (II Kings 22f.). He became more interested in the New Testament in later years and wrote an influential commentary on it, which was conservative in contrast to *Baur, but still offended the pietists by his doubts about the Bible and the rationalists by his negative views of the role of reason in religion.

Dewey, John (1859–1932)
American philosopher and educationalist. Born in Burlington, Vermont, the son of a grocer, he studied at the university of Ver-

mont and Johns Hopkins and became professor at Chicago and Columbia universities. On encountering the philosophy of *Hegel and the biological theories of T. H. *Huxley, he became convinced that everything was interrelated, and opposed dualism. Influenced by William *James, he also became interested in educational theory, stressing the importance of the role of the learner in acquiring learning. A pragmatist, he saw philosophy as a theory of logical and ethical analysis: in *Reconstruction in Philosophy* (1920) he argued that philosophy clarifies ideas in science, art and culture through criticism of beliefs. In *Experience and Nature* (1925) and *The Quest for Certainty* (1929) he presented human beings as more than spectators, who are in a position to change the world in which they live. Influenced by the idea of evolution, he was critical of traditional religion but argued in favour of a natural piety or 'religious attitude'. His views have been influential on Christian educational theory.

Dhorme, Édouard Paul (1881–1966)
French biblical scholar. First professor at the École Biblique in Jerusalem, he later taught in Paris at the École des Hautes Études and the Collège de France; he retired in 1951. He wrote much on Semitic languages and cultures, biblical poetry and religion. His commentary on *Job* (1926, ET 1967) is one of the finest on that book and also one of the great twentieth-century commentaries.

Dibelius, Martin Franz (1883–1947)
German New Testament scholar. Born in Dresden, after study at various German universities and a teaching post in Berlin he became professor at Heidelberg. Initially interested in comparative languages, he came to concentrate on the New Testament, being one of the pioneers of form criticism; he argued from the assumed needs of the earliest Christian community to the forms of the material contained in the Gospels (*From Tradition to Gospel*, 1919). He made a major contribution to the understanding of 'Luke' as an author in *Studies in the Acts of the Apostles* (1951). He also contributed towards the formation of the ecumenical movement as a leader of Faith and Order.

Dickie, Edgar Primrose (1897–   )
Scottish theologian. After studying at Edinburgh, Oxford, Marburg and Tübingen, he served in the First World War, gaining the Military Cross. He became professor at St

Andrews. His writings include *Revelation and Response* (1938) and *God is Light* (1954). His translation of Karl *Heim introduced his work to the English-speaking world and he offered a balanced critique of the early writings of Karl *Barth.

Diderot, Dennis (1713–84)
French encyclopaedist. Born at Langres and educated by the Jesuits, he became a Paris publisher's hack. His intellectual gifts brought him into a circle of advanced thinkers, and he was influenced by *Locke. Following a bookseller's suggestion, he embarked on what became his famous *Encyclopédie* (1751–72), which as well as collecting available knowledge sought to promote deism and enlightened ideas. His work had a considerable influence on Christian thinking.

Didymus the Blind (c.313–98)
Theologian. Blind from his youth, he nevertheless became head of the catechetical school in Alexandria. Though a supporter of orthodox theology as defined at the Council of Nicaea, he was influenced by *Origen and this led to his subsequent condemnation (in 553).

Dillistone, Frederick William (1903–)
English theologian. After study in Oxford he was in charge of a parish in Oxford and then became professor first at Wycliffe College, Toronto, and then at the Episcopal Theological School in Cambridge, Mass. In 1952 he returned to England to become chancellor of Liverpool cathedral and later dean. A man with sympathies as wide as his reading, he has written many books, particularly on Christianity and symbolism and Christianity and the arts. Of these perhaps the most important are *Christianity and Symbolism* (1955) and *The Christian Understanding of the Atonement* (1968).

Dillmann, Christian Friedrich August (1823–94)
German Lutheran orientalist. He became interested in Ethiopic studies and worked on manuscripts in Paris, London and Oxford, before holding various chairs in Germany. He produced an Ethiopic grammar and lexicon, and also wrote commentaries on some Old Testament books.

Dilthey, Wilhelm (1833–1911)
German professor of philosophy. Born near Wiesbaden, he studied under *Ranke and became professor at Basle, Kiel, Breslau

and Berlin. His writings, mostly in articles and not widely available in translation, have been influential in hermeneutics and the humanities. In *The Structure of the Historical World in the Humanities* (1910–27), he stressed the difference between the methods of the human sciences and those of the natural sciences, being particularly hostile to empirical psychology. His main interest was the philosophy of history in the light of the modern historical consciousness. The founder of 'the philosophy of life', he was interested in the non-rational aspects of life and culture rather than logical abstractions. His interest in hermeneutics and culture also led him to write a life of *Schleiermacher (1870).

Diodore of Tarsus (died c.390)
Bishop and theologian. He studied in Antioch and Athens, became a monk and taught in Antioch, having *Theodore of Mopsuestia and John *Chrysostom as his pupils. After a period of banishment for his views he became bishop. Little of his work remains because he was condemned in 499 as the originator of what became *Nestorianism.

Dionysius the (Pseudo-)Areopagite (fifth century)
Syrian mystic. He is named after Paul's convert in Athens (Acts 17), to whom his works were originally attributed. They combine Neoplatonist ideas with Christian thought and made a substantial impact on mediaeval theology, being an influence on, for example, *Hugh of St Victor, *Albertus Magnus, *Thomas Aquinas, *Dante and *Milton. They comprise *The Celestial Hierarchy*, on the mediation of God by angels to men; *The Divine Names*, on the attributes of God; *The Ecclesiastical Hierarchy*, on the sacraments and the three ways of spiritual life; and the *Mystical Theology*, on the ascent of the soul to God.

Dippel, Johann Konrad (1673–1734)
German pietist. Son of a Lutheran pastor, he studied at Giessen and then left orthodox Lutheranism for pietism. He wrote a good deal in defence of his new views, contrasting Christianity with the church and stressing its decline since Constantine. Banned from writing further by the authorities, he studied chemistry in Berlin (inventing Prussian blue), but had to flee for his religious views and took a degree in medicine at Leiden. Again he had to leave, going first to Denmark (where he was imprisoned) and then to

Sweden (where his views gained acceptance but were opposed). He fled to Germany, where he died.

Dix, Gregory (1901–52)
Anglican Benedictine monk and liturgical scholar. He studied at Oxford and taught there. After ordination, he entered the Anglican Benedictine abbey at Nashdom, eventually becoming prior. His *The Shape of the Liturgy* (1945), a major study of the eucharist, was widely influential.

Dodd, Charles Harold (1884–1973)
English New Testament scholar. Born in Wrexham, North Wales, after studying classics in Oxford and Berlin he became a Congregationalist minister and was then professor in Manchester and Cambridge. He had a firm belief that God is Lord of history and that the word of God must be discovered through historical criticism. In opposition to *Schweitzer, in *The Parables of the Kingdom* (1935) he interpreted Jesus' teaching in terms of 'realized eschatology' (i.e. that the kingdom of God was already present in Jesus' ministry); in *The Apostolic Preaching and its Development* (1936) he popularized the term *kerygma*, proclamation, a standard form of which he detected through the New Testament. His views left their mark on the New English Bible, the translation of which he chaired. He wrote two notable books on the Gospel of John, *The Interpretation of the Fourth Gospel* (1953) and *Historical Tradition in the Fourth Gospel* (1963), and attracted widespread attention for his popular *The Founder of Christianity* (1971).

Doddridge, Philip (1702–51)
Hymn-writer. The twentieth child of a prosperous London merchant, he refused training for the Anglican ministry and became a nonconformist minister in Leicestershire. He was subsequently appointed principal of a theological academy and founded a school and an infirmary. He was active in arranging the distribution of Bibles and was concerned to unify the nonconformists. He wrote many hymns, including 'Hark the glad sound, the saviour comes'. He died in Lisbon, where he had gone for health reasons.

Döllinger, Johann Joseph Ignaz von (1799–1890)
German Roman Catholic church historian. He spent most of his life as professor at Munich. Originally a strong supporter of the papacy, he progressively grew more liberal out of a distaste for modern Catholic institutions; a vigorous critic of Vatican I, he was excommunicated in 1871 when he refused to accept papal infallibility. He shared in the foundation of the Old Catholic Church and defended Anglican orders. He wrote important works on mediaeval history.

Domingo de Guzman (Dominic, 1170–1221)
Founder of the Dominican order. Born of an ancient family from Castile, he studied at Palencia, where during a famine he is said even to have sold his books for food for the poor. After ordination, as canon of Osma he founded a community of which he became head until, as chaplain to his bishop, in 1203 he went to the south-west of France, where the spiritualist Albigensian movement was very active. Feeling challenged to combat it, Dominic and some volunteers stayed on and with papal permission went round preaching barefoot, adopting a life of ascetical poverty to further the conversion of the Albigensians. It was against this background that he founded religious communities, first a convent for women at Prouille and then one for men at Toulouse. Refusing a bishopric three times, Dominic consolidated and expanded his new order, but never forgot that its nature was to be a mendicant preaching order.

Donne, John (1571–1631)
English poet. Originally a Roman Catholic, the son of a London ironmonger, he studied law and joined the Lord Chancellor's household. However, his elopement with the latter's niece led to his dismissal and unemployment. When all else failed he took Anglican orders and for his last decade was Dean of St Paul's. His poetry and sermons are among the great classics of English literature.

Dorner, Isaac August (1809–84)
German Lutheran theologian. Son of a pastor, he studied at Tübingen under F. C. *Baur and became professor there, after chairs at many other German universities finally becoming professor in Berlin. He sought to reconcile idealist philosophy with Lutheranism and wrote influential histories of christology and theology which are still significant.

Dostoievsky, Feodor Michaeolovich (1821–81)
Russian novelist. Son of a retired military surgeon, after private education he trained at the College of Military Engineering in St

Petersburg, but resigned after three years. He was condemned to death for revolutionary activities, reprieved at the very last moment, and did four years' forced labour in Siberia with only a Bible as reading matter before returning to the army. This led to a religious crisis and a conversion. From 1859 he was a journalist and devoted himself to writing. His experiences in Siberia are vividly reflected in *The House of the Dead* (1861). Impoverished and in debt through gambling, emotionally disturbed, and a victim of epilepsy, he produced novels like *Crime and Punishment* (1865) and *The Idiot* (1868). Along with *Kierkegaard, he proved immensely influential on existentialism and dialectical theology. He vividly brings home the problem of the individual torn between evil, the existence of which haunts him, and a quest for God through a faith which is quite detached from reason. Of all his famous novels, *The Brothers Karamazov* (1880), with its story of 'The Grand Inquisitor', representing the church as a falsifier of Christ, has been widely used in theology.

Douglas, Mary (1921–)

English social anthropologist. After studying at Oxford she did fieldwork in the Belgian Congo, returning to teaching in London, Oxford and Northwestern University, Evanston. The focus of her study has been symbols, and the lack of common symbols in our time, which she interprets as indicating the lack of a sense of belonging in an ordered society. In arriving at this conclusion she uses two factors, 'group' and 'grid', the former being the experience of a bounded social unit and the latter the rules relating one person to another on an ego-centred basis. In Western society, grid has come to eclipse group. Her views have had some influence on theology and biblical studies. Important books are *Purity and Danger* (1966) and *Natural Symbols* (1970).

Driver, Godfrey Rolles (1892–1975)

English biblical scholar and philologist. After studying at Oxford he taught there, becoming professor of semitics; with C. H. *Dodd he was closely involved in the production of the New English Bible. Several of his editions of Semitic documents have become standard texts. He was the son of

Driver, Samuel Rolles (1846–1914)

English biblical scholar. Of Quaker descent, after studying at Oxford he taught there, becoming Professor of Hebrew. He did much to mediate the approach of German Old Testament criticism and helped to establish critical scholarship in the Church of England. He wrote commentaries on many books of the Old Testament and an *Introduction to the Literature of the Old Testament* (⁹1913) which was the standard textbook in its day; with C. A. *Briggs he edited the still-standard Hebrew lexicon.

Drummond, James (1835–1918)

Unitarian theologian. After studies in Dublin and Manchester, he became a pastor in Manchester and then Principal of Manchester College, London (it later moved to Oxford). He valued Unitarianism for its freedom rather than its denials, and this led to the expression of unexpected views in his books, like the possibility of miracles and the resurrection. His books include *Via, Veritas, Vita* (1894) and *Studies in Christian Doctrine* (1908).

Duchesne, Louis (1843–1922)

French Catholic church historian. After ordination he studied in Rome and travelled in Greece and Asia Minor before becoming professor of church history at the Catholic Institute in Paris. He had to resign at one point because of his critical view of church doctrine, and his *Early History of the Christian Church* (1906–1910) was banned, partly because of its scepticism over traditional legends. From 1895 until his death he was head of the French school in Rome.

Duhm, Bernhard (1847–1928)

German Old Testament scholar. Born in Friesland the son of a brewer, he studied in Göttingen under *Ewald, *Ritschl and *Wellhausen and became professor there, later moving to a chair in Basle. He is particularly important for his work on the prophets. He identified 'Deutero-Isaiah' (chs. 40–55) and 'Trito-Isaiah' (chs. 56–66) as later compositions than Isaiah 1–39, and wrote a major work on the prophets (1916), seeing them as poets and individuals and stressing their experience. He wrote major commentaries on *Isaiah* (1892), *Jeremiah* (1901), *Job* (1897) and *Psalms* (1899).

Duns Scotus, John (c.1266–1308)

Scottish theologian. Little is known of his life; he was born at Duns, near Roxburgh, and became a Franciscan, later studying and teaching in Oxford and Paris. At the end of his life he was moved to Cologne. Critical of the philosophy of *Thomas Aquinas and its attempt to harmonize *Aristotle and

Christianity, he argued that faith cannot be established by any rational process, thus separating it from philosophy, a division which was to have far-reaching effects. In philosophy he made important contributions by restoring intelligibility to the individual (by his concept of *haecceitas*, 'thisness') in contrast to stress on the universal. His early death left his writings in disarray, and only recently have the genuine been distinguished from the inauthentic. As well as notes from his Paris and Oxford lectures there is a *Treatise on the First Principle* and discussions of Aristotle. He was also the first major theologian to defend Mary's immaculate conception. As a tribute to the complexity of his thought the church officially named him 'the subtle doctor'; Protestants found his ideas so obscure that they used his name as an insult: 'dunce'.

Durkheim, Émile (1858–1917)
French sociologist. Born in Épinal, Lorraine, he studied in Paris and decided to devote his career to sociology with the aim of establishing an intellectually respectable science of society. He subsequently became professor in Bordeaux and Paris. Influenced, among others, by Herbert *Spencer, he came to argue that social laws should not be inferred from biological laws. He is best known for his theory of 'collective consciousness', understanding human societies as *sui generis*, and his distinction between 'normal' and 'pathological' social types. In the sphere of religion he wrote a pioneering classic, *The Elementary Forms of the Religious Life* (1912), in which he saw religion, and particularly ritual, as a symbolic representation of a social bond.

Dussel, Enrique (1934–   )
Argentinian Catholic liberation theologian. He studied in Madrid, Paris and Mainz, but on his return home had to flee Argentina as a political refugee and now lives in Mexico, where he is professor in the autonomous university. His particular concern is with the history and philosophy of liberation theology; he is author of the first one-volume *History of the Church in Latin America* (1981) and *Philosophy of Liberation* (1985).

Ebeling, Gerhard (1912–   )
German Lutheran theologian. Professor at Tübingen and Zurich, he has been particularly concerned in relating the theology of the Reformers, especially *Luther, to modern thought. He argues that both must be held together and that theologians must stand up to the tension between historical and dogmatic method, theology and proclamation. He wrote a major study of *Luther* (1970); his systematic thought is represented by *Word and Faith* (1963) and *The Study of Theology* (1979).

Eck, Johann (Johann Meier of Eck, 1486–1543)
German theologian. He studied at Heidelberg, Tübingen and Freiburg and became professor at Ingolstadt. Originally influenced by humanism, he wrote some works which were almost opposed to Scholasticism, but proved an excellent apologist for Catholicism. He challenged the mediaeval prohibition of interest. Until the controversy over indulgences arose, he was on good terms with *Luther, but has gone down in history as the one largely responsible for Luther's excommunication in 1530.

Eckhart, Johannes ('Meister', 1260–1327)
German mystic. Born in Hochheim, he became a Dominican and studied in Paris, after which he was made provincial in Saxony and reformed the monastic houses in Bohemia. Returning to Paris, he taught there and made a name as a preacher and mystical teacher. In the last year of his life he was accused of heresy, but died before he was finally condemned. His spirituality centred on the creation and leads to creativity; he saw the soul as a divine spark: the divine Word is generated in the soul, producing a constant creative energy. His powerful imagery was influenced by *Hildegard of Bingen and *Mechthild of Magdeburg, and

he in turn influenced such diverse figures as *Luther, *John of the Cross, *Julian of Norwich and George *Fox. As a result of his condemnation his thought went underground, but its effect has lasted over the centuries to modern times.

Eddington, Arthur Stanley (1882–1944)
English astrophysicist. Born in Kendal, after studying in Cambridge he became chief assistant at Greenwich observatory, and was made professor at Cambridge in 1913. He influenced contemporary religious thought by his attempts to show that *Heisenberg's indeterminacy principle implies freedom of the will and that reality is structured in such a way as to imply that God is the fundamental principle of the universe. His books include *The Nature of the Physical World* (1928) and *The Philosophy of Physical Science* (1939).

Eddy, Mary Baker (1821–1910)
Founder of Christian Science. Born of a Congregationalist family in New Hampshire, she was subject to convulsions and had two ill-fated marriages. Cured by hypnosis, she worked out for herself a new understanding of Christianity as divine healing. She healed her invalid third husband and took his name when he died, thereafter founding her church. Her belief was that mind or God is the only reality and sin, evil, sickness and death are not real.

Edwards, Jonathan (1703–58)
American Calvinist theologian and philosopher. A precocious child, he had a deep interest in nature. He was educated at Yale, and then became a pastor in Northampton, Mass., where there was a revival, but was dismissed after a controversy because he admitted to communion only those with a conversion experience. He then became a missionary pastor in Stockbridge, on the frontier; later he was appointed president of Princeton, but died soon afterwards. He was instrumental in two revivals, including the Great Awakening. Strict in his *Calvinist views, he also rejected the idea of freedom (*The Freedom of the Will*, 1754). However, he kept his wonder at the divinity of nature, and also held that Calvinism fitted science better than other theological positions. His writing took on depth from the way in which he brought English empirical philosophy to bear on personal mystical knowledge of God; he was widely influential.

Eichhorn, Johann Gottfried
(1752–1827)
German biblical critical and orientalist. Son of a pastor, after studying at Göttingen he became professor at Jena and then at Göttingen. An important figure in the origins of biblical criticism, he became the first major source critic of the Pentateuch by identifying criteria for distinguishing these sources, and argued that the Babylonian exile was the background to Isaiah 40–55. He introduced the classical concept of myth to biblical studies.

Eichrodt, Walther (1890–1978)
Swiss Old Testament scholar. He studied at Greifswald and Heidelberg, and after the First World War taught at Erlangen before becoming professor in Basle, where he spent the rest of his life. In reaction against historicism, his main work was a much-read *Theology of the Old Testament* (1933–9, ET 1961, 1967), which used the idea of the covenant as its organizing principle. He also wrote a major commentary on Ezekiel (1965, ET 1970).

Einstein, Albert (1879–1955)
Physicist. Born in Ulm, Germany, he became a naturalized Swiss citizen in 1900 and an American in 1940. He was professor at Zurich, Prague and Berlin, being awarded the Nobel Prize in 1921. He left Germany in 1933 and spent the rest of his life at Princeton. His major achievement was the formulation of the special and general theories of relativity which totally changed views of space and time and laid the foundations of modern physics. He is of interest theologically because he accepted the concept of God, though not as understood in Judaism and Christianity. He expressed his views on God in his autobiographical *Out of My Later Years* (1950).

Eissfeldt, Otto (1877–1973)
German Old Testament scholar. A pupil of *Wellhausen and *Gunkel, he became professor at Halle. He was uninterested in theology, and his approach was that of comparative religion. He was particularly interested in source criticism and produced a synopsis of the Hexateuch. He wrote a long-lived introduction, *The Old Testament. An Introduction* (ET 1965), which grew increasingly large with successive revisions.

Eliade, Mircea (1907–86)
Romanian phenomenologist. Born in Bucharest, after studying there he did doctoral

work on yoga at Calcutta university and was then made professor in Bucharest. During the war he was cultural attaché in London and Lisbon and then held posts in various European universities before becoming professor in Chicago in 1957. Particularly interested in myth and symbol, he seeks above all to understand their meaning, which he sees as archetypes. He has been deeply interested in the philosophy of *Jung. A major book is *The Myth of the Eternal Return* (1949, ET 1954), which looks at the conceptions of primitive societies with no notion of historical time; *Myths, Dreams and Mysteries* (1957, ET 1960) discusses the relationship between imagination and the unconscious to religious structures. His last major work was a three-volume *History of Religious Ideas* (ET 1979–86).

Eliot, George (Mary Ann Cross, née Evans, 1819–80)
Novelist and translator. Daughter of the agent for a Warwickshire estate, she had her religious views broadened by Charles Bray, a Coventry manufacturer, and she translated *Strauss's *Life of Jesus* and *Feuerbach's *Essence of Christianity*. In 1854 she went to live with George Henry Lewes, a prolific writer, and did so until his death. At this point her talent as a novelist emerged. Her novels, particularly *Middlemarch* (1871–2) and *Daniel Deronda* (1874–6), also brilliantly illustrate the religious sensibility of her time. She married John Walter Cross in the last year of her life.

Eliot, Thomas Stearns (1888–1965)
American/English poet and critic. Born in St Louis, he was educated at Harvard, the Sorbonne and Oxford. Originally a Unitarian, in 1927 he became an Anglican and took British citizenship. His poetry, with its indirect allusions to and influence from the mystics, especially *Four Quartets* (1944), has been particularly attractive to modern theologians. He specifically reflected on religion in *The Idea of a Christian Society* (1939).

Ellul, Jacques (1912–   )
French theologian. Born in Bordeaux, of a Greek Orthodox father and a Protestant mother, he discovered the thought of *Marx at an early stage and became active in politics, organizing small groups committed to social change. He also had a conversion experience. In 1938 he was appointed professor of law at Strasbourg, but was re-moved two years later by the Vichy government and spent the rest of the war farming and working in the Resistance. After the war he became deputy mayor of Bordeaux but found his concern for change constantly frustrated; he then attempted to secure change through the Reformed Church and the World Council of Churches, but broke with the latter over what he considered its naivety towards Third World revolution movements. A professor of law and sociology at Bordeaux university since the war, he has continued to be involved locally with both the church and social issues. He has written many books on both sociology and theology; these include *The Technological Society* (1954), *The Meaning of the City* (1970), *The Ethics of Freedom* (1976).

Emerson, Ralph Waldo (1803–82)
American transcendentalist. Descended from a long line of ministers, he too became a Unitarian pastor in Boston after studying at Harvard, largely disliking his ministry. Resigning after the death of his wife and two brothers, he went to Europe, where he met *Coleridge, Wordsworth and *Carlyle, who were a great influence on him. He then re-married and settled in Concord, Mass., staying there as a lecturer for the rest of his life. His books were largely based on his lectures, beginning with his influential *Nature* (1838). He stressed the 'beauty, dignity and infinite importance of the human soul' and combined a rational critique of traditional Christianity with mysticism. He believed in the divinity of human beings, but was stronger on the individual than on the collective. However, he was no democrat, and only reluctantly supported the abolition of slavery.

Engell, Ivan (1906–64)
Scandinavian Old Testament scholar. Professor of Old Testament at Uppsala, he reacted against source criticism and laid particular stress on oral tradition. He also emphasized the role of myth and ritual in ancient Israel, as evidenced by his major book *Studies in Divine Kingship in the Ancient Near East* (1943).

Ephraem Syrus (c.306–73)
Syrian church father and poet. Perhaps the son of a pagan priest, after ordination he settled in Edessa where he spent the rest of his life, of which virtually nothing is known. His writings are ascetical and polemic and are mostly in verse. He is a valuable witness

to the Syriac tradition and his poetry can be rich and vivid.

Epictetus (c.50–c.130)
Stoic philosopher. Born a Phrygian slave in Hierapolis, he was given his freedom and taught in Rome until expelled by Domitian in 90, when he moved to southern France. He wrote nothing, and his teachings were collected by his pupil Arrian (*Discourses*). His views are closer to Christianity than those of most Stoics, including the Fatherhood of God and the brotherhood of man.

Epicurus (342–270 BCE)
Greek philosopher. He believed that the senses provide the sole criterion of truth, denying e.g. immortality. Human beings should seek pleasure, since genuine pleasure is lived with prudence, honour and justice. Gods exist, but they have no relevance to human life. His philosophy became, with Stoicism, widely influential in the Roman world.

Epiphanius (c.315–403)
Defender of orthodoxy. Born in Palestine, he founded a monastery in Judaea before being made bishop of Salamis on Cyprus. Rigid in his orthodoxy and unable to understand other positions, he rejected learning, criticism and theological speculation. His *Panarion* (Refutations of all the Heresies) is important for the information it contains, among all its polemic.

Erasmus, Desiderius (c.1469–1536)
Dutch humanist. The illegitimate son of a Dutch priest, after schooling he reluctantly became a monk and was ordained. Encouraged by the bishop of Cambrai he was able to travel, and studied in Paris, Oxford, Louvain and Turin. On the accession of Henry VIII (1509) he returned to England, and became professor at Cambridge, being the first to teach Greek there. He next went as royal councillor to the court at Brussels, and, after being relieved of all monastic obligations, settled in Basle until the Reformation arrived in 1529. He spent his last years in Freiburg im Breisgau. A great scholar, he produced an edition of the Greek New Testament which later became the basis of the standard text and editions of texts of many church fathers. His own works were read widely, the best known being *In Praise of Folly* (1509, against evils in the contemporary church and state) and *On the Freedom of the Will* (1524, against Luther). A complex person,

he was his own man, remaining a Catholic and refusing many prestigious offers in order to keep his freedom.

Erigena, John Scotus (810–77)
Irish theologian. Moving to France, under royal patronage he was head of the palace school at Laon. A philosopher in the Neoplatonist tradition, with a knowledge of Greek rare in the West of his time he was able to interpret Greek thought. In his *On the Divisions of Nature* (subsequently condemned for its suggestions of pantheism) he tried to reconcile Platonic emanation with the Christian view of creation and in his *On Predestination* he asserted that God could not know evil and that evil was simply absence of good, bringing its own punishment.

Erskine, Thomas (1788–1870)
Scottish theologian. Trained as a lawyer, on inheriting the family estates in Angus he devoted himself to theology, developing liberal opinions. He supported John McLeod *Campbell in the controversy over universalism and contributed towards the liberalizing of theology. He wrote several books, including *Internal Evidence for the Truth of Revealed Religion* (1820), and his letters are classics.

Eudes, St John (1601–80)
French missioner. Born and educated in Normandy, as an Oratorian (*see* *Bérulle, *Philip Neri) he became involved in pastoral care and missionary work, founding an order for the rehabilitation of prostitutes. In 1643 he left the Oratory to found his 'Congregation of Jesus and Mary' to run seminaries. He is associated with Marguérite Marie *Alacocque in beginning devotion to the Sacred Heart of Jesus.

Eusebius (c.265–339)
Church historian. Probably born in Palestine, he came to be associated with *Pamphilus, founder of the theological school in Caesarea, and later became bishop of Caesarea. He attended the Council of Nicaea under suspicion of *Arian sympathies and offered a compromise creed which was rejected for not containing *homoousios*. But his main fame is as author of a uniquely valuable *Church History*, the main source for the history of Christianity before him apart from the Acts of the Apostles. It is more important for its source material than its judgments, which are influenced by his ideology. He was an apologist for the new

development of Christianity under *Constantine, whose life he wrote.

Eustathius of Antioch (died c.337)
Theologian. Bishop of Beroea and confessor before becoming bishop of Antioch, he was a vigorous opponent of *Arianism at the Council of Nicaea and incurred the hostility of *Eusebius. As a result of his defence of the orthodox line, he was deposed and banished to Thrace; followers who continued to support him caused a schism.

Eutyches (c.378–454)
Monophysite theologian. Head of a large monastery at Constantinople, he was also influential at the court there. He is generally held to be the founder of monophysitism, the view that in Christ there was only one nature, the divine nature. He was a powerful opponent of *Nestorius, who was condemned for going to the opposite extreme, but was himself condemned at the Council of Chalcedon (451).

Evagrius Ponticus (346–99)
Spiritual writer. Born in Pontus, he became a noted preacher in Constantinople, but in 382 went into the Libyan desert to live a monastic life, which he did until his death. He was the first monk to write extensively, and through his work passed on the teaching of *Origen, by whom he was much influenced.

Evans-Pritchard, Edward Evan (1902–73)
Social anthropologist. Born in Crowborough, after studying at Oxford and under the great English anthropologist Malinowski at the London School of Economics, he did field work in the southern Sudan. He then became professor in Oxford. His studies of Nuer religion (1940–56), based on his expeditions, became classics; they provided confirmation of existing anthropological theories as put forward e.g. by Durkheim, and demonstrated how there could be rationality in apparent mysticism and order in apparent anarchy. In 1944 he was converted to Christianity, and his views altered significantly: going back on his earlier approach he argued that comparative sociology was impossible and laws for human social behaviour could not be established.

Ewald, Heinrich Georg August (1803–75)
German Old Testament scholar and orientalist. He spent much of his life as professor in Göttingen, being twice dismissed from his chair, and taught *Duhm and *Wellhausen. He was the author of a pioneering Hebrew Grammar and a five-volume *History of the People of Israel* (1843–55).

Faber, F. W. (1814–63)
English hymn writer. Born in Yorkshire and brought up as an Evangelical, at Oxford, where he studied and taught, he was influenced by the high church movement and after six years as an Anglican priest became a Roman Catholic. He joined *Newman's Birmingham Oratory and then, on Newman's prompting, founded the London Oratory. Concerned to bring spiritual life to the people of London, he was also open to science, natural beauty and secular culture. His many hymns include 'My God, how wonderful thou art'.

Fairbairn, Andrew Martin (1838–1912)
Scottish Congregational theologian. At work before he was ten and largely self-educated, he eventually went to Edinburgh university and after Scottish ministries became principal of two nonconformist Oxford colleges. Open to the German liberal theology of the time because of visits there, he was a popular preacher and lecturer, also in the United States, and did much to further popular education.

Fanon, Frantz (1925–61)
French revolutionary writer. Born in Port-de-France, Martinique, he served in the Second World War and then studied medicine and psychiatry. His first book, *Black Skin, White Masks* (1952, ET 1967), analysed the impact of white colonialism on blacks. He then became head of a psychiatric hospital in Algeria and was a supporter

of the Algerian revolution. His best-known book, *The Wretched of the Earth* (1961, ET 1964), argued the need for revolution in the Third World generally and is a work much noted by liberation theologians and Black theologians. Ambassador of the provisional Algerian government to Ghana, he died of leukemia in the United States.

Farmer, Herbert Henry (1892–1981)
English theologian. He was professor at Westminster College and Cambridge. His distinctive approach was to argue that the interpretation of religion as personal encounter must be extended to areas often seen impersonally, like miracles. His main books were *The World and God* (1935) and *Revelation and Religion* (1954).

Farrar, Frederick William (1831–1903)
Dean of Canterbury. After study at King's College, London, under F. D. *Maurice, and at Cambridge, he became a distinguished schoolmaster (writing a classic school story *Eric: Or Little by Little*, 1858) and churchman. Devout, broad-minded and capable of writing for a wide audience, he was enormously influential. He wrote a best-selling *Life of Christ* (1874); his controversial *Eternal Hope* (1877) attacked the doctrine of eternal punishment.

Farrer, Austin Marsden (1904–68)
Brought up a Baptist, he became an Anglican at Oxford, where he taught all his life, finally being made Warden of Keble College. A brilliant and imaginative author, he wrote books of New Testament interpretation characterized by much typology; however, he was primarily a philosophical theologian. His works explored the nature of personal belief and include *Finite and Infinite* (1943) and *The Glass of Vision* (1948).

Febronius, Justinus *see* **Hontheim, Johann Nikolaus von**

Fénelon, François de Salignac de la Mathe (1651–1713)
French Catholic mystic and quietist. Born in Périgord, he studied at Cahors and in Paris before ordination, and subsequently was involved in mission to the French Protestants in Saintogne. He then became tutor to the grandson of Louis XIV, and in 1695 was made archbishop of Cambrai, by which time he had met Madame *Guyon and become her defender. Two years later he was deposed, following attacks by *Bossuet on his book defending mystical spirituality, and never returned to court favour. A distinguished preacher and spiritual director, he wrote letters of spiritual counsel which were published after his death and much read.

Feuerbach, Ludwig Andreas (1804–72)
German philosopher. He was born in Landshut and studied theology at Heidelberg, but in Berlin was persuaded by *Hegel to change to philosophy. For most of his life he had no teaching post. His most celebrated work is *The Essence of Christianity* (1841), which was extremely influential, not least on *Marx. Denying transcendence, he saw religion as being the projection of human qualities and hopes on to a fictitious God. Theology is anthropology writ large.

Fichte, Johann Gottlieb (1762–1814)
German philosopher. He studied Protestant theology at Jena and Leipzig, but then encountered *Kant's philosophy and went to Königsberg to meet him. He became professor of philosophy at Jena, but was dismissed for atheism (he in fact argued that God is not a supreme being but the essence of all that is); however, ten years later he was appointed professor in Berlin. As well as writing philosophical works in the Kantian tradition, he was also influential on the development of German nationalism.

Ficino, Marsilio (1433–99)
Italian humanist. Born near Florence, the son of Cosimo de' Medici's physician, under Cosimo's patronage he had leisure to translate many Platonic works into Latin, and founded the Platonic Academy. At the age of forty he became a priest and later was a canon of Florence. Seeing a close link between Platonic philosophy and Christianity, he became widely influential well beyond the Renaissance and made a lasting mark on European thought.

Fiorenza, Elisabeth Schüssler (1938–)
American feminist theologian. Professor at Notre Dame university and then at Harvard Divinity School, she has been a pioneer in feminist studies. She is known for her comprehensive study of Christian origins, *In Memory of Her* (1983) and *Bread not Store. The Challenge of Feminist Biblical Interpretotion* (1985).

Flacius, Matthias Illyricus (1520–75)
German Lutheran theologian. He takes his second name from his birthplace on the Adriatic. He wanted to become a Catholic monk, but his uncle sent him to study in the Protestant universities of Basle, Tübingen and Wittenberg. After a spiritual crisis he was converted through *Luther and became a professor of Hebrew. However, he was forced on a long series of travels because of his controversial theology (he had an extremely pessimistic view of human depravity). Dogmatic and strongly dualist in his thought, he wrote a famous *Key* to the scriptures, and the *Magdeburg Centuries*, an influential anti-papal church history.

Fleury, Claude (1640–1723)
French church historian. Born in Paris, he had a Jesuit education and studied for the Bar. There he met many prominent figures, including *Bossuet, and subsequently offered himself for ordination. As well as becoming a royal tutor and confessor, he was abbot of a Cistercian monastery in Brittany and then prior of Notre Dame d'Argenteuil, near Paris. He wrote a twenty-volume church history, the first on such a scale.

Flew, Antony Garrard Newton
(1923–)
English philosopher. Son of a Methodist professor, he studied at Oxford and taught there and in Aberdeen before becoming prcfessor successively in Keele and Reading in England, and Calgary and Toronto in Canada. He is now simultaneously professor at Reading and Bowling Green State University, Ohio. An analytical philosopher, with Alasdair *MacIntyre he edited *New Essays in Philosophical Theology* (1956), an influential collection highlighting the philosophical challenge to theology; his many philosophical works include *God and Philosophy* (1966), a vigorous attack on the logic of Christian belief.

Forsyth, Peter Taylor (1848–1921)
Scottish theologian. Son of a postman, he went to university in his home city of Aberceen and studied under *Ritschl in Göttingen. After ordination into the Congregationalist church he held several church posts before becoming principal of Hackney College, London. At first interested in critical theology to the point of becoming suspect, he increasingly came to stress 'gospel truths' because he believed that liberal theology had no power, and wrote vigor-

ously about sin and atonement. His greatest book, *The Person and Place of Christ* (1909), anticipated much that came a generation later, and he has been called 'a Barthian before *Barth'.

Fosdick, Harry Emerson (1878–1960)
American liberal preacher. Ordained a Baptist, after a pastorate in New Jersey he taught homiletics at Union Theological Seminary, New York. In 1918 he was called to a Presbyterian church but resigned over a sermon he preached against fundamentalism. Thereafter he was minister of Riverside Church, New York. He was an influential preacher and became a much-read author, through his works on personal religion, psychology and biblical criticism. Among his best known books are *The Manhood of the Master* (1913) and *The Meaning of Prayer* (1915).

Foucault, Michel (1926–84)
French philosopher. Born in Poitiers, he studied at the École Normale Supérieure and then taught in Clermond-Ferrand and Paris, being appointed professor at the Collège de France. He made his name in 1961 with the publication of *Madness and Civilization*, exploring the need of culture to define what lies outside it. Suspicious of any universals, instead he examined the role played by such concepts in history, exploring the ways in which they have been used in society. For him, knowledge is power and it is important to see how that power is used. Other major works are *The Archaeology of Knowledge* (1972) and *The History of Sexuality* (1976ff.).

Fox, George (1624–91)
Founder of the Society of Friends. Son of a Leicestershire Puritan weaver, being disillusioned with the religion around him he became an itinerant preacher, suffering imprisonment and beatings. His mission proved successful in north-west England, where he gained the patronage of a local judge, whose widow he later married. Thereafter he went on many missionary journeys abroad. He was led by personal experience to belief in guidance by the inner light, the Holy Spirit within. A charismatic figure, he also had considerable organizing ability and developed those who accepted his teaching into an identifiable society. He wrote a famous *Journal*, published posthumously (1694).

Foxe, John (1516–87)
Protestant historian. Born in Boston, Lincolnshire, he studied and taught at Oxford before becoming a tutor to the nobility, in which role he became interested in history. On the accession of Mary he escaped to the continent and made many contacts there. On his return, in collaboration with a London printer, with whom he worked for the rest of his life, he published his famous *Book of Martyrs* (1563), a great influence on the religious feeling of his time.

Francis of Assisi (1182–1226)
Founder of the Franciscan order of Friars. Son of a wealthy cloth merchant, he was converted after a wild youth and embraced a life of total poverty. As an itinerant preacher he attracted followers and in 1209 formed an order, the Friars Minor (so called because the pope insisted they should take minor orders), centred on Assisi. (A women's order was founded three years later, called the Poor Clares, after a local heiress influenced by Francis.) In 1223 Francis handed over leadership of the order and spent the rest of his life as a hermit. His simple faith, humility and love of nature made him a popular saint, and his devotion was so deep that he is said to have received the marks of the crucified Jesus on his body (stigmatization).

Francis de Sales (1567–1622)
Catholic bishop and devotional writer. Born in the Savoie of noble family, after studying at Annecy, Paris and Padua he gave up a brilliant career to become a priest. He had been haunted by the prospect of damnation, but a vision of Jesus dispelled his fear. At first he did missionary work near Geneva, but was then sent to Paris, where he met *Bérulle and under his influence proved to have deep spiritual gifts. Returning to Geneva as bishop he preached and acted as spiritual director, also writing his most important works, *An Introduction to the Devout Life* (1608) and *Treatise on the Love of God* (1616). His works were important in furthering the practice of spirituality outside the cloister.

Francis Xavier (1506–52)
Catholic missionary. From an aristocratic Spanish family, he trained in Paris, where he met *Ignatius Loyola, with whom he took vows of poverty and chastity and dedication to missionary work. Arriving in Goa, he first engaged in traditional mission, but came to realize the need to perceive the nature of the culture of the people among whom he was working. His work in Japan and India was highly successful and he made many converts.

Francke, August Hermann (1663–1727)
German pietist. Born in Lübeck, after studying philosophy and theology he lectured in Leipzig, where he was attracted to pietism. After objections were made to his evangelical activities, he became professor at the newly founded university of Halle where his enthusiasms could be realized. His social concern led to his founding schools, an orphanage, and various industries to train his pupils and finance his work.

Frazer, James George (1854–1941)
Scottish anthropologist. Born in Glasgow, he studied classics, but then became interested in social anthropology through reading the works of *Tylor. Without firsthand experience, he drew on a wide range of sources to produce his multi-volume work *The Golden Bough* (1890). Approaching religion in evolutionary terms, he saw it as a form of primitive science, the first stage after magic. He proved to be more of an influence on those outside his discipline than on fellow anthropologists.

Frei, Hans Wilhelm (1929–89)
Born in Breslau, Germany, he emigrated to the United States in 1938. After studies at North Carolina State University and Yale he served as a Baptist minister. He then taught at Wabash College and the Episcopal Seminary of the South West, Austin, Texas, before becoming professor at Yale. His main work, *The Eclipse of Biblical Narrative* (1974), shed fascinating new light on the history of biblical interpretation by demonstrating how during the eighteenth and nineteenth century it lost a sense of narrative realism.

Freire, Paulo (1921–   )
Brazilian educationalist. Born in Reçife, he was secretary of education and general coordinator of the Brazilian national plan for adult literacy, but was forced into exile in Chile in 1964. There he worked as consultant to UNESCO and with the World Council of Churches, as well as being a visiting professor at Harvard. He is now professor of education at the Catholic university of São Paulo. Believing that education can be used to maintain the *status quo* as well as to

liberate, through his programmes of 'conscientization' he has sought to develop a form of education which fulfils the human potential and changes society. His most famous book is *The Pedagogy of the Oppressed* (1952).

Freud, Sigmund (1856–1939)
Founder of modern psychoanalysis. Born a Jew in Pribor, Czechoslovakia (then Freiburg, Moravia), he studied medicine in Vienna and specialized in neurology. He developed a method of dealing with hysterical disorders which eventually became what he himself termed psychoanalysis, and then went on to apply the method to himself. This led to two important books, *The Interpretation of Dreams* (1900, ET 1913) and *Three Contributions to Sexual Theory* (1905, ET 1910), which outlined his famous theories of infantile sexuality and libidinal development; from here he moved to the notion of repression and explanations of the nature of neurotic disorder. His books were burnt in Berlin when Hitler came to power and after the Nazi occupation of Austria he moved to London, where he died. An atheist, and implacably hostile to religion in general and Christianity in particular (e.g. *The Future of an Illusion*, 1927), he seems to have accepted Enlightenment views of science and its powers of explanation: however, his analysis of himself may be seen as a quest for self-discovery in a godless world and thus not alien to theological enquiry. Precisely what he achieved by his psychotherapy is still a much-debated question within psychology and psychiatry, but his figure is an important focal point in modern culture.

Fromm, Erich (1900–80)
German/American psychoanalyst. Born in Frankfurt, he trained in Germany but emigrated to the United States after the Nazi rise to power. Pointing to the danger of a desire for collective rather than individual responsibility in his *Escape from Freedom* (1941), he argued that individuality was a development that took place at the Renaissance. His concern was to construct a faith by which people could live, and for this he drew on *Marxism and the human capacity for love. His views, expressed in *The Art of Loving* (1956) and *To Have or to Be* (1976), have proved attractive to theologians.

Fuchs, Ernst (1903–83)
German theologian. Born in Heilbronn, he studied at Tübingen and Marburg, being influenced by both *Schlatter and *Bultmann. He then served as a pastor in Württemberg until 1949, though he was temporarily expelled from his parish by the Nazis. He was subsequently professor in Tübingen, Berlin and Marburg, becoming director of a new institute of hermeneutics. Following in Bultmann's footsteps, he was interested in hermeneutics and in the question of the historical Jesus. His work is represented in English by *Studies of the Historical Jesus* (1960).

Fulbert of Chartres (c.970–1028)
French bishop. Born in Italy, probably near Rome, he studied in Reims and Chartres. He was a brilliant teacher, and made the Chartres school famous, not least through the wide range of his knowledge. He later became bishop of Chartres, and after the destruction of the cathedral by fire, spent his last eight years rebuilding it. He made important contributions to the cult of the Virgin Mary and wrote the hymn 'Ye choirs of new Jerusalem'.

Gabler, Johann Philipp (1753–1826)
German biblical scholar. A pupil of *Eichhorn and *Griesbach, he was professor in Altdorf and Jena. He applied myth to Old Testament interpretation, but his main significance lies in being the first to distinguish between 'biblical' and 'dogmatic' theology. His *On the Proper Distinction between Biblical and Dogmatic Theology and the Special Objectives of Each* (1787) was first translated into English in 1980 in the *Scottish Journal of Theology*.

Gadamer, Hans-Georg (1900–   )
German philosopher. Born in Marburg, he studied in his home city under *Bultmann and *Heidegger and went on to teach there before going to Leipzig. After the Second World War he became rector of the university and supervised its reconstruction under Russian occupation. He then became professor in Frankfurt and finally in Heidelberg. His *magnum opus Truth and Method* (1960) is a classic of hermeneutics, being influential not only in theology but in the social sciences and in literary criticism. It explores how truth emerges outside the natural sciences, examining the place of truth in the experience of art, its place in the humanities generally and its relation to language, and discusses the relation of tradition and prejudgment to language, arguing that the meaning of works emerges only through history.

Galilea, Segundo (1928–   )
Chilean liberation theologian. He works as advisor to the Catholic church Hispanic Apostolate in New York. He has been particularly concerned with spirituality for the poor, having as its model the life and teaching of Jesus. This is expressed in his books *Following Jesus* (1984) and *The Way of Living Faith* (1989).

Galileo Galilei (1564–1642)
Italian astronomer. Born in Pisa, he was educated at a monastery near Florence and at the university of Pisa, where he then taught mathematics. He subsequently moved to Padua, where he became professor. He invented a telescope, and after observing Jupiter's moon came to support *Copernicus's theories of a universe centred on the sun. He had a long-drawn-out conflict with the Inquisition as a result, which led to his condemnation and recantation in 1616, and a second condemnation and house arrest in 1632. He is also important for theology because of his attempts to reconcile his findings with biblical statements ('Letter to Christina of Lorraine'), which mark one of the beginnings of biblical criticism.

Geddes, Alexander (1737–1802)
Scottish Roman Catholic priest. He was a pioneer in the textual and literary criticism of the Old Testament, but his translations of the Bible led to his suspension.

Gerhardt, Paul (1607–76)
Lutheran poet and hymn writer. He was a tutor in Berlin before being ordained, and subsequently became pastor in Berlin and archdeacon of Lübben. Though he was an uncompromising Lutheran, his devotional hymns show the influence of Catholic mysticism. They include 'O sacred head sore wounded', and 'The duteous day now closes'.

Gerson, Jean (1363–1423)
French Catholic theologian. Born in the Ardennes, he studied under *D'Ailly in the university of Paris, taught there and eventually became chancellor. Living in a time of schism, he worked for reform in the church, through prayer and self-sacrifice, but the strain proved excessive and he left Paris to become dean of a church in Bruges. He later returned to Paris, and took part in the Council of Constance which condemned *Hus, at the same time incurring the hostility of the Duke of Burgundy by his views against tyrannicide, in which the Duke had been an accomplice. Barred from Paris, he lived in exile near Vienna before returning to France to spend his last days in spiritual and pastoral work. He was a vigorous exponent of the view that a general council was superior to the pope, and in this way began the move towards a nationalist Catholicism in France (Gallicanism). Known as the 'most Christian doctor' in the Catholic church, he saw the church as the mystical body of Christ and held a mystical doctrine of identity between the soul and God in prayer.

Gesenius, Heinrich Friedrich Wilhelm (1786–1842)
German orientalist. Son of a doctor, he studied at Helmstedt and taught in the theological seminary at Göttingen, later becoming professor at Halle. He was an outstanding Hebraist, and his Hebrew Lexicon and Hebrew Grammar, translated into English and updated at the end of the century, are still in print today. They were in a very specific sense his life's work.

Gibbons, James (1834–1921)
American Catholic archbishop. The son of Irish immigrants, he became archbishop of Baltimore and then a cardinal. He sought to spread the influence of Roman Catholicism at a time when there was much hostility to it and became a symbol of 'Americanism', which had positive effects, including the creation of the Catholic University of America, but drew criticism from Rome.

Gilkey, Langdon (1919–   )
American theologian. After studying at Harvard, Columbia and Union Theological Seminary, he taught at Vassar College and Vanderbilt University. He became professor at Chicago Divinity School. He is interested in correlating Christian theology with the physical sciences as well as with myth and philosophy. His publications include *Maker of Heaven and Earth* (1959), *Naming the Whirlwind. The Renewal of God Language* (1969), and *Religion and the Scientific Future* (1970).

Gilson, Étienne Henry (1884–1978)
French philosopher and church historian. Son of a Paris merchant, he studied philosophy in Paris and was professor at Lille and Strasbourg, before returning to Paris for the remainder of his career. He was simultaneously Director of the Pontifical Institute of Mediaeval Studies in Toronto. Standing in the philosophical tradition deriving from *Thomas Aquinas (Thomism), he regarded it as the best creative basis for interpreting modern culture. His mediaeval studies include a history of mediaeval philosophy and works on many of the principal figures of the period.

Gogarten, Friedrich (1887–1967)
German Protestant theologian. Born in Dortmund, he was a Lutheran pastor before becoming professor at Breslau and Göttingen. He reacted against liberalism from a Lutheran, not a Calvinist background and saw existentialist interpretation of history as fulfilling *Luther's insights. He joined *Barth and others in dialectical theology, but parted company when he became a member of the Nazi-related German Christians; after the war he showed a growing interest in secularization. Major works include *Demythologizing and History* (1955) and *Christ and Crisis* (1970).

Goguel, Maurice (1880–1955)
French Protestant New Testament scholar. He spent most of his teaching career in Paris as professor in the Protestant faculty of theology and Director of the École des Hautes Études. He was the main French representative of the critical study of Christian origins, claiming to adopt a strictly historical approach and mediating current German scholarship to France. He is particularly known for his *Jesus of Nazareth: Myth or History* (1925) and his *History of Primitive Christianity* (1934).

Gollwitzer, Helmut (1908–   )
German Protestant theologian. Born in Bavaria the son of a Lutheran pastor, he studied theology under *Barth in Basle and in Bonn; towards the end of his time in Bonn he became involved in the Confessing Church in Prussia. Conscripted into the army, he was captured on the Eastern front in 1945 and remained a prisoner of war in Russia till 1950, a period which he described in the best-selling *Unwilling Journey* (1953). He was appointed professor in Bonn even before his release; subsequently he was professor in Berlin. Always a left-wing socialist, he was much involved in political issues and the peace movement. His *The Existence of God as Confessed by Faith* (1964), written at the time of the debate over John *Robinson's *Honest to God*, shows the influence of dialectical theology.

Goodspeed, Edgar Johnson (1871–1962)
American New Testament scholar. Born in Illinois, he studied at Yale, Chicago and Berlin and returned to teach in Chicago and Los Angeles. He did pioneer work on collating New Testament manuscripts and studying papyri, and as a committee member was a great influence on the production of the Revised Standard Version. Of his many books, *An Introduction to the New Testament* (1937) and *History of Early Christian Literature* (1942) were widely read.

Gore, Charles (1853–1932)
Anglo-Catholic bishop. A brilliant scholar, he rose through Oxford and Westminster to become bishop of Worcester, the first bishop of Birmingham and bishop of Oxford before resigning to devote himself to writing. He was editor of *Lux Mundi* (1889), a collection of essays which made high churchmen take account of historical criticism, and provided his own provocative contribution. He also had a deep concern for social justice. He was founder of the Anglican Community of the Resurrection at Mirfield in Yorkshire. His trilogy, combined as *The Reconstruction of Belief* (1921–24), was widely influential.

Görres, Johann Joseph von (1776–1848)
German Catholic author. Born in Coblenz, after initial enthusiasm for the Enlightenment and the French Revolution he moved in the direction of Romanticism and Catholic mysticism. He was an ardent German nationalist in the Napoleonic wars and

founded the first important German newspaper. Accepting a professorship in Munich in 1817, he became the centre of a group of Catholic scholars including *Döllinger and *Möhler. His major work was a four-volume study of *Christian Mysticism* (1836–42).

Gottschalk (c.803–69)
Theologian, poet and monk. Count Bruno, his father, forced him to be a monk in Germany; subsequently he was moved to France. Devoting himself to theology, he seems the first to have taught double predestination (the elect predestined to bliss, the damned to punishment). After surreptitious ordination he travelled round Europe preaching his doctrines and was opposed by *Rabanus Maurus, condemned, beaten and imprisoned for life. However, he continued his controversies to the end. He wrote good lyric poetry.

Gottwald, Norman Karol (1926–   )
American biblical scholar. Professor at New York Theological Seminary, he is notable for taking into account the significance of anthropology and sociology for the study of the Old Testament. In his *The Tribes of Yahweh* (1979) he studies the structural formations accompanying the radical social change which is also liberating social change as evidence in the biblical accounts of the exodus and conquest. His *The Hebrew Bible. A Socio-Literary Introduction* (1985) shows how his basic approach can be extended to the rest of the Old Testament.

Graf, Karl Heinrich (1815–69)
German schoolmaster. He recognized that a foundation document ('P') was the latest stratum of the Pentateuch; this came from after the exile, so that in fact the prophets preceded the law. His theory was taken up and developed by *Wellhausen in the hypothesis which bears their names.

Graham, William Franklin
(Billy, 1918–   )
American revivalist. Born in North Carolina, he studied at Bob Jones University Florida Bible Institute and Wheaton College. After a brief pastorate he became an evangelist, but it was when he was President of Northwestern College, Minneapolis, that his fame began as a result of a crusade in Los Angeles. He founded the Billy Graham Evangelistic Association and a successful crusade in 1954 made him a world-famous figure.

Gratian (died c. 1159)
Little is known of his life other than that he was a Catholic monk who taught at Bologna. In his *Concordance of Differing Canons*, which came to be known as 'Gratian's Decree' (*Decretum Gratianum*), he collected a vast number of patristic texts, conciliar decrees and papal pronouncements, with the aim of resolving all their contradictions. It soon became a basic textbook, and Gratian is regarded as the father of church (canon) law.

Gregory of Nazianzus (330–89)
Church theologian. Son of the bishop of Cappadocia, he studied in Caesarea, where he met *Basil. Together they went on to study in Athens. He became a monk and later his father had him ordained priest against his will, but he twice avoided being made bishop. He defended the Nicene faith against *Arianism at the Council of Constantinople (381) and then returned home. His best known work is his *Theological Addresses*, which culminate in an argument that the Holy Spirit is of the same substance (*homoousios*) as the Father and the Son. With Basil he compiled a collection of Origen's works (the *Philokalia*). He, Basil and *Gregory of Nyssa are known as Cappadocian fathers.

Gregory of Nyssa (c.330–95)
Church theologian. Younger brother of *Basil of Caesarea, he became a teacher of rhetoric, which displeased Basil. Penitent, Gregory became a monk and in 371 unwillingly accepted Basil's invitation to become bishop of Nyssa. He played a leading role at the Council of Constantinople (381) and then disappears into obscurity. Superior to Basil in intellect, he made a more original contribution to theology. Under the influence of *Origen, his thought was open and wide-ranging with a universalist hope; he was one of the first to link a theology of the sacraments with incarnational theology. He became known as the 'Father of Fathers'. As well as writing polemic against *Apollinarius and others in his *Catechetical Orations*, he expounded the doctrines of Trinity, Incarnation and redemption, and the nature of baptism and the eucharist.

Gregory Palamas (c.1269–1359)
Greek theologian. Probably born in Constantinople to a noble family, he became a

monk and went with his two brothers to Mount Athos where he became acquainted with the Hesychast tradition of silent, inner, mystical prayer. Political difficulties caused by the Turks disturbed his life at times, delaying his installation as Archbishop of Thessalonica; he was even imprisoned by them. He taught that human nature is a unity of body and soul and that the divine light ('uncreated light') could be seen physically, hence the inclusion of physical exercises in his spirituality. He is one of the most important theologians of the Greek church. His major work is *Triads in Defence of the Holy Hesychasts* (1336).

Gregory of Rome ('The Great') *see Popes of Rome*

Gregory Thaumaturgus (c.213–70)
Greek theologian. Born in Neocaesarea in Pontus of a noble family, he trained as a lawyer. On a visit to Palestine he was converted by *Origen; returning to his native city five years later he became its bishop. He owes his name, which means 'wonderworker', to the miraculous answers to his prayers related in legends. A practical churchman, he was concerned to use all that was best in paganism.

Gressmann, Hugo (1877–1927)
German orientalist. Born near Lübeck, the son of a station master, he studied theology at Greifswald and then Old Testament and oriental languages at Göttingen under *Wellhausen, who was a great influence on him, and at Marburg and Kiel. His range of scholarship was wide: his doctoral work was on Eusebius of Caesarea, and he qualified as a teacher with a study of music and musical instruments in the Old Testament. One of the founder members of the history of religions school, he produced a controversial work on *The Origins of Israelite and Jewish Eschatology* (1905). His interests moved into mythology; he also edited a collection of ancient Near Eastern texts and pictures which was long standard. He reorganized the important Institutum Judaicum in Berlin. A vigorous opponent of *Barth and *Brunner, like *Harnack he failed to understand them. He died in Chicago on a visit arranged by the New York Jewish Institute.

Griesbach, Johann Jakob (1745–1812)
German New Testament scholar. A pupil of *Semler, he became professor at Jena. He

was a pioneer textual critic, and became the first to break from the text of the New Testament which had previously been accepted as the norm (the 'received text'), producing his own, based on critical study of a variety of manuscripts. He also produced the first synopsis of the Gospels, setting Matthew, Mark and Luke side by side in parallel columns. He argued from the result that Matthew came first and Mark was dependent on Matthew and Luke ('Griesbach hypothesis').

Griffiths, Bede (1906–   )
English mystic. After becoming a Benedictine, and later Prior of Farnborough Abbey, in 1955 he went to India to found a contemplative community; from 1968 he has been at Sacchidananda ashram in Tamil Nadu, a Christian community following the pattern of a Hindu ashram. Although still a Christian, he seeks the mystery beyond all doctrinal formulations and revelations. Major books are *Return to the Centre* (1976) and *Marriage of East and West* (1982).

Grosseteste, Robert (1175–1253)
English bishop. He was born into a poor Suffolk family, and his life is obscure until he became chancellor of Oxford, where he had studied, and bishop of Lincoln. He was a close personal friend of *Adam of March and a supporter of the Franciscans. He gained great fame as a teacher, and as well as being a vigorous reformer of his diocese had a wide range of scholarly interests, including astronomy and mathematics. His scientific experiments probably influenced Roger *Bacon, and he played a part in regaining the legacy of antiquity from the Islamic world, which had been in many respects its custodian.

Grotius, Hugo (Huig de Groot, 1583–1645)
Dutch lawyer and theologian. Born in Delft into an influential family, he was an infant prodigy: he was at the university of Leyden by the age of eleven and practising law at sixteen. Two years later he began to hold important state posts. However, his irenic views involved him in conflict with the *Calvinists, and he escaped life imprisonment only by being smuggled in a box of books to Paris. There, in poverty, he produced his famous *On the Law of War and Peace* (1625), which earned him the title 'father of international law'; it dissociated law from theology, and established the principle of justice in an unalterable law of nature. After a return to Holland,

banishment, and further travels, he became Swedish ambassador in Paris, and never subsequently returned to his native land. His main religious work, *On the Truth of the Christian Religion* (1622), was written as a manual for sailors to refute pagans and Muslims, presenting a natural theology based on trust in providence and following the teaching of Christ; it was valued by Christians of all traditions. He was also a pioneer in biblical criticism. In modern times he has become known for his phrase *etsi deus non daretur*, ordering life 'as if there were no God'.

Grundtvig, Nikolai Frederik Severin (1783–1872)
Danish Lutheran. Two conversion experiences brought him first to Christian faith and later to an inability to accept orthodox views of the Bible. In his view the scriptures had now been destroyed by rationalism, so that faith had to be based, rather, on 'the living Word' confessed down the ages'. His championship of freedom in church and society led him to an educational reformer. For much of his life he was preacher at the Vartov Hospital in Copenhagen and was latterly given the title 'bishop'. He was also the author of many hymns. All this left a deep mark on the Danish church.

Gunkel, Hermann (1862–1932)
German biblical scholar. A pastor's son, born near Hanover, he taught at many German universities, most notably at Giessen and Halle. In an early work, *Creation and Chaos in Primal Time and End Time* (1895), he examined the popular mythology underlying ideas of the beginning and end of the world; in his commentaries on *Genesis* (⁵1922) and *Psalms* (1925) he pioneered the method of form criticism, stressing the long period of oral history during which much Old Testament material had been handed down and the way in which that had shaped this material through a variety of forms. He was

the first to talk about the 'setting in life' (*Sitz im Leben*) of the material. He was also a leading member of the history of religions school.

Gutiérrez, Gustavo (1928–   )
Founding father of liberation theology. A Peruvian priest of Indian descent, after studying in Louvain and Lyons he returned to Peru, where alongside being professor at the Catholic University in Lima he has involved himself with the poor. He has been consultant to the Episcopal Conference of Latin America and lives and works in Rimac, a Lima slum. His theology, including a political interpretation of the Exodus and Jesus, is that salvation cannot be seen in any kind of dualistic approach as distinguishable from liberation. In his view Marxist philosophy is not incompatible with Christian theology, and the established violence of Latin American dictatorships may, if necessary, be responded to by violence. His major books are *Theology of Liberation* (1971, ET 1973) and *We Drink from our Own Wells* (1984).

Guyon, Jeanne-Marie Bouvier de la Motte (1648–1717)
French mystic and champion of Quietism. Married to a much older rich husband and widowed, Madame Guyon (the name by which she is known) spent the rest of her life communicating her spiritual experience. For her, Christian life was one of contemplation of God in which the soul loses all concern for itself. Always controversial, and sure of being in the right, when she gained prominence in Paris she was imprisoned on suspicion of Quietism. Though soon released, she was twice condemned by the church and sent to the Bastille for a longer period, despite the support of Archbishop *Fénelon, on whom she was a great influence. On submitting to discipline, she was released and spent her last years in Blois. Her teaching is recorded in *A Short and Very Easy Way of Praying* (1685).

Habermas, Jürgen (1929–   )
German philosopher. Born in Düsseldorf, after studies at Bonn and Marburg he became an assistant at the Institute for Social Research in Frankfurt, and then taught philosophy in Heidelberg. In 1964 he returned to Frankfurt, where he has been both professor and director of the Max Planck

Institute for Psychological Research. A member of the Frankfurt school, he has worked mostly in epistemology, and has especially studied the relationship between knowledge and the knower. This makes him critical of positivism and empiricism. He argues that there is no fixed standpoint which can form the basis of criticism; even science is not neutral in its approach. Titles translated into English include *Knowledge and Human Interests* (1972); *Communication and the Evolution of Society* (1979); *Theory of Communicative Action* (1985).

Hamann, Johann Georg (1730–88)
German theologian. Born in Königsberg, after an unconventional education he became a tutor and then worked for a merchant in Riga. He had a religious experience on an unsuccessful business trip to London. On his return he became a minor customs official to have time for study. He is noted for his attack on the Enlightenment and his influence on Romanticism, being known as one of the founders of the Sturm und Drang ('storm and stress') movement. Finding inspiration in *Luther, he aspired to a personal faith wider than the current Protestant scholasticism. He was an influence on *Herder, *Kierkegaard and *Schleiermacher and in some respects may be seen as a forerunner of *Tillich. His best known book, *Golgotha and Schlebimini* (1784), is a defence of Christianity against the rationalism of Moses *Mendelssohn.

Hamilton, Patrick (c.1504–28)
Scottish martyr. At thirteen he was made abbot of Fern; he studied in Paris, where he encountered the works of *Luther, and at St Andrews, and in 1527 visited Wittenberg, where he met Luther and *Melanchthon, going on to the new Protestant university in Marburg. There he wrote his one work, *Patrick's Pleas*. On his return to Scotland he was accused of heresy, but converted *Alesius, who had been appointed to convince him of his errors. He was burnt as a heretic.

Harnack, Adolf von (1851–1930)
German church historian. Son of a Lutheran scholar, after studying at Leipzig he became professor at Giessen, Marburg and Berlin (though because he had become suspect to it, the church denied him all recognition in this last post). A man of immense learning, he wrote major works on church history (*History of Dogma*, 1886–9; *The Mission and Expansion of Christianity*, 1902, enlarged 1924) as well as (in more conservative vein) on the New Testament. His theological views were popularized in his 1900 lectures *What is Christianity?*: for him, Christianity was about the Fatherhood of God, the infinite worth of the individual soul and the commandment to love. In his old age he clashed with Barth, who was hostile to him for his liberal views and his support of the First World War. This was an encounter of total mutual incomprehension.

Haroutunian, Joseph (1904–68)
American Presbyterian theologian. He was educated at Columbia and Union Theological Seminary, New York, and taught at Wellesley College, McCormick Theological Seminary and Chicago University. Interested in the essential nature of human life as being-in-community, he developed a 'transpersonal' understanding of Christianity. The author of several books, including *God with Us* (1965), he held that human life is fulfilled in the experience of love.

Harris, James Rendel (1852–1941)
English biblical scholar. Born in Plymouth and educated in Cambridge, he emigrated to the United States and taught at Johns Hopkins university, from which he was dismissed for his protests against vivisection. Eventually returning to England, he finally became keeper of manuscripts at the John Rylands Library in Manchester. An eccentric but prolific scholar, he edited many ancient texts; a liberal Christian, he was also concerned for human and animal life.

Hartmann, Eduard von (1842–1906)
German philosopher. His 'transcendental realism' was a combination of *Hegelian idealism with *Schopenhauer's philosophy of the will. Idea and will are the attributes of a metaphysical being active in the unconscious. In his recognition of the importance of the unconscious he anticipated *Freud.

Hartshorne, Charles (1897–)
American philosopher. After study at Haverford and Harvard, Freiburg and Marburg, he became professor in Chicago and at Emory, and at the university of Texas. A 'process' philosopher, who is much indebted in his thought to *Whitehead but differs from him in approach, he has been a leading advocate of a new view of God, characterized by

the term 'panentheism', the doctrine that all is in God (this differs from pantheism by holding that God's reality is not exhausted by the fact that God includes the world). The most important difference between panentheism and the classical view of God is that it introduces change, temporality and relationality into the being of God. This view is claimed to have a close affinity to the biblical view of God. His major works include *Man's Vision of God* (1941), *The Divine Relativity* (1948), and *A Natural Theology for Our Time* (1967).

Harvey, Van Austin (1926–   )
American theologian. Born in Hankow, China, he studied at Occidental College, Yale and Marburg. After teaching at Princeton and at Perkins School of Theology at Southern Methodist University, he became professor in the university of Pennsylvania, Philadelphia and in 1977 at Stanford. His major work *The Historian and the Believer* (1966) is an influential account of the impact of modern historical critical study on religious belief; he is also known for his work on the nineteenth century and his *Handbook of Theological Terms* (1964).

Hastings, James (1852–1922)
Scottish minister. After studies at Aberdeen university, he was a minister in the Free Church and held several pastoral posts before retiring to do editorial work. He founded and edited the *Expository Times* and also edited a *Dictionary of the Bible* (1898–1904), and the *Encyclopaedia of Religion and Ethics* (1908–26); he remained a splendid preacher, always preaching without notes.

Hatch, Edwin (1835–89)
Anglican scholar. After studies at Oxford he held a variety of posts in Canada and England, finally teaching church history at Oxford. A controversial book on *The Organization of the Early Christian Churches* (1881) argued that the episcopate derived from the financial administrators of Greek religious associations (*episkopoi*), and subsequently he developed this view further. However, his name has gone down to posterity as editor of a Greek concordance to the New Testament, still used, which was completed after his death by H. A. Redpath.

Headlam, Arthur Cayley (1862–1947)
Anglican theologian. Born in Durham, after study at Oxford he became professor in London and Oxford, and later bishop of Gloucester. Originally a New Testament scholar and co-author (with W. Sanday) of a long-lived commentary on *Romans* (1895), after the First World War he became an influential figure with a concern for the reunion of the Christian churches. He was opposed to any formation of ecclesiastical parties.

Hefele, Karl Joseph (1809–93)
Catholic church historian. After being professor at Tübingen he became bishop of Rottenburg and was involved in the preparations for Vatican I. He was one of those most opposed to the definition of papal infallibility, but remained obedient after the event. He wrote a nine-volume history of the councils of the church (1855–90).

Hegel, Georg Wilhelm Friedrich (1770–1831)
German philosopher. Born in Stuttgart, he studied theology in Tübingen and while tutor in Switzerland wrote a life of Christ, seeing him not as a moral teacher but as one in whom virtue and vice were transcended in an infinite life. After various teaching posts he became professor of philosophy first in Heidelberg and then in Berlin, succeeding *Fichte. In the idealist tradition, he is well known for his view of historical development as a threefold process of thesis, antithesis, synthesis, representing a dialectical evolution of Spirit, i.e. God in process. Truth is a totality, rather than the perquisite of individual disciplines. He also applied this approach to Christianity. His views were very influential, not least on *Baur, *Feuerbach, *Marx and *Strauss. Many of his best known books arose out of lecture courses in Berlin, including *Philosophy of History*, *Philosophy of Religion* and *Aesthetics*.

Hegesippus (second century)
Church historian. Little is known of him, but he seems to have been a converted Jew from Palestine. *Eusebius preserves extracts from his *Memoirs*, which as well as being a historical survey were an attack on the Gnostics.

Heidegger, Martin (1889–1976)
German existentialist philosopher. Son of a Catholic sexton in Baden, after studying at a Jesuit seminary he studied at Freiburg

university under *Husserl. He lectured there, and then became professor of philosophy at Marburg, but returned to Freiburg in 1929 as Husserl's successor. He remained there until the end of the Second World War, when he came under justified suspicion for sympathies with the Nazi regime. Subsequently he lived in seclusion in the Black Forest. In his most important work, *Being and Time* (1927, ET 1962), he analysed the distinctiveness of human existence as care, characterized by possibility, facticity and fallenness, seeing human beings as thrown into a world in which they have to cope with death and are faced with the alternatives of authentic and inauthentic existence. This existentialist philosophy was welcomed as a vehicle for the communication of Christianity in the modern world, especially by *Bultmann in his programme of demythologization. There is argument over how Heidegger's later philosophy relates to his early work, but it too has been influential on theology.

Heiler, Friedrich (1892–1967)
German theologian. Originally a Roman Catholic, after studying at Munich, he became a Lutheran in Uppsala, being influenced by *Söderblom. In 1922 he was made professor of comparative religion in Marburg. He is best known for his book on *Prayer* (1918), which classifies types of prayer and illustrates them from many religions. He distinguished between mystical and prophetic spirituality. Under the influence of *von Hügel, he came to be more sympathetic to Catholicism and was also involved in the ecumenical movement.

Heim, Karl (1874–1958)
German Lutheran theologian. Born in Württemberg, and a lifelong pietist, he studied in Tübingen and then was a pastor and schoolmaster before becoming professor in Münster and, in 1920, in Tübingen. Differing markedly from *Barth and *Bultmann, who overshadowed him, he sought to reconcile the whole of human existence in the modern world with faith in Christ. Though he vowed never to write a dogmatic theology, in his long life he covered most aspects of Christian theology, writing more than the books on theology and natural science for which he was latterly known. In his apologetic he was influenced over the years by many thinkers including *Husserl and *Buber (whose distinction between I-Thou and I-It was taken up into his idea of a 'God dimen-

sion' which is the presupposition of meaningful living). Though differing with Barth over natural theology, he too was an opponent of National Socialism. Perhaps more than any other, he was the average German pastor's theologian.

Heisenberg, Werner (1901–76)
German physicist. Born in Würzburg, after studying in Munich he taught in Göttingen; he was professor at Leipzig from 1927 and then directed the German project to build an atomic bomb. After the war he helped to rebuild scientific research in Germany, becoming director of the Max Planck Institute in Göttingen. His discovery of the 'principle of indeterminacy', that at the most microscopic levels it is impossible to produce a measurement in terms of space and time, showed up the limits of classical physics and was seized on by philosophers and theologians as support for their theories.

Heitmüller, Wilhelm (1869–1926)
German New Testament scholar. Born near Hanover, he was professor in Marburg, Tübingen and Bonn and was *Bultmann's teacher. A member of the history of religions school, he argued that the sacraments should be seen in the context of Hellenistic religion. Most of his work was in article form.

Hendry, George Stuart (1904–   )
American theologian. He studied in his home city of Aberdeen and also in Edinburgh, Tübingen and Berlin, and was then a parish minister in Scotland for twenty years. In 1949 he became professor of systematic theology at Princeton Seminary. He was interested in relating Reformed theology to contemporary concerns. His writings include *The Gospel of the Incarnation, The Holy Spirit in Christian Theology* (1957) and *The Theology of Nature* (1980).

Hengel, Martin (1926–   )
German New Testament scholar. After war service and working in the family textile business he became professor in Erlangen and Tübingen, making his name with *Judaism and Hellenism* (ET 1974), which demonstrated that Hellenistic influence on Palestine after Alexander the Great was much greater than usually assumed. Subsequent studies have focussed more directly on the New Testament and have combined great historical scholarship with a conservative and pietistic approach.

Hengstenberg, Ernst Wilhelm
(1802–69)
German Old Testament scholar. After studies in Bonn he taught in Berlin. Though brought up a rationalist, he was influenced by pietism and became a spokesman of Lutheran orthodoxy, vigorously opposing biblical criticism. He wrote commentaries on many biblical books.

Henry, Carl F. H. (1913–   )
American theologian. Born in New York City of immigrant parents, he grew up on Long Island. After working as a journalist for a time he was converted and went to study at Wheaton College and Northern Baptist Seminary, Chicago. He spent some time in the pastorate, returning to Wheaton as professor. He then moved to Fuller Theological Seminary, Pasadena. From 1956 to 1971 he was editor of *Christianity Today*; he was then appointed professor at Eastern Baptist Seminary, Philadelphia, but went on to work full time as evangelist, writer and lecturer. A prolific writer, as well as producing a six-volume apologetic *God, Revelation and Authority* (1976–83) he has been a spokesman on social and ethical issues for evangelical Christianity; his views are expressed in two major books, *The Uneasy Conscience of Modern Fundamentalism* (1947) and *Christian Personal Ethics* (1956).

Henry, Matthew (1662–1714)
Biblical interpreter. Son of an evangelical minister, he studied law in London. He was then ordained a Presbyterian minister, first serving in Chester and then in Hackney. He made exposition of the Bible his main concern, producing a lengthy spiritualized exposition. This led to a seven-volume commentary which is still held in esteem, though it is hardly in the critical tradition.

Herbert of Cherbury, Edward
(1583–1648)
English philosopher. After an eventful youth he became ambassador to Paris, where he wrote (in Latin) a philosophical treatise attacking empiricism. He went on to write on religion. A forerunner of deism, he defended a rational religion based on innate ideas, namely that there is a God, who ought to be worshipped, principally through virtue; that repentance is a duty and that there is another life with rewards and punishments. He was the first Lord Herbert of Cherbury.

Herbert, George (1593–1633)
English poet. Younger brother of Edward *Herbert, he studied classics at Cambridge and was also a gifted musician. He became public orator at Cambridge, though he spent most of his time at court. The death of King James I and his patrons led him to be ordained five years later, and he spent the last years of his life as a parish priest near Salisbury. He wrote an account of the English clergyman, *A Priest to the Temple*, published posthumously; he is best known for his poems, full of Anglican spirituality.

Herder, Johann Gottfried von
(1744–1803)
German writer and philosopher. After study in Königsberg, in due course he became court preacher in Weimar. A disciple of *Kant and *Hamann, he reacted to eighteenth-century rationalism: the focal point of his thought was 'humanity', of which religion is the highest expression. In his book *The Spirit of Hebrew Poetry* (1782), by empathy he sought to understand the Bible in a human way. He proved to be a forerunner of *Schleiermacher and the history of religions school.

Hermas (second century)
Roman Christian writer. All we know of him is from his book *The Shepherd*, which says he was a freedman who made money by sometimes shady means, lost it in a persecution and with his family had to do penance. This book is an apocalyptic work concerned with the need for penance and indicating the possibility of the forgiveness of sins at least once after baptism.

Herrmann, Johann William (1846–1922)
German theologian. After teaching at Halle, he became professor at Marburg. In the Idealist tradition, influenced by *Kant and *Ritschl, he saw God as the power of goodness and Jesus as an exemplary man; even if Jesus never existed, his portrait was still valid. His book *The Communion of the Christian with God* (1886) was regarded as almost a paradigm of the liberal theology against which *Barth and dialectical theology reacted.

Heyne, Christian Gottlob (1729–1812)
German classical scholar. He analysed myth, distinguishing it from poetry. His approach led to the abandonment of the idea that the biblical authors were deliberately deceptive in their writing.

Hick, John Harwood (1922–   )
English philosopher of religion. He studied in Edinburgh, Oxford and Cambridge, becoming professor in Birmingham (where he was deeply involved in race relations) and Claremont. A United Reformed Church minister, he was twice indicted for heresy in the United States. He became well known through his *Evil and the God of Love* (1966), offering an alternative, *Irenaean approach to the predominantly *Augustinian interpretation of evil and remained in the public eye through his editorship of *The Myth of God Incarnate* (1977), questioning the doctrine of the Incarnation, and *The Myth of Christian Uniqueness* (1989), and arguing for religious pluralism, in which with others he 'crossed the Rubicon' of claiming that Christians may believe that salvation need not necessarily be exclusively through Christ. In his philosophical work he introduced the idea of 'eschatological verification' as a way of justifying Christian beliefs.

Hilary of Poitiers (c.315–67)
French theologian. Born of a prominent family, after a classical education he was converted and made bishop of Poitiers by popular acclaim. Banished to Phrygia for his defence of *Athanasius in the anti-*Arian disputes, he had an opportunity to get to know Eastern theology, which influenced him, to the degree that his christology is almost monophysite (suggesting that Christ had only one, divine, nature). For his stance he became known as the 'Athanasius of the West'. Chief among his works, which are not easy to understand, is *On the Trinity*.

Hildegard of Bingen (1098–1179)
German mystic. Born of a noble family at Böckelheim on the river Nahe, and experiencing visions from childhood, she was brought up by a recluse called Jutta, who formed a Benedictine community. At eighteen she joined the community, and twenty years later became its abbess. She described her visions in her main work *Scivias*, which has an apocalyptic flavour. Her correspondence and travels in Germany and France made her influential and she also wrote on medicine and natural history, created an alphabet and language of her own, and composed music.

Hillel (active c.20 BCE–15 CE)
Liberal Pharisee. He worked in Jerusalem and was the founder of a school of rabbis which became dominant after the destruction of the Jerusalem temple in 70 CE (his opponent was *Shammai). He interpreted the law in a liberal way and wrote seven rules for scriptural interpretation (Middoth).

Hilton, Walter (died 1396)
English mystic. Little certain is known of his career; he studied at Cambridge and became an Augustinian canon in Thurgarton, Nottinghamshire. He is particularly remembered for *The Scale of Perfection*, a mystical work which describes the journey of the soul to the heavenly Jerusalem.

Hippolytus of Rome (c.170–236)
Roman churchman. Little is known of his life, probably because he was involved in disputes with the mainstream church (including one over the terms on which sinners could be readmitted to the church, in which he took a hard line) and because he wrote in Greek. This led to later confusion over his identity. He was the last major Eastern church writer working in Rome, and his *Apostolic Tradition* gives an important picture of church life there in the second century, particularly its liturgy; his *Refutation of all Heresies* is the longest of the anti-Gnostic treatises. His *Commentary on Daniel* is the oldest to come down to us in its entirety; he was the first to construct a scheme for calculating Easter independent of Judaism.

Hobbes, Thomas (1588–1679)
English political philosopher. Son of a clergyman, he travelled abroad a great deal as a tutor and was influenced by Francis *Bacon and *Galileo. Unpopular with both sides during the Civil War for his political views, he went into exile, and was tutor to the future Charles II in Paris. In 1651 he returned to England and accepted the Commonwealth government. His *magnum opus*, *Leviathan*, appeared the same year. It is a defence of political absolutism: the state is the 'mortal god' which alone stands between human beings and nature. The church is subordinate to the secular state and the creed is said as an act of obedience to state law.

Hocking, William Ernest (1873–1966)
American philosopher. He was professor at Harvard. In the Idealist tradition, he was a critic of the traditional missionary enterprise: missionaries were to foster inter-cultural relations in a way which would lead to a synthesis of religions. He was concerned to interpret the knowledge of God in terms

of the meaning of religion in historical and personal experiences, and he developed this interest in *The Meaning of God in Human Experience* (1912).

Hodge, Charles (1797–1878)
American Calvinist theologian. He was born in Philadelphia, son of an army surgeon, and educated at Princeton, where he remained for the rest of his life. He was a great controversialist, upholding traditional *Calvinism with rigorous arguments, in a system which he believed to be faithful to the Westminster Confession and the Reformation. He defended a supernaturally inspired Bible. This approach came to be known as Princeton theology and was a great influence on American Presbyterianism. He wrote a three-volume *Systematic Theology* (1871–73).

Hodgson, Leonard (1889–1969)
English theologian. After studying at Oxford, he was ordained and returned to teach there until 1925, when he became professor at General Theological Seminary, New York. He returned to become, successively, a canon of Winchester cathedral, professor at Oxford and warden of William Temple College, Rugby. He exercised considerable influence on a generation of later Anglican theological critics (including Dennis *Nineham) with his rigorous insistence on the need to take historical consciousness seriously. His approach is best exemplified by his 1955–1957 Gifford Lectures, *For Faith and Freedom*, with their memorable question, 'What must the truth have been and be if that is how it looked to men who thought and wrote like that?'

Höffding, Harald (1843–1931)
Danish philosopher. He was professor in the university of Copenhagen. He saw religion as evaluation rather than explanation: religious and scientific explanation cannot be reconciled and this constantly creates problems, but religion plays a vital role in the conservation of values, thus encouraging the moral life. His works include a *History of Philosophy* (1894, ET 1900) and a *Philosophy of Religion* (1901, ET 1906).

Hofmann, Johann Christian Konrad von (1830–77)
German Lutheran theologian. Born in Nuremberg, he studied at Erlangen and taught there most of his life. He was particularly concerned to relate biblical theology and

dogmatics in the form of a 'salvation history' (*Heilsgeschichte*), in which prophecy and fulfilment were related. Hence the title of his most important work: *Prophecy and Fulfilment* (1841–44).

Holl, Karl (1866–1926)
German church historian. He was born in Tübingen, where he was professor before moving to Berlin. Concerned with exact historical and philological study, with *Harnack he edited an edition of the Greek fathers; his writing on *Luther, especially *The Cultural Significance of the Reformation* (ET 1959), was a great influence on neo-orthodoxy.

Holland, Henry Scott (1847–1918)
English theologian. Born in Herefordshire, after studying at Oxford he taught there, and then became a canon of St Paul's; he returned as professor in 1910. He was associated with the contributors to *Gore's *Lux Mundi* (1889) in a liberal approach and was also a strong advocate of social reform. The same year he founded the Christian Social Union with *Westcott as president. Most of his books were collections of sermons.

Holtzmann, Heinrich Julius (1832–1910)
German New Testament scholar. Born in Karlsruhe, he studied in Berlin, and after a pastorate in Baden became professor at Heidelberg and then Strasbourg. He developed a hypothesis based on the presupposition that Mark was the earliest of the Gospels at a time when the priority of Mark was hardly accepted. He went on to develop a two-stage interpretation in Jesus' career, of success followed by failure. His liberal views involved him in church controversies.

Hontheim, Johann Nikolaus von (1701–90)
He was born in Trier, where, after study at Louvain, he spent most of his life, being ordained priest and later becoming assistant bishop. In 1742 he began to investigate the historical basis of the papacy and in the Latin work which resulted, *The State of the Church and the Legitimate Authority of the Roman Pontiff* (1763), while recognizing the pope as head of the church, attacked the power the papacy had gained in the Middle Ages. He argued that church affairs should be basically under the control of bishops and civil authorities. The book was banned, but the pseudonym under which it was published, Justinus Febronius, gave its

name to a movement, Febronianism. Hontheim later published a recantation, but with little change of view.

Hooke, Samuel Henry (1874–1968)
English orientalist. After study at Cambridge he later became professor of Old Testament in the university of London. He wrote widely on biblical topics and Near Eastern religion, and a representative collection of his studies appeared in *The Siege Perilous* (1956). However, it was as editor of a volume of essays entitled *Myth and Ritual* (1933) that he became prominent. The authors, influenced by British anthropology, argued that there was a fundamental pattern underlying all Near Eastern religions to which Israelite religion conformed. This gave rise to a myth and ritual school, which came to extend to Scandinavian scholarship (*see* *Engnell).

Hooker, Richard (1553–1600)
Anglican churchman. Born near Exeter, he studied at Oxford, where he became a professor, though he spent most of his life in charge of parishes and as a chaplain to lawyers in London. He was a skilful champion of Anglicanism; his great work is the *Treatise on the Laws of Ecclesiastical Polity* (1594–97, some books appeared posthumously), which defended the Church of England against Puritan criticism with an appeal to natural law and common consent. However, he had a markedly low-church view of the sacraments, reflected both in his eucharistic doctrine and his denial of the need for episcopal ordination.

Hopkins, Gerard Manley (1844–89)
English poet. Born in Stratford, Essex, and brought up as an Anglican, he was received into the Roman Catholic church by *Newman when studying at Oxford (where he was a pupil of *Jowett and a follower of *Pusey). He then became a Jesuit. After ordination he held several teaching posts and in 1884 became professor of Greek in Dublin. His sensitive and often agonized poetry, the most noted of which is 'The Wreck of the Deutschland', was collected by Robert *Bridges and published posthumously (1918)

Horkheimer, Max (1895–1973)
German social theorist. Born in Stuttgart, he became director of the Institute for Social Research in Frankfurt in 1930 and was a leading member of the Frankfurt school. He left Germany with the Institute on the rise of Hitler, and went to the United States, returning after the war. He laid down the basic principles of the school, based on the view that modern civilization is so corrupted that only a complete transformation of theory and practice can save it. He attacked the positivist views of the Enlightenment, and the use of knowledge for domination, particularly of nature. What was needed was a new 'critical theory'. Major works are *Dialectics of Enlightenment* (with *Adorno, 1947, ET 1972) and *Eclipse of Reason* (1947).

Hort, Fenton John Anthony (1828–92)
English New Testament scholar and theologian. He was educated at Rugby school under Thomas *Arnold and at Cambridge; his life alternated between Cambridge teaching (including two professorships) and a country parish not far away. A distinguished New Testament scholar, he produced a classic edition of the Greek text (with *Westcott). However, his interests ranged far wider. He was concerned with the real purpose of biblical study, with the relationship between theology and science, and above all with social matters, being sympathetic to *Kingsley and F. D. *Maurice.

Hoskyns, Edwyn Clement (1884–1937)
English New Testament scholar and baronet. Educated in Cambridge and Berlin, where he met *Harnack and *Schweitzer, he spent his life teaching in Cambridge apart from serving as an army chaplain in the First World War. A pioneer of the biblical theology movement, he was deeply affected by translating *Barth's *Commentary on Romans* (1933). He himself wrote a seminal book *The Riddle of the New Testament* (1931), with his pupil Noel Davey, on the relationship between Jesus and the church, and a magisterial *The Fourth Gospel*, unfinished at his death and completed by Davey (1940).

Hromadka, Josef Luki (1889–1969)
Czech Reformed theologian. Born in Moravia, he was professor in Prague before spending the war at Princeton. On his return he played an important role in interpreting the life of the church in Communist areas to the churches in the non-Communist world and urging reconciliation between Christians and Communists. His views are contained in the posthumous *Thoughts of a Czech Pastor* (1970).

Huck, Albert (1867–1942)
German New Testament scholar. He spent his life as a pastor, but left his mark on New Testament studies with his *Synopsis of the Gospels* (1892), presenting the Greek texts of Matthew, Mark and Luke in parallel columns. Revised many times, it is still a basic text.

Hügel, Friedrich von *see* **Von Hügel, Friedrich**

Hugh of St Victor (died 1142)
Theologian. Little is known of his life, but he probably came from Lorraine or the Low Countries. He was the most distinguished of the Victorines, scholars living at the Abbey of St Victor in Paris, a kind of chaplaincy to university students, and he was called a 'second Augustine'. He sought to integrate the new learning that was developing into the content of and introduction and guide to Bible study, in the process pioneering a new approach to scripture. He wrote on a wide range of topics, including biblical commentaries (on those books in which he was interested), history, grammar and geometry. He had a vivid imagination and a scientific curiosity; he learned Hebrew and talked with Jews. His interests were taken further by his pupil *Andrew (see also* **Richard of St Victor***)*.

Hume, David (1711–76)
Scottish philosopher and historian. He was born and educated in Edinburgh and held several administrative posts in England and abroad. His philosophy follows on from that of *Locke and *Berkeley and attacks reason by making it a product of experience: on the basis of experience the facts of reality can be established only with a degree of probability. This led, for example, to a challenge to belief in miracles. Since belief in God cannot be proved by reason, it must be a matter of faith. His major works in this area were *Philosophical Essays Concerning Human Understanding* (1748) and the posthumous *Dialogues Concerning Natural Religion*. His approach is regarded as one of the most basic attacks on theology in modern times.

Huntingdon, Selina, Countess of (1707–91)
English religious leader. She joined the *Wesleys' Methodist society and at the age of forty, on her husband's death, devoted herself to its cause, opening Trevecca House as a Methodist seminary. Legal objections to her appointing Methodist ministers as her chaplains led her to register her own chapels as dissenting. In the disputes between John Wesley and *Whitefield, she sided with the latter; this led to a split and the formation of the Calvinistic Methodist 'Countess of Huntingdon's Connexion'.

Hus, John (1369–1415)
Bohemian reformer. Born of a peasant family, he studied at Prague university, where he eventually became dean. He gained his influence as preacher of the Bethlehem chapel there. Attracted by *Wycliffe's doctrines, he attacked the morals of the clergy, a hierarchical and propertied church and the sale of indulgences. He was excommunicated in 1412 and went into exile, but was lured by promise of safe conduct to the Council of Constance, which condemned him and burnt him at the stake. He became a national hero.

Husserl, Edmund (1859–1938)
German philosopher. Born a Jew in Prostejov, Czechoslovakia (then Prossnitz, Moravia), he studied in Leipzig, Berlin and Vienna (under *Brentano) and later became professor at Halle, Göttingen and Freiburg. Criticism of his work on the philosophy of mathematics led him to a descriptive psychology which he called phenomenology. This began as a descriptive analysis of subjective processes, but later moved in a more metaphysical direction with a quest for 'essences'. He became a Christian in 1887. His major works include *Investigations in Logic* (1900) and *Experience and Judgment*, published posthumously.

Hutchinson, Anne (1591–1643)
American colonist. An emigrant to Massachusetts, her Calvinism and criticism of existing practices, and her belief in pure grace, brought her into conflict with the leaders of the colony. She was banished and excommunicated because of claims to direct and immediate revelations, and moved to Rhode Island, later to Long Island, where she was killed by Indians.

Hutter, Jacob (died 1536)
Moravian Anabaptist leader. He became leader of disparate Anabaptist groups in 1529 and united and organized them with a view to communal production and consumption. This aroused fierce Roman Catholic

opposition and he was burnt at the stake, but he succeeded in founding a tradition which has lasted to the present day.

Huvelin, Henri (1838–1910)
Roman Catholic priest. Immensely gifted, he spent his time on the staff of a Paris parish. He counselled many: ordinary people, as well as *Brémond, *De Foucauld and *Von Hügel. His spiritual teaching was unconventional, attaching importance to intellectual integrity and following the promptings of conscience; with this went a capacity for understanding the needs of different types of personality.

Huxley, Aldous Leonard (1894–1963)
English writer. Born in Godalming, Surrey, he was descended from the *Huxley and *Arnold families. He first expressed his views on the world in a series of novels, most noted of which is *Brave New World* (1932), in which he warned of the danger that scientific progress could lead to totalitarianism. In the 1940s he became deeply interested in mysticism, as evidenced by his *The Perennial Philosophy* (1945). He died in Hollywood.

Huxley, Thomas Henry (1825–95)
A Londoner, he studied medicine and then joined the Navy on an expedition to the southern tropics, later becoming a lecturer at the Royal School of Mines before holding administrative office. His campaigns on behalf of science, after the publication of *Darwin's *Origin of Species*, brought him into conflict with the church. On the basis of his knowledge he argued that God is unknown and unknowable and that our primary duty is the relief of suffering. His collected works ran to nine volumes.

I

Ibas of Edessa (active 435–57)
Bishop and theologian. He was involved in controversies over christology at the time of the Council of Chalcedon and adopted a mediating position between the Nestorians and the views advocated by *Cyril, being sympathetic to *Theodoret. He is known for a theological letter written in 435; deposed at the Robber Synod of Ephesus, he was reinstated, but condemned again in the next century.

Ignatius of Antioch (c.35–c.107)
Martyr bishop. Little is known of his life; he was probably born in Syria and was one of the first bishops of Antioch. He was sent under escort to Rome, where he was executed. His letters, written from Smyrna while he was staying with *Polycarp, and from Troas, are important evidence for the early church: in them he pleads for a unity of the church which is not only spiritual but bodily in the face of a threatened division through a heresy which seems to be some form of Gnosticism.

Ignatius Loyola (1491–1556)
Founder of the Jesuit Order. Son of a Spanish nobleman, he had a career in the court and the army, but at the age of thirty was wounded. During his convalescence he was converted to an ideal represented by *Francis of Assisi and *Dominic, and in a period of prayer and extreme austerity began writing his *Spiritual Exercises*. After an abortive attempt to settle in the Holy Land he studied theology and philosophy at Barcelona, Alcala and Salamanca; from there he went on to Paris and then, again prevented from going to Palestine, with the group of companions who had meanwhile gathered round him, put himself at the service of the pope. The Jesuit order was given papal recognition by *Paul III in 1540, with Ignatius as its reluctant superior general, and he spent the rest of his life organizing it.

Illich, Ivan (1926–   )
Catholic educationalist. Born in Vienna, after studying in Rome and Salzburg he was ordained and went to the United States as assistant priest in a New York Irish–Puerto Rican parish. He later became vice-rector of the Catholic University of Puerto Rico. He was a co-founder of the Center for Intercultural Documentation in Cuernavaca, Mexico, and for many years

directed research seminars on 'Institutional Alternatives in a Technological Society'. His *Deschooling Society* (1971) questioned much in current educational thinking, and his *Limits to Medicine* (1976) brought out the disadvantage of professional control over medicine. He argues that people need to be more involved in decision-making in matters which affect their lives, from education and health to transport and religion.

Inge, William Ralph
(1860–1954)
Dean of St Paul's cathedral, London. Born in Yorkshire, after study at Cambridge and teaching in Oxford he was vicar of a London parish; he then became professor in Cambridge. However it was at St Paul's cathedral that he became widely known. A theologian with deep knowledge of spirituality in the *Platonic tradition, he was even more successful as a popular writer on many subjects, for years contributing a column to a daily newspaper. His many books include *Christian Mysticism* (1899), *Faith and its Psychology* (1909) and *The Philosophy of Plotinus* (1918).

Irenaeus (c.115–90)
Church father. Born in Asia Minor and acquainted with *Polycarp, he studied in Rome before going to Lyons, of which he became bishop. His encounter with Gnosticism led him to write his *Against the Heresies* in five books, which now survives only in Latin. He is particularly known for his doctrine of recapitulation (Greek *anakephalaiosis*), that all those men and women who had lived before the saving work of Jesus were taken up into Christ and summarized in such a way that Adam could be saved. His less

dark view of sin and evil is often contrasted with that of Augustine.

Irving, Edward (1792–1834)
Scottish minister. He was born in Dumfriesshire and studied in Edinburgh. After being assistant to Thomas *Chalmers in Glasgow, he went to London, where he was so successful with a blend of Catholicism and Pentecostalism that a new church was built for him. But his popularity wore off and he became more extreme, turning to millenarian ideas among others, and these were a contributory factor to his downfall. He was excommunicated on the grounds of his belief that Christ's human nature was sinful, and removed from office. His followers constituted a new Catholic Apostolic church (they are also known as 'Irvingites', though he did not found the church). Irving returned to Scotland until he was expelled from there, returning to a minor role in the sect which had grown from him.

Isidore of Seville (560–636)
Spanish scholar. Of a noble family, he had a monastic education and succeeded his brother as archbishop of Seville. He was famous for his holiness and learning, and his works, some of them meant as textbooks for cathedral schools, proved a storehouse of information for later ages, preserving the essentials of ancient learning until later mediaeval revivals.

Ivo of Chartres (1040–1115)
He studied in Paris and at Bec (under *Lanfranc), and became prior at Beauvais and then bishop of Chartres. His three substantial treatises on canon law were of great importance for later developments, and surviving letters are a source of information about conditions in his time.

James, William (1842–1910)
American psychologist and philosopher. He was born in New York, the son of a *Swedenborgian theologian and brother of the novelist Henry James, and studied at Harvard and in Europe. He was originally a medical student, but his interests turned to psy-

chology and philosophy, and after teaching at Harvard, in 1885 he became professor of philosophy there; he also lectured widely in America and Europe. He had a popular style; his psychological interests are expressed in his classic *The Varieties of Religious Experience* (1902), in which he analysed conversion and distinguished between 'once-born' and 'twice-born' believers. His philosophical interests are expressed in his *Pragmatism* (1907). He saw truth as something to be made and remade on the basis of experience; the truth of religion lay in the fact that it was virtually a universal experience.

Jansen, Cornelius Otto (1585–1638)
Belgian theologian. Born in Utrecht, the son of the bishop of Ghent, he studied at Louvain and in Paris, where he worked with *Saint-Cyran, and then became director of a newly-founded college in Louvain. In 1636 he was made bishop of Ypres. His *magnum opus* was *Augustinus* (1640), about grace and human freedom, based on Augustine and against scholasticism. It became the basis of the religious reform movement of Jansenism, to which Jansen gave his name. Jansenists had the pessimistic view that human beings cannot perform God's commands without his grace, and grace is irresistible.

Jaspers, Karl (1883–1969)
German philosopher. Born in Oldenburg, he studied medicine and lectured in psychology in Heidelberg. He then turned to philosophy and became professor there. He had a Jewish wife and was suspended by the Nazis in 1937. After the Second World War he became professor in Basle. In the existentialist tradition, he was influenced by *Dilthey and *Husserl. He saw philosophy not as science but more as an alternative to religion and sought to interpret the crisis of Germany after the First World War. Regarding Christianity as one religion among many, he identified an 'axial point' in history between 800 and 200 BCE, when the key figures (religious, ethical and prophetic) in shaping humanity lived; for him history was shaped by countless individual decisions, not by an overriding purpose. His major books are *The Perennial Scope of Philosophy* (1948) and *The Origin and Goal of History* (1949).

Jenkins, David Edward (1925–   )
British theologian. Born in London, after war service in India he studied at Oxford and later taught there; after working with the World Council of Churches in Geneva, he became professor in Leeds and in 1984 bishop of Durham. Concerned with social and political issues, but hardly a radical theologian, he came to prominence as bishop through his statements on virgin birth and resurrection and his outspoken criticism of the government of the day. Of his works, *The Glory of Man* (1967) and *The Contradiction of Christianity* (1976) are important.

Jeremias, Joachim (1900–79)
German New Testament scholar. Born in Dresden, he was professor at Greifswald and then in Göttingen, where he did remarkable pastoral work under the Nazi régime. He is particularly known for his work on the Jewish background to the life of Jesus, which influenced more than one generation of scholars. His *Jerusalem in the Time of Jesus* (1937, ET 1969) is built up from detailed examination of Jewish sources; his *Eucharistic Words of Jesus* (1935, ET 1966) seeks to discover the form of the last supper; and his *The Parables of Jesus* (1947, ET [3]1972) takes further the work of *Jülicher. His work on Jesus was summed up in the first volume of an unfinished *New Testament Theology* (1971). His approach proved particularly congenial to British readers for its positive qualities.

Jerome (Eusebius Hieronymus, 348–420)
Hermit and biblical scholar. He was born on the Adriatic coast, educated in Rome, and after much travelling ultimately settled in Bethlehem, where he founded a monastery and devoted the rest of his life to biblical study. Mastering Greek and Hebrew, he translated the Bible into Latin, and this Vulgate, as it is known, influenced the church down to modern times; he also wrote commentaries on most biblical books. An ascetic and a great controversialist, he wrote, among others, against *Augustine, *Origen and *Pelagius. His letters are particularly important.

Jewel, John (1522–71)
English Reformer. He studied and then taught at Oxford before having to flee to Frankfurt in the reign of Queen Mary. After going on to Strasbourg and Zurich he returned to England under Queen Elizabeth, who made him bishop of Salisbury. He wrote the first defence of the Church of England against the Church of Rome, the *Apology for the Church of England* (1562), and was the teacher of *Hooker.

Joachim of Fiore (1132–1202)
Italian mystic. Little is known of his life; after a pilgrimage to the Holy Land he became abbot of a Cistercian house in Calabria. However, a few years later he left to found

his own congregation in Fiore. Allegedly on the basis of a vision in his youth, he interpreted history in terms of the Trinity: the Old Testament was the age of the Father; the New Testament the age of the Son, which would end soon after his day; he identified the new age of the Spirit then to come with the millennium of the biblical book of Revelation. Some of his views were subsequently condemned, but his ideas of the new age caught the imagination of revolutionary groups. His main works were the *Book of Concord of the Old and New Testament*, *Psalter of Ten Strings*, and a commentary on Revelation.

John XXIII *see Popes of Rome*

John Climacus (c.570–649)
Spiritual writer. A monk on Sinai, he became a hermit and later was abbot of Sinai. His writing *The Ladder* (Greek *climax*, hence his name) *of Paradise* presented the achievement of Christian perfection as climbing thirty steps of a ladder, to correspond to the years of Jesus' supposed age.

John of the Cross (Juan de Yepis y Alvarez, 1542–91)
Spanish mystic. Son of a poor family of noble origin, he became a Carmelite, studied theology at Salamanca, and was ordained priest. With the help of *Teresa of Avila he sought to reform his order, but this led to opposition, resulting in a split between calced and discalced Carmelites (those who did or did not wear sandals). Prior of several monasteries of the discalced, he eventually fell out with the vicar general and was banished to Andalusia, where he died. An unusually perceptive mystic, he is best known through *The Spiritual Canticle* (1578), the *Ascent of Mount Carmel* (1579), and *The Living Flame of Love* (1583). He is particularly noted for his account of 'the dark night of the soul'.

John of Damascus (675–749)
Greek theologian. After serving as a Christian representative in the court of the caliph of Damascus, he moved to Jerusalem, where he became a priest. A traditionalist and systematician, in the controversy over icons he defended their use. His *Feast of Wisdom*, covering philosophy, heresies and orthodox belief, became a textbook in the Orthodox church, but was long unknown in the West. He is regarded as the last of the great Eastern church fathers. He also wrote famous hymns, including 'The Day of Resurrection, earth tell it out abroad'.

Jones, Rufus Matthew (1863–1948)
American Quaker theologian. He studied at Haverford, Heidelberg, Oxford and Harvard, and returned to be professor of philosophy at Haverford for forty-one years. A leader in the Society of Friends, he gave his efforts to interpreting the value of the Western mystical tradition in ways which were consistent with contemporary thought. Noted as a leading authority on Christian mysticism, he wrote more than sixty books, including *Social Law in the Spiritual World* (1904), *Studies in Mystical Religion* (1907), *The Inner Life* (1916), and *A Preface to Christian Faith in a New Age* (1932).

Josephus, Flavius (37–100)
Jewish historian. Son of a Palestinian priestly family, he lived in the desert with a hermit before becoming a Pharisee. He took part in the Jewish War and was captured by Vespasian, whose favour he won by prophesying that he could become emperor. Freed when this happened, Josephus became a Roman citizen and had a pension which enabled him to devote his time to literary work. He is the most important primary source for Palestine in the New Testament period. His main works are *The Jewish War*, a personal account; *Jewish Antiquities*, a twenty-volume history of the Jews from creation; and his autobiography.

Jowett, Benjamin (1817–93)
Born in London, he proved a brilliant scholar; he became a fellow of Balliol College while still an undergraduate and rose to be Master. He was also professor of Greek at Oxford, where he spent his life. A theological liberal, he contributed one of the most controversial essays, on 'The Interpretation of Holy Scripture', to *Essays and Reviews* (1860), which caused a national scandal in nineteenth-century England, arguing that the Bible should be interpreted as any other book. Subsequently, under suspicion, he turned to classics, translating Plato and Aristotle, and was a major figure in Oxford university.

Julian the Apostate (331–63)
Roman emperor. He was born in Constantinople, the nephew of *Constantine. After an eventful career, which included banishment and imprisonment, and attempts to win him to Christianity, he turned to Platonism and the mystery religions. As emperor, he pro-

moted paganism and weakened Christianity, with increasing severity. He was a prolific author, writing orations, letters, and a work *Against the Christians*.

Julian of Norwich (c.1342–1420)
English mystic. She lived in a cell beside St Julian's church in Norwich, from which she may have taken her name. Little is known of her life, but reflection on her visions is contained in her *Revelations of Divine Love*, one of the great spiritual classics, which emphasizes the love of God and contains the great assurance 'all shall be well'.

Jülicher, Adolf (1857–1938)
German New Testament scholar. After a pastorate near Berlin he became professor at Marburg; from 1925 he was almost blind. He was the founder of the modern study of the parables, in his two-volume *The Parables of Jesus* (1888–9) breaking with traditional allegorical interpretation and arguing that Jesus' parables were originally told to illustrate one point only. He was also an expert on the Old Latin versions of the Bible.

Julius Africanus, Sextus (160–240)
Historian. He was born in Jerusalem and travelled widely; his work involved reorganizing the imperial library in Rome for Alexander Severus. He wrote a history of the world, which was used by *Eusebius, arguing that the world would last 6000 years, Christ being born in 5500.

Jung, Carl Gustav (1875–1961)
Swiss psychologist. Born in Thurgau canton, Switzerland, he studied in Basle and then worked in the Zurich psychiatric clinic. This led to collaboration with *Freud, but in 1913 a break came with Freud's essentially sexually-orientated theories. Jung subsequently worked in Zurich, developing his own views under the name of analytic psychology. He postulated a collective unconscious common to all human beings through history, expressed through basic forms of archetypes. On this basis he saw the human psyche in terms of the shadow, the *animus* and the *anima*, which are projections from the archetypes. He regarded his analytical philosophy as friendly to religion, seeing religion as a mythological description of how the psyche works and as a way of bringing healing to the psyche, but he was uninterested in the foundations of theology. His writings range widely and are collected in twenty volumes; his *Memories, Dreams, Reflections* (1963) is a particularly important expression of his views.

Jüngel, Eberhard (1932–   )
German systematic theologian. A pupil of Ernst *Fuchs and interpreter of *Barth and *Bultmann, he has been professor in Zurich and Tübingen. With an approach centred on the person of Christ, and influenced by Fuchs' hermeneutics, his writings have covered the Trinity, anthropology and a restatement of natural theology, concerned to distinguish between a human God and his human creation. His major work is *God the Mystery of the World* (ET 1983).

Justin Martyr (c.100–65)
Roman apologist. Born of pagan parents in Shechem, Palestine, he studied the leading philosophies before being converted to Christianity. He taught in many great cities, and spent some time in Rome, where *Tatian was one of his pupils. He was denounced as a Christian and beheaded. He is important for his Christian interpretation of the Old Testament and the way in which he uses the Gospels as providing confirmation of the fulfilment of prophecy. He argued that Christianity was not immoral and compatible with the best of Greek philosophy. His major works are his *Apology* and a dialogue with the Jew Trypho.

Justinian (483–565)
Roman emperor. He did much to extend the empire and built many basilicas, notably in Ravenna and Constantinople (Santa Sophia). His lawyers drafted the basic code of Roman law. As a Christian he championed Chalcedonian orthodoxy and was concerned for collaboration between church and state in one body.

Juvencus, Caius Vettius Aquilinus (fourth century)
Spanish poet. A priest of noble descent, he made a name by writing a poetic harmony of the Gospels in Latin verse, aimed at showing that Christianity could produce as good poetry as paganism.

Kaftan, Julius Wilhelm Martin
(1848–1926)

German Protestant theologian. Born in Schleswig, he taught in Basle and Berlin, and was strongly influenced by *Ritschl. Stressing personal experience, he interpreted the atonement in mystical and ethical categories, and argued that Paul's theology grew out of his experience on the Damascus road. His main works were *The Essence of Christian Religion* (1881), *The Nature of Christian Religion* (1888) and a *Dogmatics* (1897).

Kagawa, Toyohiko (1888–1960)

Japanese social reformer. From a wealthy family, he was brought up a Buddhist. When he was converted to Christianity, his family disinherited him. He studied at the Presbyterian seminary in Kobe, and then, becoming aware of the social dimensions of Christianity, went to work in the slums. From 1914 he spent three years at Princeton Theological Seminary learning modern methods of social welfare and then returned to work among the poor. He helped to establish churches, schools and missions, and founded the first Japanese trade union and peasant union. Imprisoned during the Second World War, afterwards he became a democratic leader and member of the Japanese House of Peers. He wrote many books, including *The Religion of Jesus* (1931) and *Christ and Japan* (1934).

Kähler, Martin (1835–1912)

German systematic theologian. Born in Prussia the son of a Lutheran pastor, after university studies he spent his life as professor at Halle. Though he wrote a major book on Christian doctrine, he is best known for his collection of essays *The So-Called Historical Jesus and the Historic, Biblical Christ* (1892, ET 1964), in which he rejected the nineteenth-century quest for the historical Jesus; the real Christ is the Christ of preaching, as he is encountered in the church. Kähler's recognition that the Gospels are made up of units, each reflecting Christ in a variety of aspects, anticipated the form criticism of *Bultmann and *Dibelius.

Kant, Immanuel (1724–1804)

German philosopher. He was born and died in Königsberg in Prussia and never went outside Prussia. Influenced by *Hume, he sought to demonstrate the role of reason in the gaining of knowledge. He undermined the metaphysical basis of orthodox and rationalist dogmatics by his argument that human beings do not know 'things in themselves', with the aim of 'removing knowledge to make room for faith'. The classical proofs for the existence of God were untenable. With these views, expressed in his *Critique of Pure Reason* (1781), he set the agenda for nineteenth-century theology, influencing such different figures as *Schleiermacher, *Ritschl, *Feuerbach and *Barth. His *Critique of Practical Reason* (1788) discussed the problem of morality and its implications for theism; his other major work was *Religion within the Limits of Reason Alone* (1793). For a century until 1929 his works were banned in the Roman Catholic church.

Käsemann, Ernst (1906–   )

German New Testament scholar. Born in Bochum, and a pupil of *Bultmann at Marburg, he taught as professor in Mainz, Göttingen and Tübingen. Always a controversial figure, he was active in the Confessing Church and at one point was imprisoned by the Nazis; he was also active in the post-war reconstruction of the Protestant church in Germany, being attacked by the conservatives for his radical views. He encouraged a new approach to many issues: the New Testament canon, the unity of the New Testament, the role of apocalyptic in early Christianity, the nature of the Gospel of John (which in *The Testament of Jesus*, 1966, he argued was Greek and docetic) and the consolidation of the primitive church into early Catholicism. His 1953 lectures on the historical Jesus are seen as the beginning of the 'new quest'. They and other important writings can be found in *Essays* *on New Testament Themes* (ET 1964) and *New Testament Questions of Today* (ET 1969). His *magnum opus* is a magisterial commentary on Romans (1973, ET 1980). In latter years he also became a vigorous opponent of nuclear armament.

Keble, John (1792–1866)
English tractarian and poet. Son of a clergyman, after a distinguished career at Oxford, culminating in his appointment as professor of poetry, he spent most of his life in a country parish near Winchester. A leading figure in the nineteenth-century Oxford Movement, which aimed at restoring high church ideals (*Newman regarded the 1833 Assize sermon which he preached as its start), he was a champion of apostolic succession in the church and of the centrality of the eucharist in worship. As well as writing many tracts, he joined Newman and *Pusey in editing a library of the church fathers, which were then being rediscovered. But his best-known work is *The Christian Year* (1827), poems for Sundays and holy days, the source of many hymns.

Kempe, Marjorie (c.1373–1430)
English mystic. Born in Norfolk, she married a local official by whom she had fourteen children. Then after a pilgrimage to Canterbury, she and her husband took vows of chastity; she later went on pilgrimage to Europe and Palestine. She is known from *The Book of Margery Kempe*, an account of her travels and mystical experiences, which included visions and revelations; she was an acquaintance of *Julian of Norwich.

Ken, Thomas (1637–1711)
Anglican bishop. He went to school at Winchester College, where he returned to teach after studying and teaching at Oxford, and looking after several parishes. He became a royal chaplain to Charles II, refusing to offer hospitality to Nell Gwynne; as a result of this principled stand the king made him bishop of Bath and Wells. His principles also emerged in his refusal to sign either James II's Declaration of Indulgence which allowed freedom of worship to Nonconformists or the oath of allegiance to William of Orange. As a 'non-juror' he was thereupon deposed and spent the rest of his life in retirement. He lived an ascetic life, and wrote an exposition of the catechism and many hymns, including 'Glory to thee, my God, this night'.

Kepler, Johann (1571–1630)
German astronomer. Educated at Tübingen, he became professor in Graz and then court astronomer in Prague. Familiar with the work of *Copernicus, he was led by mystical Neoplatonist doctrines to discover the laws of planetary motion for which he is known. Though basically pantheistic, he accepted the traditional authority of the Bible and worked out a new theory about the star of the Magi.

Kermode, Frank (1919–   )
English scholar. After studying at Liverpool university he served in the British Navy during the Second World War and then taught in Newcastle and Reading before becoming professor in Manchester, Bristol, London and Cambridge. His books *The Classic* (1975) and *The Genesis of Secrecy* (1979) have proved important for the development of literary criticism of the Bible, and with Robert Alter he edited the influential *A Literary Guide to the Bible* (1988).

Khomiakoff, Alexei Stepanovich (1804–60)
Russian philosopher. A member of the gentry, he was educated at Moscow university before travelling as a cavalry officer. Retiring to his estates, he tried to improve conditions for his serfs, ultimately campaigning to abolish serfdom. His intellect was stimulated by winters in the Moscow salons. Seeing the Orthodox Church as a guiding light and critical of Protestantism and Roman Catholicism, he believed that Russia had a mission to save Western civilization and that Russian moral superiority was evidenced by *sobornost*.

Kierkegaard, Søren Aaby (1813–55)
Danish philosopher. The son of a wealthy Lutheran hosier, he spent his life in Copenhagen. He was melancholy in disposition, with much unhappiness in his life, and his works are introspective and individualistic. But he was a great influence on subsequent philosophy and theology, particularly existentialism and dialectical theology, and a major figure of the nineteenth century. As indicated by his famous remark 'truth is subjectivity', he took as his focal point the individual in his existence, relegating reason to the lowest level of human activity. He saw the need to rise from being a mere spectator, through responsible decision and a sense of failure, to belief in Christ. Among his many works are: *Either/Or* (1843), *The Concept of*

Dread (1844) and *Concluding Unscientific Postscript* (1846); these were succeeded by more 'Christian' works, including *Training in Christianity* (1850); he also wrote a *Journal*.

King, Martin Luther, Jr (1929–68)
American civil rights leader. Born in Atlanta, after gaining a doctorate at Boston university he became a Baptist pastor in Alabama, then was co-pastor with his father in Atlanta. He became prominent in the movement to secure equal rights for Blacks by nonviolence, organized the Southern Christian Leadership Conference, led the 1963 March on Washington and was awarded the Nobel Peace Prize. He was assassinated by a white man in Memphis, Tennessee. A moving orator and preacher, he also wrote books, including *Stride toward Freedom* (1958) and *Why We Can't Wait* (1964).

Kingsley, Charles (1819–75)
English novelist and social reformer. He was born in Devon and educated at King's College, London and Cambridge. After being vicar of a country parish he was made professor of modern history at Cambridge before going to canonries at Chester and Westminter. Influenced by F. D. *Maurice, he became associated with the Christian Socialist movement in a concern for reform in education and hygiene, as evidenced in his best-known novel *The Water Babies* (1863); he also wrote *Hereward the Wake* (1866) and many other novels. No great intellectual, he became associated with the phrase 'muscular Christianity'. He was a vigorous opponent of the high-church Oxford Movement, and an ill-considered insult to *Newman led the latter to write his *Apologia pro Vita Sua*.

Kirk, Kenneth Escott (1866–1954)
English moral theologian. Apart from a period in the army during the First World War, he spent his life in Oxford, eventually as professor of moral theology and then bishop. He was an outstanding moral theologian; his greatest book was *The Vision of God* (1931).

Kittel, Gerhard (1888–1948)
German biblical scholar. Born in Breslau, he taught at several universities before becoming professor of New Testament at Tübingen. Notorious for his Nazi sympathies, he was removed from his post in 1945. He is known for beginning a gigantic multivolume *Theological Dictionary of the New Testament*, not finished until the 1960s, which traced the secular use of each word as well as its occurrence in biblical literature, adopting an approach devastatingly criticized by James *Barr. He was son of

Kittel, Rudolf (1853–1929)
Born in Swabia, he studied at Tübingen before becoming Professor of Old Testament in Breslau and Leipzig. As well as writing commentaries and works on Israelite history and the Near East he produced a critical edition of the Hebrew Bible, *Biblia Hebraica*, which, through subsequent revisions, has remained the standard scholarly text.

Klopstock, Friedrich Gottlieb (1724–1823)
German religious poet. Son of a lawyer, he studied theology at Jena and Leipzig. At school he conceived the plan of a religious epic, *The Messiah*, inspired by *Milton's *Paradise Lost*, which he did not complete until 1773. Given a pension by the king of Denmark to enable him to complete the work, he lived first in Copenhagen, then in Hamburg. Its publication was a landmark in German literature. He also wrote other works and latterly devoted himself to philosophy.

Knox, John (1514–72)
Scottish Reformer. Born in Haddington and educated at St Andrews, he was ordained and served as a tutor before being converted to Protestantism. Captured in a drive against heretics, he was sent as a galley slave to France. On his return to England, he continued his protests, and had to flee to the continent in the reign of Queen Mary, where at *Calvin's prompting he became pastor to the English congregation in Frankfurt. Further disputes took him to Geneva, where he wrote *The First Blast of the Trumpet against the Monstrous Regiment of Women*, arguing against female sovereignty. In 1559 he returned to Scotland, where he was instrumental in shaping the Kirk of Scotland through the Scots Confession and the Book of Common Order. He also wrote a history of the Reformation in Scotland.

Knox, John (1900–   )
American Methodist and Episcopalian theologian. In a long career he taught at Emory and Fisk Universities, Hartford Theological Seminary, Chicago University, Union Theological Seminary, New York and the Episcopal Theological Seminary of the Southwest.

A gifted popular writer, he has combined a deep sense of the church with a critical view of the New Testament. Important among his many books are *Chapters in a Life of Paul* (1950) and *The Death of Christ* (1954).

Knox, Ronald Arbuthnott (1888–1957)
Catholic apologist. Son of an evangelical bishop of Manchester, he had a brilliant career at Oxford and there became an extreme Anglo-Catholic. He was made a college chaplain and taught there, but in 1917 was converted to Roman Catholicism and ordained. He taught at a Catholic seminary and then returned to Oxford as Roman Catholic chaplain to students. In 1939 he resigned to devote himself to translating the Bible; his version became famous and was authorized for public use in the Catholic church. The best known of his other works is a study of *Enthusiasm* (1950).

Koester, Helmut (1926–   )
New Testament scholar. Born in Hamburg, he was a pupil of *Bultmann, *Bornkamm and *Käsemann, and became professor at Harvard Divinity School. He has done a good deal to introduce Bultmann's history of religions approach to North America, arguing that the New Testament must be seen as part of the wider cultural environment of its time and that to focus on the canonical writings without taking this wider world into account introduces serious distortion. This approach is reflected in his two-volume *Introduction to the New Testament* (1982), which is divided into the history, culture and religion of the Hellenistic age and the history and literature of early Christianity, and his *Ancient Christian Gospels* (1990).

Koyama, Kosuke (1929–   )
Japanese missionary theologian. Born in Tokyo, he was in Japan to experience the atomic bombing of Hiroshima and Nagasaki. He studied in Tokyo and at Princeton Theological Seminary and was then a missionary in Thailand. He was made Dean of the South East Asia Graduate School of Theology in Singapore and taught at Otago University before becoming professor at Union Theological Seminary, New York. His theology shows a concern for the indigenization of Christianity; his *Waterbuffalo Theology* (1974), based on his Thai missionary experience, discusses the new forms which Christianity must take; *Mount Fuji and Mount Sinai* (1984) is a study of idols in Japanese and Christian spirituality.

Kraemer, Hendrik (1888–1966)
Dutch missioner. After training in oriental languages, he was sent by the Netherlands Bible society to serve in Indonesia, where he wrote his most famous book, *The Christian Message in a Non-Christian World* (1938), which argued that the Christian revelation is incomparable and *sui generis*, and that co-operation with non-Christian religions is a betrayal of truth. In 1937 he became professor of religion in the University of Leiden and in 1948 the first director of the World Council of Churches Ecumenical Institute at Bossey. His thought was very influential on the WCC.

Krause, Karl Christian Friedrich (1781–1832)
German philosopher. He studied at Jena under *Hegel and *Fichte. He developed the view that the universe is a divine organism: God includes nature and humanity in his being but transcends both. For this view, which is more than pantheism, he coined the term panentheism; the term has been used widely in modern philosophy and theology, e.g. by Charles *Hartshorne and John A. T. *Robinson.

Krauth, Charles Porterfield (1823–1883)
American Lutheran theologian. Born in Martinsburg, Virginia, he served congregations in Maryland, Virginia and Pennsylvania, ultimately becoming professor of philosophy at the university of Pennsylvania. The editor of several Lutheran journals, he was concerned to bring about a sacramental and liturgical renaissance among American Lutherans and did much to achieve this.

Kuenen, Abraham (1828–1891)
Dutch biblical theologian. Born at Haarlem, he became professor of the New Testament, ethics and Old Testament at Leiden. With *Graf he did pioneering work on the sources of the Pentateuch which made *Wellhausen's historical criticism possible. His major works were *The Hexateuch* (1861–5, ET 1886) and *The Religion of Israel* (1869–70, ET 1873–5).

Kümmel, Werner-Georg (1905–   )
German New Testament scholar. He studied in his home city of Heidelberg and in Berlin and Marburg, and then became professor in Zurich, Mainz and Marburg. He is particularly known for his basic textbooks, an *Introduction to the New Testament* (ET ²1975), a *Theology of the New Testament*

(ET 1974) and a history of New Testament interpretation (*The New Testament*, ET 1973). His *Promise and Fulfilment* (ET 1957) was an important study of the future expectations of Jesus.

Küng, Hans (1928–   )
Roman Catholic theologian. Born near Lucerne, Switzerland, he studied widely in Rome, Paris, Berlin, London, Amsterdam and Madrid. His first major book, *Justification* (1957), which argued that Karl *Barth's doctrine of justification and that of the mediaeval Council of Trent were virtually the same, caused a sensation and made him a marked man. After a brief period as a parish priest he became professor in the Catholic faculty of the University of Tübingen. Two further books, *The Council, Reform and Reunion* (1960) and *Structures of the Church* (1962), criticizing existing church structures and calling for reform, just antedated the Second Vatican Council, the open atmosphere of which prevented action being taken against him. However, the situation deteriorated after publication of *The Church* (1967) and *Infallible? An Inquiry* (1970). His *On Being a Christian* (1974) and *Does God Exist?* (1978) became international best-sellers, reaching vast audiences, but provoked an unprecedented declaration that Küng could no longer be considered a Catholic theologian or function as such. However, his influence has continued to grow, and his interests now extend to inter-faith dialogue. His significance lies above all in his ability to present theological questions clearly and comprehensively.

Kutter, Hermann (1869–1931)
Religious socialist. A Swiss pastor, with *Ragaz he was the most significant defender of religious socialism at the beginning of the century. His 'theocentric theology' was an important preliminary to Barth's 'dialectical theology'.

Kuyper, Abraham (1837–1920)
Dutch Reformed theologian and politician. Son of a minister, at Leiden university he rebelled against the orthodoxy in which he had been brought up. However, he was unsatisfied emotionally by critical theology, and so turned to *Calvinism in his first parish at Beesd. After moving to Utrecht and then Amsterdam, he was involved in politics and became leader of the Anti-Revolutionary Party. Elected to Parliament, he mobilized the Calvinists for political support and drafted a programme of reform. He founded a Free University of Amsterdam and taught in its seminary, and led an exodus from the Reformed church to form a new branch of it. Ultimately he became Prime Minister of the Netherlands in 1901. He remained an influential figure all his life.

L

Laberthonnière, Lucien (1860–1932)
French Roman Catholic Modernist. Ordained priest, he spent his life teaching in Paris. He followed *Blondel's 'philosophy of action' and developed a pragmatic view of religious truth, called moral dogmatism. He was a considerable influence on *Tyrrell. His books were banned in 1906 and he was prohibited from writing in 1913.

Lachmann, Karl Konrad Friedrich Wilhelm (1793–1851)
German philologist. Born in Brunswick, he studied at Leipzig and Göttingen, and after serving in the Prussian army became professor of classics in Berlin. He published the first critical text of the New Testament based entirely on early manuscripts, dating from the fourth century (1831), as opposed to the 'received text', and proposed the priority of Mark on the grounds that the order within his Gospel was the best (1835).

Lacordaire, Jean-Baptiste Henri Dominique (1802–61)
French Roman Catholic liberal. Originally a deist, after practising law he was persuaded of the truth of Christianity by reading *Lamennais, though he parted company with him later. He was ordained, and then became a revolutionary, arguing for separation of church and state and freedom of religion

and the press, though theologically he supported the authority of Rome (i.e. he was an Ultramontanist). He later became a Dominican and did much to revive the order in France.

Lactantius, Lucius Caecilius Firmianus
(c.240–320)
African Christian apologist. Appointed by the emperor Diocletian teacher of rhetoric in Nicomedia, he was converted to Christianity, whereupon he lost his job. Later *Constantine made him tutor to his son. His *Divine Institutions* (304–11) commend Christianity to educated people and are a first attempt in Latin to set out the main articles of Christian faith. His *The Deaths of the Persecutors* is an important source on the persecutions of the period.

Lagarde, Paul Anton de (Paul Bötticher, 1827–91)
German biblical scholar and philologist. (At eighteen he changed his name to that of his mother's family.) He was a schoolmaster in Berlin and then professor at Göttingen. Opposed to liberalism and materialism, and vigorously antisemitic and nationalistic, he was an important influence on subsequent developments in Germany. He wrote many learned works on the Greek Bible and ancient history.

Lagrange, Marie Josèphe (1855–1938)
French biblical scholar. Born in Burgundy, he studied in Paris, Salamanca and Vienna. He became a Dominican, and after teaching in Salamanca and Toulouse founded the École Biblique in Jerusalem and the Catholic journal *Revue Biblique*. His work paved the way for the Jerusalem Bible. In the circumstances of his time he did much to encourage historical criticism of the Bible in the Roman Catholic church. He wrote substantial commentaries on the four Gospels.

Lake, Kirsopp (1872–1946)
English biblical scholar. After studying at Oxford, he became professor in Leiden and at Harvard. He was a controversial scholar. His *Historical Evidences for the Resurrection of Christ* (1907) cast doubt on the empty tomb and his book on *The Earlier Epistles of Paul* (1911) stressed the influence of Hellenism on Christianity. He was joint editor of the unfinished five-volume *The Beginnings of Christianity* (1920–1933), which was widely influential.

Lamennais, Hugo Felicité Robert de
(1782–1854)
French political and social theorist. Born in St Malo, Brittany to a well-to-do Catholic family, he read widely, losing his faith under the influence of the works of *Rousseau. He became a mathematics teacher at a local church college at the age of twenty-two and in the same year was converted to Catholicism by his brother. Like his brother, he too became a priest; he retired to his grandfather's country house and founded a religious congregation and a journal, *L'Avenir* (The Future, 1830). After a first book demonstrating the futility of reason and calling for systematic organization of the clergy, which got him into trouble with Napoleon, he wrote his main work *Essay on Indifference in the Matter of Religion* (1817–23), arguing that the individual depends on the community for knowledge of the truth. His ideas developed and became more radical as time went on: first he called for a theocracy, with the pope as supreme world ruler, then for the separation of the church and education from the state with freedom for the press. Pope Gregory XVI, initially favourable, later condemned these views, expressed in *L'Avenir*, and Lamennais left the church, turning towards politics, seeing the future of society in liberal democracy and denying Catholicism and the supernatural. He was an important influence on later social and political ideas.

Lampe, Geoffrey William Hugo
(1912–80)
English churchman and theologian. After studying at Oxford he was ordained and taught as a schoolmaster before service as a chaplain in the Second World War, in which he was awarded the Military Cross. He returned to Oxford to teach and in 1953 became professor of theology at Birmingham, moving in 1959 to Cambridge. A distinguished patristic scholar, he devoted much of his life to the editing of *A Lexicon of Patristic Greek* (1969), the authoritative work on the Greek of the church fathers. His own major works include a study of early Christian baptism, *The Seal of the Spirit* (1969), and *God as Spirit* (1977), which sought to replace traditional incarnational doctrine with a Spirit christology.

Lanfranc (c.1010–89)
Scholastic theologian. Born of a well-to-do family in Pavia, he studied in northern Italy and then became an itinerant scholar. In

1042 he entered the then newly-founded abbey of Bec in Normandy, and was later made its prior. He subsequently became an abbot in Caen and archbishop of Canterbury. He wrote biblical commentaries and a major work *On the Body and Blood of the Lord*, criticizing the eucharistic teaching of *Berengarius and coming near to a doctrine of transubstantiation. However, he is most important as an organizer: he made Bec famous and exerted considerable influence through his pupils, who included *Anselm.

Las Casas, Bartolomé de (1474–1566)
Spanish Catholic missionary. Born in Seville, he studied law in Salamanca. He went to Haiti as legal adviser to the governor, and was ordained priest there. Disturbed at the treatment of the natives, from 1517–22 he travelled between Spain and America, seeking authority from the king to set up projects to improve their lot. His plans failed, and he became a Dominican; he continued his campaigning for the rest of his life, often in the face of bitter opposition from the colonists. He became bishop of Chiapa in Mexico before retiring to Spain, where he wrote many books. The best known is *A Brief Relation of the Destruction of the Indies* (1552), published on his return to Spain.

Latourette, Kenneth Scott (1884–1968)
Church historian. Born of a Baptist family in Oregon, he studied at Yale and taught in China until invalided home. From then on he devoted his time to writing missionary history, later returning to Yale, where he spent the rest of his life. Of his many books, his seven-volume *History of the Expansion of Christianity* (1937–45) and five-volume *Christianity in a Revolutionary Age* (1958–62) are particularly notable.

Law, William (1686–1761)
English mystic. Born in Northampton, he studied and taught at Cambridge but lost his post on refusing to give the oath of allegiance to George I (i.e. became a non-juror). After a decade in London as a tutor he retired to Northampton, where he led a simple life and engaged in charitable work. His best known book is *A Serious Call to a Devout and Holy Life* (1728), inspired by *Ruysbroeck and *Thomas à Kempis, which argues that all everyday virtues must be directed towards the glorification of God, in meditation and an ascetic life. Later in life he discovered Jakob *Boehme, who influenced his last books. His writings were deeply influential on the thought of John *Wesley during his early development.

Leclerc, Jean (Clericus, 1657–1736)
Biblical scholar. Born in Geneva, he studied at Grenoble and Saumur as a strict Calvinist, but later became an *Arminian. In 1684 he was made professor of philosophy in Amsterdam. He explained the traditional Christian doctrines on rational lines and wrote many biblical commentaries. He denied that Moses wrote the Pentateuch and generally held very advanced views for his time.

Leeuw, Gerhardus van der *see* **Van der Leeuw, Gerhardus**

Lehmann, Paul Louis (1904–   )
American theologian. After teaching at Harvard and Princeton Theological Seminary he became professor at Union Theological Seminary, New York. A specialist in Christian ethics, in his *Ethics in a Christian Context* (1963) he presented an account of ethics in the context of the Christian community and in his *The Transfiguration of Politics* (1974) a study of types of revolution.

Leibniz, Gottfried Wilhelm von
(1646–1716)
German philosopher. A precocious child, born in Leipzig, he entered university at fifteen to study law, but became interested in philosophy and mathematics. He spent his life in service to local rulers, mostly the Duke of Brunswick in Hanover, whose historian/librarian he became, meeting many of the great intellectual figures of the day. Dissatisfied with the dualistic views of *Descartes, *Locke and *Newton then current, in his *Monadology* (1714) he produced an optimistic account of the world as consisting of an infinite number of 'monads', each mirroring the universe in its own way. His conclusion that the world was 'the best of all possible worlds' was satirized by *Voltaire in his *Candide*. He defended the proofs for the existence of God and was the first to use the word theodicy, the justification of God's ways to man. He also discovered calculus and was active in seeking to further international peace.

Leith, John Haddon (1919–   )
American Presbyterian theologian. Born in South Carolina, he studied at Erskine College, Columbia Theological Seminary, Vanderbilt and Yale. After serving a church in

Auburn, Alabama, he became professor of theology at Union Theological Seminary in Virginia, where he introduced and enlivened the theology of the Reformers to many. His best known books are *Creeds of the Church* (³1983) and *Introduction to the Reformed Tradition* (1977).

Leo the Great *see Popes of Rome*

Leo X *see Popes of Rome*

Leontius of Byzantium (480–543)
Monk and theologian. He was probably from Palestine, but little is known of his life. He defended the orthodox teaching of the Council of Chalcedon against the monophysites (those who believed that Christ had only one, divine, nature), and made use of the Greek word *enhypostatos*: the humanity of Christ is neither impersonal nor a separate personality but is made personal by union with the deity.

Lessing, Gotthold Ephraim (1729–81)
German philosopher and dramatist. Born in Saxony the son of a Lutheran pastor, he studied at Leipzig and then made a name for himself as a playwright and critic (he has been called the father of German literature). He became interested in philosophy and theology and later was librarian to the Duke of Brunswick. His late play *Nathan the Wise* (1779) presents his view of religion as humanitarian morality through the figure of an ideal Jew. He was opposed to any historical revelation, as evidenced by his famous phrase, 'Accidental truths of history can never become the proof of necessary truths of reason.' He was a key figure in the Enlightenment, and his *The Education of the Human Race* (1780) was an important work for later German Protestant liberalism. *Schweitzer saw Lessing's publication of by *Reimarus ('the Wolfenbüttel fragments', 1774–8) as the beginning of the quest for the historical Jesus.

Levinas, Emmanuel (1905–   )
Jewish philosopher. Born in Lithuania, he studied in Strasbourg, Fribourg and Paris and became director of the École Normale Orientale. In 1964 he was made professor in Poitiers and subsequently moved to Nanterre and the Sorbonne. In the existentialist tradition, and influenced by *Husserl and *Heidegger, he has developed further *Buber's thinking about I-Thou, and is particularly concerned with the dimensions of encounter between persons. His works include *Totality and Infinity* (1961) and *Beyond Essence* (1974).

Lévi-Strauss, Claude (1908–   )
French social anthropologist. Born in Brussels, he studied in Paris and was soon appointed professor of sociology at São Paulo, Brazil; in 1938 he led an extended anthropological expedition to central Brazil. He spent the war years in the United States, returning to Paris in 1948, since when he has held various academic posts in France, finally being professor at the Collège de France. A key figure in structuralism, his work focusses on the relationship of culture to nature, based on the human capacity to communicate through language; he gave a new methodology to ethnology, based on communication (*The Elementary Structures of Kinship*, 1969). His four-volume *Introduction to the Science of Mythology* (1964–72, ET 1970–9) presents a structuralist account of myth, seeing myths as attempts to resolve problems of human existence and social organization rather than as explanations of natural phenomena.

Lévy-Bruhl, Lucien (1857–1939)
French philosopher. A Parisian, he became professor at the Sorbonne, where he studied primitive societies. In *How Natives Think* (1910, ET 1926) he argued that much of their mentality was prerational, without logical thought, so that they could accept contradictions, and that they followed a law of mystical participation (*Primitive Mentality*, 1922; *The 'Soul' of the Primitive*, 1923). Later in his life he revised these views, but developmental psychologists have by no means rejected his insights.

Lewis, Clive Staples (1898–1963)
English novelist and apologist. Born in Belfast, he became an atheist, and after serving in the First World War studied, then taught for many years, at Oxford. He then became professor of English at Cambridge. However, he achieved fame as a gifted writer of popular books on Christianity and novels. Having returned to Christianity at the end of the 1930s, he wrote *The Screwtape Letters* (1941); thereafter, broadcasting and more books made him a household name. His *Chronicles of Narnia* became children's classics. Other books include *The Great Divorce* (1945) and *Mere Christianity* (1952), and a trilogy of novels beginning with *Out of the Silent Planet*, which presented Christian-

ity in science-fiction terms as a cosmic myth. His perceptions as an apologist generally reinforced traditional orthodox Christian belief.

Lietzmann, Hans (1875–1942)
German church historian. He studied in Jena and Bonn, returning to Jena as professor; in 1924 he succeeded *Harnack in Berlin. A scholar of wide learning, he wrote commentaries on some of Paul's letters, but is best known for his book *The Mass and the Lord's Supper* (1926) and a four-volume history of the early church which was long a standard work.

Lightfoot, Joseph Barber (1828–89)
Born in Liverpool, he studied at Cambridge where he taught for many years, later becoming professor. For the last decade of his life he was bishop of Durham. Immensely learned, he planned with *Hort and *Westcott a multi-volume commentary on the New Testament. Though the project was never completed, he did produce three commentaries on Paul's letters. However, his most important work was a classic study of the Apostolic Fathers, in which he demonstrated the authenticity of the letters of *Ignatius, then under dispute. As bishop of Durham he distinguished himself by his work as an administrator.

Lightfoot, Robert Henry (1883–1953)
English New Testament scholar. Born in Wellingborough, he studied at Oxford, returning there in due course to teach and become a professor. He was instrumental in introducing form criticism to England, and a pioneer in drawing attention to the theological and literary tendencies of the Gospels in two important books: *History and Interpretation in the Gospels* (1935), and *Locality and Doctrine in the Gospels* (1938).

Liguori, Alphonsus *see* **Alphonsus Liguori**

Lindbeck, George Arthur (1923–)
Lutheran systematic theologian. Born in China, he studied at Gustavus Adolphus College, Minnesota and at Yale, to which he returned to teach. He is particularly known for his views on doctrine, put forward in *The Nature of Doctrine* (1984), which to a great degree immunize belief-systems from truth-questions.

Lipsius, Richard Adelbert (1830–92)
German Protestant theologian. After studying at Leipzig he became professor at Jena. He tried to reconcile scientific principles with philosophy and theology, by arguing that while science can provide objective knowledge of the world, real understanding of values requires subjectivity, and subjective experience shows the unity of the world in God. This brought him much opposition from the Lutheran church. He also made major contributions to the study of early church history, doing particularly important work on the apocryphal acts of apostles; he was co-editor of the standard edition of these works.

Locke, John (1632–1704)
English philosopher. Born to a Somerset family of minor gentry, after studies at Oxford, where he was influenced by *Descartes and Robert *Boyle, he became secretary to Lord Ashley, first Earl of Shaftesbury. Thereafter his career had its ups and downs, involving much forced travelling as he fell foul of the authorities; from 1691 he lived quietly in a manor house in Essex. He was the first major British empiricist philosopher and perhaps the most influential, and also helped to lay the foundation for liberal democracy. He combined his empiricism with a Christian rationalism. He argued that knowledge comes from experience alone, and that reality as such cannot be grasped by the human mind. However, the existence of God can be arrived at by reason, and Christianity has a secure rational base. In this area his major works are *An Essay Concerning Human Understanding* (1690) and *The Reasonableness of Christianity* (1695). A defender of free enquiry and toleration, he pleaded for religious freedom for all but Roman Catholics (because they owed allegiance elsewhere) and atheists (as a danger to the state). His *Two Treatises of Government*, published in 1690 but largely written earlier, defended constitutional rule and the freedom of the individual when both were threatened.

Lohmeyer, Ernst (1890–1946)
German New Testament scholar. He was born in Westphalia and in 1920 became professor in Breslau (from where he was dismissed for being anti-Nazi) and Greifswald. The night before the university reopened after the war he was arrested by the Russians and never seen again. He wrote

commentaries on several New Testament books and a study of *The Lord's Prayer* (published 1952).

Loisy, Alfred Firmin (1857–1940)
French Catholic Modernist. From a farming family in the Marne, he trained at the Catholic Institute in Paris, to which, after parish work, he returned to teach, later becoming professor. His critical work aroused suspicion and he was dismissed. After being chaplain to a Dominican convent and further teaching, he was forced to resign and excommunicated for his critical views. He spent the rest of his working life as professor of the history of religions in the secular Collège de France. His *The Gospel and the Church* (1902), written in answer to *Harnack's *What is Christianity?*, which argued that the church did not develop according to a plan of Jesus ('Jesus preached the gospel and the church came'), and critical studies of John and the Synoptic Gospels paved the way for his excommunication. His subsequent works, culminating in *The Birth of Christianity* (1933), are widely regarded as erratic.

Lonergan, Bernard (1904–85)
Canadian Roman Catholic theologian. Born in Buckingham, Quebec, he trained as a Jesuit and became professor at the Gregorian university in Rome. Influenced by *Husserl, his theology employed a 'transcendental method' of reflecting, enquiry into enquiry, intellectual awareness, understanding of one's self-consciousness. He argued that understanding has a unified structure, regardless of what is understood (*Insight*, 1957) and this leads to a unified method for all theology (*Method in Theology*, 1972).

Loofs, Friedrich Armin (1858–1928)
German Lutheran church historian. He studied at Leipzig under *Harnack and Göttingen under *Ritschl, then teaching at Leipzig and Halle. He also played a major part in church affairs. Of his patristic studies, works on *Paul of Samosata and *Nestorius are the most important.

Lossky, Nicolai (1870–1965)
Russian philosopher. He studied at St Petersburg where he became professor; from 1921 he spent the rest of his life in Western Europe and America. Influenced by *Leibniz and *Bergson, he believed in an Absolute (which he interpreted as God),

towards which all things moved, and in human freedom. His works include *The World as an Organic Whole* (1917) and *The Freedom of the Will* (1927). He was father of

Lossky, Vladimir (1903–58)
Russian lay theologian. He began his studies in St Petersburg, but was expelled in 1922 after his father's departure from Russia, and completed them at Prague and the Sorbonne. He spent the rest of his life in Paris and the United States, expounding Eastern Orthodox theology to the West; he was an opponent of *Bulgakov. His best-known book is perhaps his *Essay on the Mystical Theology of the Eastern Church* (1944).

Lotze, Rudolf Herrmann (1817–81)
German philosopher. Born in Bautzen, he studied at Leipzig and taught there before becoming professor in Göttingen and Berlin. He tried to reconcile philosophy with the natural sciences, without resorting to vitalism or idealism; for him, fact, law and value are separated only in our minds. The human mind is a microcosm of God. He was an important influence on *Ritschl. His views were presented most simply in his *Microkosmus* (3 vols, 1856–64).

Lovejoy, Arthur Oncken (1873–1962)
American philosopher. Born in Berlin, he studied at Berkeley and Harvard, and then taught at Johns Hopkins university. He originated the study of the history of ideas in the English-speaking world. By tracing in detail and analysing the assumptions and ideas of individuals and periods he broke down generalizations like romanticism and naturalism and showed how complex and often contradictory are the realities to which they refer. He founded the *Journal for the History of Ideas*; his best-known book is *The Great Chain of Being* (1936); his views are also collected in *Essays in the History of Ideas* (1948).

Löwith, Karl (1897–1973)
German historian of ideas. Born in Munich, in his writings he argued that Western civilization had lost the concept of nature and replaced it with historicism, a development for which Christianity was largely to blame by its concept of a transcendent creator. Modern historicist philosophies were a secularization of the Christian view; only in

*Nietzsche's idea of the eternal return did the older cosmology survive.

Lowth, Robert (1710–87)
English biblical scholar. After studying at Oxford he became professor of poetry there and was then bishop successively of St David's, Oxford and London. Despite pressure from King George III he refused to be archbishop of Canterbury. His main fame arises from his study of Hebrew poetry: he was the first to recognize parallelism (the characteristic verse-structure of the Psalms) as a regular device.

Lucian of Antioch (240–312)
Theologian and martyr. He was a presbyter in Antioch in the church to which *Arius belonged and Arius may have learnt his views from him. He revised the Greek text of the Bible, making it smoother and more intelligible, and his version was widely used in Syria and Asia Minor. He was martyred at Nicomedia.

Lucian of Samosata (c.115–200)
Syrian pagan satirist. He was originally a lawyer in Antioch before turning to writing and becoming an itinerant lecturer. Author of satires on many subjects, he also wrote on Christianity, particularly in *On the Death of Peregrinus*, in which he portrays Christians as being kindly but credulous.

Luckmann, Thomas (1927–)
American sociologist. Born in Jeseniče, Yugoslavia, he grew up and studied in Vienna and then moved to the United States; he has now returned to Europe as professor at the university of Constance. In an early study into German churches (*The Invisible Religion*, 1967) he argued the need for the religious dimension, but showed how in modern times values have moved away from the institutions and become privatized, and the churches face competition from other religious-type ideologies without parallel social structures. This leads to changes in the social expression of religion. However, social developments will not lead to a complete secularization of individual consciousness. With *Berger he also wrote *The Social Construction of Reality* (1966).

Ludlow, John Malcolm Forbes (1821–1911)
Founder of Christian Socialism in England. An Anglican, he studied in France, getting to know socialist pioneers there, before becoming a lawyer in London. Though he was overshadowed by *Kingsley and *Maurice, he was the real founder of the Christian Socialist movement, and was its leading organizer. He thought socialism the best form of democracy but believed that social and moral education had to go with it.

Luis of Granada (Luis Sarria, 1504–88)
Spanish spiritual writer. Born in Granada, he became a Dominican and, after studying at Valladolid, worked in Andalusia, writing on spirituality and restoring the Dominican house there. From 1555 he worked in Portugal, as spiritual director and writer; he counselled the great and refused high office. His spirituality, expressed in his *Book on Prayer and Meditation* (1554) and *Guide for Sinners* (1557), stressed the inner life, seeing outward ceremony as unimportant by comparison. This led to his books being banned.

Lull, Ramon (1232–1316)
Spanish missionary and philosopher. He was born in Majorca and educated as a knight. A vision of Christ when he was thirty made a deep impact, and he studied Arabic and Christian thought with a view towards converting Muslims. His *Book of Contemplation* was written in Arabic and translated into Catalan; he was the first mediaeval theologian not to write in Latin. In addition to teaching in Spain and France he travelled widely and wrote much. His thinking sought to arrive at a single system of language and belief to which all could adhere. His mystical theology anticipates that of *Teresa of Avila and *John of the Cross.

Luther, Martin (1483–1546)
German Reformer. Born in Eisleben, he studied at the university of Erfurt and then became a novice in the order of Augustinian Eremites. At the age of twenty-five he was transferred to the university of Wittenberg, where he later became professor, a post which he held until his death. Anxiety about his salvation led to a 'tower experience' in which he became convinced that the essence of the gospel was that justification is a gift of God through faith. This led him to deny the need for the priesthood and the church as mediator. Opposed to the indulgences (promises of forgiveness of time in purgatory) from Pope Leo X sold for renovating St Peter's, Rome, he fixed his famous Ninety-Five Theses attacking current Catholic abuses to the door of the castle church in Wittenberg. This inevitably led to conflict

and his trial in Augsburg in 1518 and a debate between him and John Eck in Leipzig in 1519. In 1520 he appeared before the Emperor Charles V in Worms and was put under the ban. He was rescued by Elector Frederick III of Saxony, the ruler of Wittenberg, and concealed in Wartburg castle. After much agonizing, he then broke with the Roman Catholic Church, calling on the German princes to reform the church themselves: this appeal was contained in *To the Christian Nobility of the German Nation* (1520); also published the same year were *On the Babylonian Captivity of the Church*, rejecting the sacrifice of the mass and transubstantiation and putting forward a eucharistic theology including communion in both kinds; and *The Freedom of the Christian*, expounding justification by faith. As a result he was excommunicated. In personal danger, he continued to be protected by the Elector of Saxony. His teaching spread widely, favoured by the religious and political situation, extending to many countries. He left a permanent mark on the German language in his translation of the Bible, and wrote many fine hymns, including 'Ein feste Burg' ('A safe stronghold'). As the Reformation proceeded he came into conflict with other Reformers, calling for the suppression of the Peasants' Revolt and opposing *Zwingli's views on the eucharist. His contribution eventually led to the confessional documents included in the Lutheran Book of Concord. He criticized *Erasmus' approach to church reform and wrote against his views in *The Bondage of the Will* (1525). That year he married Katharina von Bora, an ex-nun, and had a happy family life and home; his many volumes of biblical commentaries, sermons, etc., include his Table Talk. He died in Eisleben and was buried in Wittenberg.

Lyman, Eugene William (1872–1948)
American Congregational minister and educator. Born in Massachusetts, he studied at Yale and in Germany under *Harnack before being ordained and teaching at Oberlin School of Theology and Union Theological Seminary, New York. A theological liberal, he sought to reconcile orthodox Christian belief with modern culture. His books include *Theology and Human Problems* (1910), *The Experience of God in Modern Life* (1918) and *Religion and the Issues of Life* (1943).

Mabillon, Jean (1632–1707)
French Benedictine scholar. He was the first to treat scientifically the problems of 'diplomatics', i.e. the evaluating, dating and authorship of manuscripts. His major work is *De re diplomatica* (1681), written at a time when the authenticity of many charters was under attack. He produced many learned editions.

Macdonald, George (1824–1905)
Scottish novelist and poet. He studied at Aberdeen university and in London and became a Congregationalist minister, but left the ministry when opposition from his church to his views made life intolerable. He subsequently earned his living by writing. Many of his books have a Scottish background and he also wrote fantasy; his *Phantastes* (1858) and *Lilith* (1895) influenced C. S. *Lewis.

McFague, Sallie (1933–   )
American theologian. Born in Quincy, Maryland, she studied at Smith College and Yale, going on to be professor and dean at Vanderbilt Divinity School. A leading representative of feminist theology, she has been particularly concerned to relate theology to contemporary issues. Her books include *Speaking in Parables: A Study of Metaphor and Theology* (1982), and *Models of God: Theology for an Ecological, Nuclear Age* (1987).

Machen, John Gresham (1881–1937)
American Presbyterian scholar. Born in Baltimore, he studied at Johns Hopkins and Princeton and abroad in Marburg and Göttingen, returning to Princeton to teach. The last representative of Princeton theology, and influenced by his predecessor *Warfield, he was a staunch Calvinist and fundamentalist; in 1929 he resigned from Princeton and was a leading founder of

Westminster Theological Seminary, where he served as president till his premature death. His most notable book was *Christianity and Liberalism* (1923).

Macintosh, Douglas Clyde (1877–1948)
Canadian theologian. Born in Ontario, he studied at the university of Chicago and taught at Yale Divinity School all his life. He was the centre of a case in which he was denied United States citizenship by a majority of the Supreme Court for refusing to bear arms. His *The Problem of Religious Knowledge* (1940) was concerned with the problem of knowledge in the light of modern science and used the empirical method to defend Christian faith. Against dualism and idealism, he advocated ⌐ critical realism which assumes the existence of God.

Macintyre, Alasdair Chalmers
(1929–   )
British philosopher. After studying at Manchester and Oxford he taught in Manchester, Leeds and Oxford and then became professor of sociology in the university of Essex. In 1970 he moved to the United States, becoming professor at Boston and Vanderbilt. In addition to his early works *Christianity and Marxism* (1954) and *New Essays in Philosophical Theology* (which he edited with A. G. N. *Flew), his most recent books *After Virtue* (1981) and *Whose Justice, Which Rationality?* (1988) have been of concern to theologians because of their stress on the importance of tradition.

MacKinnon, Donald MacKenzie
(1913–   )
Scottish theologian and philosopher. Born in Edinburgh, after studying in Oxford and Edinburgh he taught for many years in Oxford, during the Second World War directing a special course in philosophy for officer cadets. He subsequently became professor in Aberdeen and Cambridge. Author mostly of articles, his main concerns are in theology, metaphysics and moral philosophy. His work is allusive, approaching topics at a tangent through historical incidents or particular texts. His influence has been much greater than the number of his publications suggests. His works include *The Stripping of the Altars* (1969) and *The Problem of Metaphysics* (1974).

Mackintosh, Hugh Ross (1870–1936)
Scottish theologian. Born in Paisley, he studied in Edinburgh, Freiburg, Halle and Marburg, and after parish work became professor in Edinburgh. A liberal evangelical, he was particularly involved in introducing continental writers to Britain. His best known book is *Types of Modern Theology*, published posthumously.

Macmurray, John (1891–1960)
British philosopher. He was professor in London and Edinburgh. In his main work, *The Self as Agent* (1957), he argued that, rather than taking the self as subject as a starting point for philosophy, it would be better to take the self as agent, since thought derives from action. He developed this line in terms of community in *Persons in Relation* (1961).

McPherson, Aimée Semple
(1890–1944)
Evangelist. Born in Canada, she was converted by the evangelist Robert J. Semple and went with him as a missionary to China. Widowed after three months, she returned home; her second marriage ended in divorce. Travelling widely with her mother through the United States, she developed her 'four-square' gospel: Christ as saviour and healer, the baptism of the Holy Spirit, speaking in tongues, and the second coming. She is supposed to have broadcast the first radio sermon. She organized the International Church of the Foursquare Gospel.

Macquarrie, John (1919–   )
Scottish theologian. He studied at Glasgow university and returned to teach there after a pastorate. In 1962 he was appointed professor at Union Theological Seminary, New York, later returning to be professor in Oxford. His first writing was on existentialism, and he translated *Heidegger's *Being and Time* into English. While in America he became an Episcopalian and this has left a mark on his subsequent theology; his major works are *Twentieth-Century Religious Thought* (1963, and twice revised), *Principles of Christian Theology* (1966), and *Jesus Christ in Modern Thought* (1990). He has proved a successful mediator between the academic world and the parishes, in producing a believing form of academic theology.

Maimonides (Moses ben Maimon, 1135–1204; known as Rambam)
Spanish Jewish philosopher. Born in Cordova, and trained by his father as a

Talmudist, he fled during a persecution and settled at Fez in Morocco, finally becoming head of the Jewish community in Cairo and physician to the sultan. His aim was to reconcile Jewish thought with *Aristotelian philosophy as presented by contemporary Arab writers, doing for Judaism what *Thomas Aquinas did for Christianity. He wrote a commentary on the Mishnah and produced a version of the Talmud classified by subject matter, but his most widely known work is his *Guide for the Perplexed*, written to reconcile reason with faith. His *Mishneh Torah* codified rabbinic law and ritual. His work influenced mediaeval thinkers like *Albertus Magnus and Thomas Aquinas and later, differently, *Spinoza. He has been called 'the second Moses'.

Malebranche, Nicolas (1638–1715)
French philosopher. After ordination he spent his life at the Oratory in Paris (*see* **Bérulle**). Seeking to reconcile the thought of Descartes with Catholic belief, he produced a highly original philosophical system. He denied that matter acted on mind, seeing sensation as a new creative act in the mind to correspond with what is the case in the empirical world. Things are known through ideas which are archetypes in the mind of God and are revealed to us supernaturally (this view is known as occasionalism). His most important works are *Search for the Truth* (1674) and *Treatise on Nature and Grace* (1680).

Mannheim, Karl (1893–1947)
Hungarian sociologist. Born in Budapest, he studied in Heidelberg, and became professor in Frankfurt. He made his name with *Ideology and Utopia* (1929, ET 1936), which showed how thought was conditioned by the social position of the group to which the thinker belonged, so that all social thought was ideological. This raised serious problems for any claims to objective knowledge. The approach was presented as the beginnings of a sociology of knowledge. However, Mannheim's career was interrupted by the Nazi rise to power, and this along with the criticism which he encountered led to a change of direction when he moved to London. His subsequent *Man and Society in an Age of Reconstruction* (1941) is about irrationalism in society and the destruction of standards.

Mansel, Henry Longueville (1820–71)
British theologian. Born the son of a Northamptonshire vicar, he studied at Ox-

ford, was ordained and became professor of philosophy there. He went on to be dean of St Paul's, but died three years later. His *The Limits of Religious Thought Examined*, delivered as lectures in 1858, argued that God cannot be known by reason alone: revelation is needed, and is above criticism. Christian dogma cannot be rationalized and philosophical theology is an impossibility.

Manson, Thomas Walter (1893–1958)
British biblical scholar. He studied at Glasgow and Cambridge, and after working as a Presbyterian minister became professor in Oxford and Manchester, largely as a result of his book *The Teaching of Jesus* (1935). He argued that 'Son of Man' had a corporate significance for Jesus until the end of his ministry, when Jesus recognized his isolation and took the full significance of the role on himself alone. His other major book is *The Sayings of Jesus* (1949).

Manzoni, Alessandro (1785–1873)
Italian poet and novelist. Initially influenced by *Voltaire, and *Diderot's *Encyclopaedia*, he returned to Christianity through *Jansenism. He wrote many sacred poems on the great events of Christianity, plays on the justice of God as opposed to human oppression, and most notably a classic novel, *The Betrothed* (1820–42), which sums up his admiration for simple faith among the poor as opposed to the ambitions of the Catholic clergy. Verdi wrote a Requiem for him.

Marcel, Gabriel (1889–1973)
French Catholic existentialist. He was born in Paris and studied at the Sorbonne, writing literary and dramatic criticism while developing his philosophy. During the First World War he served in the Red Cross. He became a Roman Catholic at the age of forty. He attempted a middle way between scholasticism and atheistic existentialism by what he called a metaphysic of hope, the response of finite human beings to the wider being of God. Working among other things with contrasts between problem and mystery, having and being, he argued the need to move from possessing to participation; when that happens problem turns into mystery and life unfolds as being. His major works were *Being and Having* (1935) and *The Mystery of Being* (two vols., 1950–51).

Marcellus of Ancyra (died 384)
Theologian and bishop. Little is known of his life, except that he became bishop of Ancyra

in Anatolia, was twice deposed for his views, and died in exile. A supporter of *Athanasius at the Council of Nicaea, he went too far, exaggerating the oneness of the Father and the Son: he believed that only the incarnate Logos is the Son and that his independent existence ends when he returns to the Father – hence the addition of 'whose kingdom shall have no end' to the creed of the Council of Constantinople (381), where he was declared a heretic.

Marcion of Pontus (died 160)
Church founder. A wealthy shipowner from Sinope in Pontus (perhaps son of a bishop there), he joined the church in Rome but was excommunicated. He formed his followers into a separate community and his movement spread across the empire. He rejected the Old Testament and reduced the New Testament to an abbreviated Gospel of Luke and ten letters of Paul (which he edited), whom he regarded as the only true apostle. This may have led by reaction to the formation of the orthodox canon. He contrasted a gospel of love to the law, and believed that the God of the Old Testament, cruel, despotic and capricious, had nothing to do with the God of Jesus Christ. He was a major threat to the second-century church.

Marheineke, Philipp Konrad (1780–1846)
German Protestant theologian. Professor in Berlin, he was also in charge of the Church of the Trinity there. He sought to explain Christian doctrines without distortion in terms of *Hegel's philosophy, for example seeking the unity of Catholics (thesis) and Protestants (antithesis) in a higher synthesis.

Maritain, Jacques (1882–1973)
French philosopher. He was born in Paris, studied at the Sorbonne where he was influenced by *Bergson, and became a Roman Catholic. Subsequently he was professor in Paris, Toronto and Princeton. In the 1920s he was a focus for the Catholic revival in art and philosophy. He was also at one time French Canadian ambassador to the Holy See; he spent the last decade of his life in Toulouse with *De Foucauld's Little Brothers of Jesus. Interested in the theory of knowledge, he sought to relate Thomistic theology to many areas of modern philosophy – moral, social, political, aesthetic and educational – and was associated with the neo-Scholastic revival in Europe. He wrote many books, of which *Art and Scholasticism* (1920) is one of the best known.

Marsilius of Padua (c.1275–1342)
Italian political philosopher. From the university of Padua he went to Paris to study medicine, became rector of the university, and after a spell in Avignon and northern Italy practised medicine there. His main work was the *Defender of the Peace* (1324); this argued that civil order must be guaranteed by the state, which derives its authority from the people. The state must have a monopoly of coercion and the church has only the rights granted by the state. This approach undermined political arguments with a theological basis and paved the way for the Renaissance and subsequent developments. He was excommunicated, and spent the rest of his life in Munich at the court there.

Martineau, James (1805–1900)
English Unitarian minister. Born in Norwich, he held various teaching posts before becoming professor of philosophy and then principal in a Manchester college. He opposed the current challenge to religious belief from science; two major works were his two-volume *Types of Ethical Theory* (1885), and *A Study of Religion* (also two volumes, 1888), developing morality as an argument for theism. He did much to organize Unitarianism in England.

Marty, Martin Emil (1928–   )
American theologian and historian. Born in West Point, Nebraska, he studied at Concordia Seminary, the Lutheran School of Theology in Chicago and Chicago University, before serving as pastor in Illinois. He became professor at Chicago Divinity School in 1963 and is also president of Park Ridge Center, Illinois. Since 1956 he has been editor and senior editor of *Christian Century* and from 1963 co-editor of *Christian History*. His wide range of experience has made him a unique figure in the study of modern American religious belief and practice, on which he has written a wide range of books, from *The New Shape of American Religion* (1959) to *Protestantism in the United States* (1985), the first volume of *Modern American Religion* (1986) and *An Invitation to American Catholic History* (1986). Consequently he often becomes the spokesman for American Protestantism. His involvement in Park Ridge also indicates his interest in health, medicine and ethics,

witnessed by his *Health and Medicine in the Lutheran Tradition* (1983).

Marx, Karl Heinrich (1818–83)

German economist. Born in Trier to a family which stood in a long line of Jewish rabbis, he studied law, history and philosophy at Bonn, Berlin and Jena, discovering the thought of *Hegel and *Feuerbach. He wrote his *Communist Manifesto* in 1847. He went to Paris during the 1848 revolution, and then returned to Cologne, from where he was expelled in 1849 after a trial for treason. He spent the rest of his life in England, where he wrote his *magnum opus, Das Kapital* (1867, ET 1887). There is an important difference between what Marx himself wrote and what later came to be developed as Marxism. His early works are particularly important for theology, containing a more complex discussion of religion than is usually supposed in the light of his saying that it is the 'opium of the people'.

Mathews, Shailer (1863–1941)

American Baptist theologian. Born in Portland, Maine, he studied and taught at Colby College, before moving to Chicago Divinity School. A champion of liberalism and the social gospel, he is regarded as the founder of the Chicago school of theology. His major work is *The Social Teaching of Jesus* (1897). He opposed a functionalist approach to current fundamentalism and was concerned that his theology should spread into the church.

Maurice, John Frederick Denison (1805–72)

English theologian. Born near Lowestoft, the son of a Unitarian, and brought up in Bristol, he studied at Cambridge. Religious objections to accepting the Anglican Thirty-Nine Articles, assent to which was then a necessary condition, prevented him from gaining a degree; unable, therefore, to teach, he spent time writing in London. In 1830 he did become an Anglican and went to Oxford, and after a country parish held a hospital chaplaincy (during which he wrote his best-known book, *The Kingdom of Christ*, 1838, which contains a survey of religious and philosophical movements and churches with the famous conclusion that religious movements tend to be right in what they affirm and wrong in what they deny). He was then made professor at King's College, London. Following the 1848 revolutions he joined the Christian Socialists, where he met *Ludlow

and *Kingsley, and later he started a Working Man's College in London. However, his theological views, particularly his rejection of endless punishment in hell, forced him to resign his chair, and after a London parish post he became professor of moral philosophy at Cambridge. Individualistic and distinctive in his approach, and putting great stress on a *living* God, he was one of the most important of English nineteenth-century theological figures.

Maximus Confessor (580–662)

Greek theologian and ascetic. As a young aristocrat he became chief secretary to the emperor, but then went to be a monk at Chrysopolis, where he was later abbot. When the Persians invaded, he fled to Africa. He was a determined opponent of monothelitism (the view that there was only one divine will in Christ), which was widespread in the East, and by his prolific writings became one of the main architects of Byzantine theology. The emphasis of his thought was that the purpose of history is the incarnation of God and the divinization of humanity by the restoration of the kingdom of God. His devotional writings include a mystical interpretation of the liturgy. His opposition to monothelitism and his sympathies with the Western church got him into trouble with the Byzantine emperor; his tongue and right hand were cut off and he was exiled to the Black Sea coast.

Max Müller, Friedrich (1823–1900)

German philologist. Born in Dessau, after studies in Leipzig and Berlin he went to Paris, and later to England, where he became professor in Oxford. He specialized in comparative religion, edited a series of Eastern religious classics and was very influential in Victorian England. His own major work was a four-volume series: *Natural Religion* (1889), *Physical Religion* (1891), *Anthropological Religion* (1892) and *Theosophy, or Psychological Religion* (1893).

Mbiti, John S. (1931–   )

Kenyan theologian. Born at Kitui, Kenya, he studied at Makerere University, Uganda; Barrington College, Rhode Island; and Cambridge. Originally a member of the African Inland Church, he was ordained an Anglican and became professor at Makerere, subsequently moving to be director of the World Council of Churches' Ecumenical Institute at Celigny, Switzerland. He is now a pastor in a Swiss Reformed Church. He is the most prolific of African theologians, and his writings cover a wide range of topics. His books challenge the traditional Western distinction between general and special revelation by stressing that God can be found in African religious traditions as much as in the Judaeo-Christian tradition. Chief among them are *African Religions and Philosophy* (1969) and *Bible and Theology in African Christianity* (1986).

Mechthild of Magdeburg (c.1210–80)
German mystic. Descended from a noble family in Saxony, she left home to join an austere community of the Beguines in Magdeburg, later moving to a Cistercian convent at Helfta. A visionary, she wrote down her visions in *The Flowing Light of the Godhead*.

Melanchthon, Philip (1497–1560)
German Reformer. His real name was Schwarzerd (Black-earth), and his name, the Greek equivalent, came from an uncle as a tribute to his linguistic skill. He studied at the universities of Heidelberg, Tübingen (where he was noticed by *Erasmus) and Wittenberg (where he became a professor and a supporter of *Luther). His *Loci communes* (1521) was the first systematic account of Lutheran theology. The leading humanist among the Lutheran Reformers, he was a moderate ready for compromise and openness, with a keen interest in education. He wrote textbooks and left his mark on schools and universities.

Meland, Bernard Eugene (1899–   )
American theologian. Born of Norwegian immigrants, he was educated at Park College, the University of Illinois, McCormick Theological Seminary and the University of Chicago. He also studied under Rudolf *Otto and Friedrich *Heiler in Marburg. After teaching at Central College, Missouri, and Pomona College, he became professor at the University of Chicago. A member of the Chicago school, he was interested in the relationship between faith and culture. His books included *Faith and Culture* (1953), *Modern Man's Worship* (1934) and *The Realities of Faith* (1962).

Melito of Sardis (died 180)
Bishop and theologian. Virtually nothing is known of his life. Though he wrote a good deal, only fragments were known until the publication in 1940 of his *Homily on the Pasch*. This Eastern sermon brings out parallels with the Passover in a polemical way; the work is markedly anti-Jewish; it also demonstrates the growing Hellenization of the Asian church at this time.

Melville, Andrew (1545–1622)
Scottish Reformed theologian. Born near Melrose, he studied at St Andrews, Paris and Poitiers; he met *Beza in Geneva and became professor there. On his return to Scotland he became principal of Glasgow university, where he carried out major reforms, and then of St Mary's College, St Andrews. Though he was a distinguished scholar, he was more significant as a churchman. He was an opponent of the imposition of episcopacy on the Scottish Kirk after John *Knox's reform, successfully advocating the system of presbyteries; conflict with King James I of England brought him imprisonment in the Tower of London. He ended his career in France, as professor in the university of Sedan.

Mendelssohn, Moses (1729–86)
Jewish philosopher. Born at Dessau, he studied widely in Berlin and then became tutor to a rich silk manufacturer, rising to become his partner. In his philosophy he utilized the thought of *Maimonides for his own day. He did not produce a system, but upheld freedom of conscience and the rights of the individual, including freedom of religion, in the state. His books include *Philosophical Conversations* (1755) and *On Evidence in the Science of Metaphysics* (1763).

Menno Simons (c.1496–1561)
Anabaptist leader. A parish priest in Friesland, he left the Roman Catholic church because of doubts over infant baptism, and after reading Luther joined the Anabaptists, then recovering from persecution. For twenty-five years he travelled round the Netherlands and Baltic Germany organizing congregations, spending his last years in Holstein. He gave his name to the Mennonites. He stressed Christianity as a closed community of believers who are 'new creatures', having entered on a spiritual resurrection with the church as a corporate new creation.

Mercier, Desiré Joseph (1851–1926)
Belgian Catholic philosopher. He studied at Malines and Louvain, and after ordination became professor of philosophy at both

places successively. A supporter of the Thomistic revival, he was interested in the relationship between the principles of the philosophy of *Thomas Aquinas and natural science. He founded a Higher Institute of Philosophy at Malines, and became Archbishop of Malines and then a cardinal. During the First World War he upheld Belgian interests against the Germans, and was a leading supporter of Christian unity in the famous Malines conversations. However, he was hostile to the Modernist movement and denounced *Tyrrell.

Merleau-Ponty, Maurice (1908–61)
French philosopher. Born at Rochefort-sur-Mer, he was a schoolteacher until the Second World War. Subsequently, he became professor in Lyons and Paris. Though influenced by *Husserl, he developed a phenomenology of his own. Rejecting a dualistic approach, he saw life as arranged in physical, biological and mental spheres; since consciousness arises out of a particular individual perspective, it is inevitably subjective, and this subjectivity is not completely overcome by the subjectivity of language. His works include The Structure of Behaviour (1942) and The Phenomenology of Perception (1943).

Merton, Thomas (1915–68)
Catholic monk. Born in Prades, France, he had an unhappy and itinerant childhood; his parents, both artists, died when he was young. He was educated in Bermuda, France and England. After studying at Cambridge, he went to Columbia University, New York. There he joined the Catholic Church and became a Trappist monk in Gethsemani Abbey, Kentucky. He died as the result of an accident at a monastic conference in Bangkok. He became world-famous for his autobiography, The Seven-Storey Mountain (1948), and followed this by a wealth of other writing, displaying increasing openness. He was an articulate interpreter of the monastic experience, experiencing tension between the solitary life and social involvement.

Mesrob (c.345–440)
Armenian patriarch. A scholar and historian, he sought to develop the American church along national lines, eliminating foreign influences. He constructed an Armenian alphabet, and was active in translating into the Bible. He also encouraged Armenian monasticism.

Methodius (c.815–85)
Born to a Greek senatorial family in Thessalonica, with his brother *Cyril he was sent to organize the Slav church in Moravia. On the premature death of his brother on a visit they paid to Rome, he was consecrated bishop and returned, only to be imprisoned through the action of hostile German bishops. His release was secured only at the price of using the Slavonic language in liturgy.

Methodius of Olympus (died 310)
Bishop in Lycia. Little is known of his life, except that he was martyred. He wrote a good deal, but most of his work is lost. He was an opponent of *Origen, particularly over the idea of a completely spiritual resurrection. He was influenced by Platonic thinking, to the point of composing dialogues: his only complete surviving work is a Symposium, praising virginity.

Metz, Johann-Baptist (1928–   )
German Roman Catholic theologian. Born in Bavaria, he is now professor in the university of Münster. He is a leading figure in political theology, seeing Christianity as a constructive critique of society and the church. His works include Theology of the World (1968) and Faith in History and Society (1980).

Meyer, Eduard (1855–1930)
German historian. He was professor of ancient history at the University of Berlin and one of the most important influences on critical study of antiquity. He wrote an eight-volume History of Antiquity and a number of works on Christianity and Judaism, including a defence of the historicity of the Acts of the Apostles.

Meyer, Heinrich August Wilhelm (1800–73)
German New Testament scholar. Born in Gotha, he studied theology at Jena and held various church posts in Hanover. His life's work was as editor of a Critical and Exegetical Commentary on the New Testament, to which he himself contributed many volumes, and which in revised form still exists today.

Michaelis, Johann David (1717–91)
German biblical scholar. Son of a professor in Halle, he studied there and afterwards for eighteen months in England. He financed himself by translating novels, but then became professor in Göttingen. He revised *Lowth's work on Hebrew poetry and pro-

duced a translation of the Bible with notes 'for the unlearned'. Primarily a philologist, he was paradoxically more of a pioneer in New Testament scholarship than in Old Testament, where he failed to see the significance of new developments.

Migne, Jacques-Paul (1800–75)

French Catholic priest and publisher. Following a disagreement with his bishop he went to Paris and after unsuccessful attempts at journalism decided to publish a universal library for the clergy. He ran a large publishing house which produced many works, but his memorial is the series of the Latin and Greek church fathers comprising the 221-volume *Patrologia Latina* (1844–1864) and the 162-volume *Patrologia Graeca* (1857–1866), the one edition which is anywhere near complete. His workshops and moulds were destroyed in a disastrous fire in 1868.

Mill, John Stuart (1806–73)

English philosopher and economist. An infant prodigy, born in London, under his father he learned Greek at the age of three, Latin at seven and philosophy at twelve. At seventeen he began work as a clerk for the East India Company, rising over thirty-five years to be head of the department. At the end of his life he became a member of Parliament. He experienced a deep crisis at the age of twenty because of his intellectual development. He made his name as a philosopher with his *System of Logic* (1843) and also wrote an influential treatise on political economy and an *Essay on Liberty* (1859). A utilitarian, he argued that religion may be morally useful without being intellectually sustainable; he saw the value of the example of Jesus, but believed that both Jesus and religion could be dispensed with (*Utilitarianism*, 1863).

Milton, John (1608–74)

English poet. Born in London, after studying at Cambridge he lived on his father's estate in Buckinghamshire and devoted himself to scholarship and literature. One of the greatest of English poets, he wrote his 'Ode on the Morning of Christ's Nativity' at the age of twenty-one. Ten years later he moved to London, where he became involved in controversy; he joined the Presbyterians and in the Civil War supported the Commonwealth. He became blind in 1651. In danger of losing his life at the Restoration, he was pardoned. His poetry culminated in his epic

Paradise Lost (1667), with its sequel *Paradise Regained* (1671), and also *Samson Agonistes*, which with its phrase 'eyeless in Gaza' reflects Milton himself. His major theological work is *On Christian Doctrine*, published posthumously, which denies that all the persons of the Trinity are equal and eternal and that creation was from nothing.

Miranda, José Porfirio (1924–   )

Mexican liberation theologian. He has long been an adviser and lecturer to groups of workers and students throughout Mexico, and has held chairs in several universities and technological institutes there. A professed communist, he is not a Marxist; he distinguishes between Marxism and the thought of Karl *Marx. His main books are about Marx: *Marx and the Bible* (1971), *Marx against the Marxists* (1979), *Communism in the Bible* (1981). He is in favour of collective ownership, but not state ownership.

Moberly, Robert Campbell (1845–1903)

Anglican theologian. Son of a bishop, after studying at Oxford he later became professor there. A high churchman, his major work was *Ministerial Priesthood* (1897), written against Roman Catholic criticisms of Anglican orders; it saw the priesthood of Christ being the determinative factor in the theology of the ministry. He also wrote a study of the atonement, *Atonement and Personality* (1901).

Moffatt, James (1870–1944)

Scottish New Testament scholar. Born in Glasgow, he studied there and then served in the ministry. Then, after teaching in Oxford and Glasgow, he became professor at Union Theological Seminary, New York. He was a pioneer in producing a colloquial modern translation of the Bible (NT 1913, OT 1924) and edited a commentary on the New Testament.

Möhler, Johann Adam (1796–1838)

German Catholic historian and theologian. He studied in Tübingen and after ordination became professor there and in Munich; finally he was dean of Würzburg cathedral. A precursor of the Modernists, he was concerned to mediate between Catholicism and Protestantism, and as a result verged on the unorthodox. His major work was *Symbolics. An Account of the Dogmatic Differences between Catholic and Protestants accord-*

ing to their Public Confessions of Faith (1832).

Molina, Luis de (1535–1600)
Spanish theologian. After becoming a Jesuit he taught in Coimbra and Evora and then spent several years writing in Lisbon; he retired to Cuenca and was appointed professor in Madrid the year he died. In his *The Concord of Free Will with the Gift of Grace* (1588), a highly controversial work, he sought to defend, against Protestantism, the doctrine that human beings are free to resist or accept grace, a doctrine which became known as Molinism.

Molinos, Miguel de (c.1640–97)
Spanish mystic. Born near Saragossa, after studying theology he was sent to Rome, where he became a distinguished confessor and spiritual director. His *Spiritual Guide* (1675), teaching that the soul achieves perfection when it abandons effort and desire and becomes lost in God, brought him fame, but because of the consequences drawn from this by the nuns he directed, he was condemned and sentenced to life imprisonment.

Moltmann, Jürgen (1926–   )
German Reformed theologian. Born in Hamburg, he was conscripted into the German army in the Second World War at seventeen, captured in Belgium, and held prisoner of war in England. After studying at Göttingen, where he was influenced by *Barth's theology, he served as a country pastor and became professor at Wuppertal and then at Bonn. He is now professor of theology in Tübingen. His first major book, *Theology of Hope* (1965), combined insights of *Bloch with a rediscovery of biblical eschatology and was widely influential; *The Crucified God* (1973) took up the issue of the nature of Christian belief after Auschwitz; *Church in the Power of the Spirit* (1975) sees the church as a messianic community. A systematic theology, still in process, so far comprises *The Trinity and the Kingdom of God* (1980), *God in Creation* (1985), *The God of Jesus Christ* (1989). It shows a particular concern with the significance of current ecological issues for contemporary theology.

Montaigne, Michel de (1533–92)
French essayist. Born of a noble family in Périgord, he was first made to learn Latin as a mother tongue from a German tutor. He

then went to school in Bordeaux, studied law in Toulouse and became a counsellor. After marrying a rich wife in 1565 he retired to the ancestral chateau he had now inherited, travelled, and became mayor of Bordeaux. His *Essays*, of which he wrote three books, were very influential (e.g. on Francis *Bacon and *Pascal): they presented ancient philosophy (first a form of Stoicism, later Epicureanism) in a just-Christian way, commending it as an ethical system free from religious influence. At the same time he remained a nominal Catholic.

Montalembert, Charles René Forbes (1810–70)
French Roman Catholic theologian. Born in London to an émigré family, he became a liberal who associated himself with *Lacordaire and *Lamennais. Failing to gain papal support on a journey to Rome, when he returned to France he turned to politics, and sat in the Chamber of Deputies. He continued to support liberal views, which aroused opposition. His main work was a multi-volume history of Western monasticism.

Montanus (second century)
Apocalyptic prophet. A convert to Christianity from Asia Minor, he claimed that the Holy Spirit spoke through him and that he was bringing the church into the final stage of revelation, the age of the Paraclete. He gathered a large following, the most notable among whom was *Tertullian. Returning to the pattern of the earliest church, he included a large number of women in his movement. He has proved to be of renewed interest to modern Pentecostal movements.

Montefiore, Claude Joseph Goldsmid (1858–1938)
Biblical scholar. A liberal Jew, he studied at Oxford under *Jowett, and after inheriting a considerable fortune was able to live independently. He wrote on Judaism and the Gospels, stressing the importance of the rabbinic writings for the understanding of the New Testament. A major work is his *The Synoptic Gospels* (two volumes, 1909).

Montesquieu, Charles Louis Joseph de Sécondat, Baron de la Brède et de (1689–1755)
French philosophical historian. He studied law in Bordeaux and was involved in local government there, but soon adopted a liter-

ary career. His anonymous *Letters* (1721) ridiculed Catholic church dogmas. After becoming a member of the French Academy he travelled widely in Europe and England, a journey which led to the first modern work on the philosophy of history. His *The Spirit of the Laws* (1748) attacked intolerance, seeing Christianity as a powerful moral source in society. It was banned by the Catholic church.

Moody, Dwight Lyman (1837–1899)
American evangelist. Born in Massachusetts, the son of a bricklayer, he had to work from the age of thirteen, and although he was converted to Christianity, his acceptance was delayed through lack of learning. He became a successful businessman in Chicago and organized a Sunday School, later deciding to devote himself to such work. With Ira Sankey, he had a triumphant mission to Britain, which formed the basis for equally eventful missions all over the United States. He also founded a Bible Institute in Chicago. His message was non-theological, non-denominational and conservative, prior to fundamentalistic controversies.

Moore, George Foot (1851–1931)
American scholar. He was born in West Chester, Pennsylvania, and after studying at Yale, Union Theological Seminary, New York, and in Tübingen, he served as a Presbyterian pastor. He then became professor at Andover Seminary and at Harvard. He is particularly known for his three-volume study *Judaism in the First Centuries of the Christian Era* (1927–30).

More, Hannah (1745–1833)
English political propagandist and religious writer. She spent her early life in Bristol, after which an unexpected inheritance gave her independence. By associating with literary circles in London, she came to know the evangelical Clapham sect, which encouraged philanthropic activities. She returned to the West Country, started a Sunday school and wrote religious tracts. These sought to make the poor content with their lot and not try to be revolutionaries.

More, Thomas (1478–1535)
Lord Chancellor of England. Descended from a prominent London family, after studying at Oxford he became a lawyer, entered Parliament and became Lord Chancellor under Henry VIII. His famous *Utopia* (1516)

was written early in his brilliant career: it describes an ideal community practising a natural religion and living by a natural law, and contains much satirical criticism of contemporary abuses. His career collapsed in 1532 when he opposed the king over his divorce; he later refused to forswear obedience to the pope and accept royal supremacy in religious matters. This led to imprisonment in the Tower of London (during which he wrote *A Dialogue of Comfort against Tribulation*) and execution.

Mott, Jo. Raleigh (1865–1955)
American churchman. A Methodist layman, he was born in New York; after studying in Iowa and Cornell he was converted and became involved in the YMCA. He helped to form the World Student Christian Federation and was president of the 1910 Edinburgh World Missionary Conference with its slogan 'the evangelization of the world in this generation'. For the rest of his life he was actively involved in ecumenical affairs.

Moule, Charles Francis Digby (1908–   )
English New Testament scholar. After studying at Cambridge, apart from brief pastoral appointments he remained at the university until his retirement, becoming professor there. Of a distinguished evangelical family, he remained in that tradition and his works were basically philological and exegetical. In addition to his *Idiom Book of New Testament Greek* (1953), his *The Birth of the New Testament* (1962) and *The Origin of Christology* (1977) have remained of lasting influence.

Mowinckel, Sigmund Olaf Plytt (1884–1965)
Norwegian Old Testament scholar. After studying at Oslo, Copenhagen, Marburg and Giessen he spent his life teaching at Oslo. In a six-volume series of studies on the psalms he argued that some reflect a pre-exilic liturgy of the enthronement of Yahweh, a theory which he developed in connection with messianic ideology in *He that Cometh* (1956).

Mühlenberg, Henry Melchior (1711–87)
German Lutheran clergyman. Son of a shoemaker in Hanover, after study in Göttingen and Jena he became inspector of an orphanage. He thought of going as a missionary to the East Indies, but was called to Pennsylvania, where the Lutheran church was in

decline. In his revival work, he founded the first Lutheran synod in America there and did much to strengthen American Lutheranism generally.

Münzer, Thomas (1489–1525)
German Anabaptist and radical Reformer. After studying in Leipzig and Frankfurt, he became confessor to a convent in Thuringia. Under the influence of *Hus, *Luther and others he became a Protestant preacher, calling for radical social and religious reform. He believed that the church had fallen from purity after the apostles and that purity would be restored apocalyptically in his own times. His views constantly involved him in conflict and he eventually preached open revolt. He joined the Peasants' Revolt, and when they were defeated in battle he was captured and executed.

Muratori, Lodovico Antonio (1672–1750)
Italian historian and theologian. Born near Modena, after a Jesuit education he was ordained priest. For five years he was on the staff of the Ambrosiana in Milan, one of the world's first public libraries. While there he discovered a list of New Testament writings, the oldest extant, and this bears his name (Muratorian canon). He subsequently became archivist to the Duke of Modena. He wrote many theological works, some under a pseudonym, and was accused for heresy by the Spanish Inquisition, but died before he could be brought to trial.

Neander, Johann August Wilhelm (1789–1850)
German Protestant church historian. Born David Mendel, he changed his name when he was converted to Christianity. He studied under *Schleiermacher and became professor in Berlin. He held that individuals are more important in recreating the past than institutions and that the history of the church is the history of the interpenetration of human life with the divine life of Christ. After studies of individual Christian figures he wrote a six-volume church history.

Neill, Stephen Charles (1900–84)
English New Testament scholar. He spent twenty years in India, becoming bishop of Tinnevelly. In 1944 he returned to Europe for health reasons and in 1962 became professor of missions in Hamburg and then professor in Nairobi. A gifted communicator, he lectured and wrote much; his books include *The History of Christian Mission* (1964), *The Interpretation of the New Testament 1861–1961* (1966) and *Anglicanism* (1974).

Nestle, Eberhard (1851–1913)
German biblical scholar. Professor at Ulm and Tübingen. After working on the Septuagint, the Greek Old Testament, he became editor of what proved one of the standard Greek texts of the New Testament. He also wrote many other aids to biblical study.

Nestorius (died 451)
Syrian theologian. He entered a monastery in Antioch and probably studied under *Theodore of Mopsuestia. A famous preacher, he was made bishop of Constantinople, where he was a vigorous defender of orthodoxy. However, he was opposed to the increasing use of the title *theotokos* (mother of God) for the Virgin Mary, which he thought unbalanced if left on its own. Here opinion consolidated against him, not least because of his forthright way of defending his views, and he was condemned as a heretic by the Council of Ephesus in 431. He was sent back to Antioch and later banished to Upper Egypt. Only fragments of his work survived until his *The Bazaar of Heracleides* was discovered in a Syriac translation in 1910. Whether his condemnation was a fair one in terms of the christology of the time is much disputed; at all events, bishops who found his views more satisfactory than the official line formed a Nestorian church, which has lasted to the present day.

Neusner, Jacob (1932–   )
Jewish scholar. Born in Hartford, Connecticut, he studied at Columbia university and became professor at Brown university,

where he established a notable centre for the study of Judaism. He subsequently moved to the University of South Florida. He has translated the Mishnah and many rabbinic works, and written more than 300 books.

Newman, John Henry (1801–90)
English theologian. Son of a London banker, and brought up an evangelical in the Church of England, he studied and taught at Oxford and became vicar of the university church. His sermons made him a nationally known figure. With *Keble, *Pusey and others he wrote 'Tracts for the Times'. His aim was to demonstrate that the Church of England, based on patristic tradition, held a middle place between modern Roman Catholicism and modern Protestantism. His famous Tract 90 (1841), which sought to reconcile the Thirty-Nine Articles of the Church of England with Roman Catholic doctrine (1841), was highly controversial, and he was silenced by his bishop. He had already begun to have doubts about the Anglican church, and four years later became a Roman Catholic, a move which he defended in his *Essay on the Development of Christian Doctrine* (1845). Although he later became a cardinal, his relations with the Roman Catholic church were never easy. Among his major subsequent works were *Apologia pro Vita Sua* (1864), provoked by *Kingsley; his famous poem *The Dream of Gerontius* (1865), depicting a soul going to God at the hour of death and immortalized when set to music by Edward Elgar; and *A Grammar of Assent* (1870). His subsequent influence has been very great, not so much because of his theology as because of his views on doctrinal development and his psychological and moral insights.

Newton, Isaac (1642–1727)
English mathematician and physicist. Born of a Lincolnshire farming family, he studied at Cambridge and became professor of mathematics there, later holding distinguished posts in London and serving as a member of Parliament. He is well known for formulating the universal law of gravity, discovering differential calculus, and analysing light through a prism, but it is not always recognized that the discoveries are set in a religious context. He was converted at university and believed that his discoveries were communicated to him through the Holy Spirit, which was showing him the rationality of the universe. He kept his somewhat unor-

thodox religion in the private sphere: his interests extended to church history, chronology and prophecy.

Newton, John (1725–1807)
English evangelical. The son of a shipmaster, he was press-ganged into the Navy, tried to escape, was arrested in West Africa and spent two years as the slave of a slave-trader. Converted in a storm on the voyage back home, he spent more time at sea and in the slave trade before becoming surveyor of the tides at Liverpool. Under the influence of *Whitefield he began to study and became curate of Olney, Buckinghamshire, where with the poet William *Cowper he produced a famous set of *Olney Hymns* (1779). He later moved to London as a city rector and was an influence in the evangelical revival, not least on *Wilberforce. His hymns include 'Glorious Things of Thee are Spoken' and 'How Sweet the Name of Jesus Sounds'.

Nicholas of Cusa (1401–64)
German philosopher. From Cues on the Moselle, he studied at Heidelberg, Padua and Cologne. After ordination he became dean of St Florin's, Coblenz. He did much work on behalf of Pope Nicholas V, as a result of which he was made a cardinal. Though appointed bishop of Brixen in the Tyrol, he had trouble with the local ruler, as a result of which he eventually had to return to Rome, where he spent the rest of his life. His most important work was his treatise *On Learned Ignorance* (1440), in a Platonist vein: learned ignorance is the highest stage of knowledge possible to the human intellect, since absolute truth is unknowable, knowledge being complex, relative and approximate. In this approach he was a forerunner of the Renaissance.

Nicholas of Lyra (1265–1349)
French Franciscan scholar. He studied and taught in Paris, before becoming provincial of his order. He had a range of learning rare in the Middle Ages, knowing Hebrew and reading Jewish commentaries. He produced a commentary on the Bible, *Postillae perpetuae*, in two parts, the first giving the literal sense and the second the moral sense, which was directed against the extravagances of figurative interpretation; it was the first commentary on the Bible to be printed.

Nicole, Pierre (1625–95)
French Catholic theologian. Born in Chartres, he studied in Paris and taught at

Port-Royal, defending e.g. the eucharistic doctrine of transubstantiation against *Calvinism. He was also a moderate and skilful advocate of *Jansenism (though he renounced it in a posthumous work), and an opponent of mysticism.

Niebuhr, Barthold Georg (1776–1831)
German historian. Born in Copenhagen, after studying at the university of Kiel he became private secretary to the Danish minister of finance and then entered state service. He became director of the national bank of Prussia and in 1810 was made royal historiographer and professor in Berlin, writing a famous Roman history (1812, ET 1847–51). His next post, as ambassador to Rome, was the ideal position from which to pursue his researches. He resigned in 1823 and moved to Bonn, where he died. He introduced new critical principles into the study of ancient history and was a pioneer in the assessment of sources.

Niebuhr, Helmut Richard (1894–1962)
American theologian. Born in Missouri, he studied at Eden Theological Seminary, Washington University and Yale Divinity School; after serving as a pastor he returned to Eden to teach until 1931, with a brief period as president of Elmhurst College; he then moved to Yale Divinity School and in 1938 became professor at Yale University. His thought was particularly influenced by the work of Ernst *Troeltsch. His first book, *The Social Sources of Denominationalism* (1929), attacked the church's acceptance of middle-class values; his interest in the relationship between culture and faith was continued in important books on *The Meaning of Revelation* (1941), *Christ and Culture* (1951) and *Radical Monotheism and Western Culture* (1960), all concerned with different forms of the relationship between Christianity and the modern world. The last of these books highlights the theocentric character of his theology. He was brother of

Niebuhr, Reinhold (1892–1971)
American theologian. Born in Missouri, he studied at Eden Theological College and Yale Divinity School and then for thirteen years was pastor of a Detroit church. Here he became involved in the Social Gospel movement, and his experience of industrial society shaped the rest of his life. His critical reaction to the liberal Protestantism in which he had been brought up was expressed in his first book *Does Civilization Need Religion?* (1928). His move to become professor at Union Theological Seminary, New York, virtually coincided with the beginning of the Great Depression. His classic *Moral Man and Immoral Society* (1932) argued that moral values when put into practice collectively produce behaviour which seems immoral from an individual perspective and highlighted the weakness of liberal Protestant social ethics. He was much exercised in interpreting the political developments of the 1930s; at the same time in his writing he presented Christianity as a prophetic religion and offered his own *Interpretation of Christian Ethics* (1935). His greatest book, *The Nature and Destiny of Man* (1941, 1943), opposes a biblical view of human nature to Renaissance humanism, focussing on creation and fall, atonement and the second coming of Christ. In later years his interest moved to history and the theology of history (*Faith and History*, 1949; *The Self and the Dramas of History*, 1954; *The Structure of Nations and Empires*, 1959); a stroke in 1952 hampered his activities thereafter. His prophetic approach and his political involvement made him a controversial figure whose full significance has perhaps yet to be appreciated.

Nietzsche, Friedrich Wilhelm (1844–1900)
German philosopher and philologist. Son of a Lutheran pastor in Saxony, he studied in Bonn and Leipzig, and was briefly professor in Basle before resigning for ill health. He became insane in 1889. He criticized Christianity and its ethics for otherworldliness and resented it for being a slave morality, which was condemning Europe to mediocrity. He was concerned with the will to power which can transform human values; claiming that God was dead, he saw this as the opening up of new horizons to those who accepted the challenge. In this context he envisaged the future superman, pursuing his goal without scruples, beyond good or evil, which were the values of a defunct Christianity. His ideas, prophetic and expressed in a disjointed and aphoristic way, were frequently misinterpreted, for example by the Fascists; nevertheless he has been a significant influence on twentieth-century thought. His major works include *The Gay Science* (1882), *Thus Spake Zarathustra* (1883), *Beyond Good and Evil* (1886) and *The Antichrist* (1888).

Nineham, Dennis Eric (1921–)
English New Testament scholar. After studying at Oxford he taught there, subsequently becoming professor in London, Cambridge and Bristol, and Warden of Keble College, Oxford. His approach to the New Testament has been more critical than most of his English contemporaries, taking note of developments in European scholarship; this was particularly evident in his commentary on the Gospel of Mark. Interest in the nature of biblical authority led him to a study of hermeneutics, from which he turned to an exploration of cultural relativism. Much of his work has been done in the form of articles; his major book is *The Use and Abuse of the Bible* (1976).

Nock, Arthur Darby (1902–63)
Classical scholar. Born in Portsmouth, he studied and then taught at Cambridge, in 1930 moving to the United States to become professor of the history of religions in Harvard. He wrote authoritatively on the Hellenistic background to the New Testament but is particularly known for his study *Conversion* (1933), which examined the circumstances and psychology of religious conversion in the centuries before and after Christ, questioning many current assumptions.

Norris, John (1657–1711)
English philosopher. After studying and teaching in Oxford, he spent the rest of his life in parishes in Somerset and Wiltshire. The last of the group known as the Cambridge Platonists, he was influenced by *Malebranche and wrote against *Locke and the deists.

Noth, Martin (1902–68)
German Old Testament scholar. Born in Dresden the son of a university chaplain, he studied at Erlangen, Rostock and Leipzig, where he was a pupil of *Alt and became his assistant. He was later made professor in Königsberg and, after the Second World War, in Bonn. His most important work was on the history of traditions and on the social and political structure of early Israel and the biblical books in which that is described. Thus he argued that before the monarchy the Israelite tribes were organized as an amphictyony similar to those attested in classical Greece; he also saw Deuteronomy as a prelude to a Deuteronomistic history extending from Joshua to II Kings. Although doubts were eventually cast on parts of his work, it was influential for a generation, above all in his *History of Israel* (1950). A scholar's scholar, he was uninterested in literature, politics or church affairs, but like *Barth was a devoted Mozartian. He died in Israel and was buried in Bethlehem.

Novalis (pseudonym of Friedrich Leopold von Hardenberg, 1772–1801)
German Romantic poet. From a Moravian family, he studied at Jena, Leipzig and Wittenberg. A Romantic mystic, his 'Jesus' poems contributed to the quest of the historical Jesus. His *Heinrich von Ofterdingen* records his spiritual quest in terms of a search for a blue flower.

Novatian (third century)
Roman theologian. A Roman presbyter, he became leader of a sect challenging the then pope, *Cornelius, for excessive compromise with pagan religion and was also consecrated bishop of Rome. The first theologian at Rome to write in Latin, he was later martyred.

Nygren, Anders (1890–1978)
Swedish theologian. Born in Göteborg, he studied at Lund, where after a pastorate he became professor of systematic theology and then bishop. He played a major part in the World Council of Churches and the Lutheran World Federation. His best known book, *Agape and Eros* (1953), uses a method of motif research to trace the conflict between *agape*, *eros* and *nomos* down through Christianity.

Ogden, Schubert Miles (1928–)
American theologian. Born in Cincinnati, he studied at Ohio Wesleyan University and the University of Chicago. After ordination as a Methodist minister he has taught at Perkins School of Theology, Southern Methodist

university, leaving only between 1969–72 to become professor at Chicago Divinity School. His major works are *Christ without Myth* (1961), one of the most penetrating critiques of *Bultmann's programme of demythologizing, and *The Reality of God* (1966). *On Theology* (1986) contains a criticism of any theology that does not take the doctrine of God seriously.

Oldham, Joseph Houldsworth
(1874–1969)
Ecumenist. Born in India the son of an army officer, he studied at Oxford and then went back to India with the YMCA. He was invalided home, and studied in Edinburgh and Halle before working for the Student Christian Movement and organizing the 1910 World Missionary Conference. His involvement in missions included important work in Africa, particularly in relation to education and the political future of the British colonies. He was also active ecumenically, being involved in the preparations for the World Council of Churches. His *Christian News Letter* was published throughout the Second World War.

Olier, Jean-Jacques (1608–57)
Born in Paris, he studied with the Jesuits in Lyons and at the Sorbonne. In Rome for further studies, he went blind; on recovering his sight he was converted and after ordination met *Vincent de Paul. He went on missions and in 1642 took charge of the Paris church of St Sulpice, then in decline. He used it as the base for a seminary which became a model for other dioceses; its influence spread as far as Montreal. He wrote many books on spirituality.

Oman, John Wood (1860–1939)
British Presbyterian theologian. Born in Orkney, after studies in Edinburgh and Heidelberg and a ministry in Northumberland he became professor at Cambridge and later college principal. Influenced by *Schleiermacher, whom he translated, he emphasized feeling, defining religion as the direct feeling of the supernatural. This led him to stress the inner authority of truth, contrasting the individual religious conscience over against creeds and church. His main book was *The Natural and the Supernatural* (1931).

Origen (c.185–c.254)
Greek biblical scholar. He was born in Egypt and educated in Alexandria, where his mother had to prevent him forcibly from going out to seek martyrdom in the persecution in which his father was killed. He became head of the catechetical school, leading an extremely ascetical life; he even castrated himself. He was not ordained until 230, on a visit to Palestine; his own bishop deposed and exiled him because of the irregularity of his ordination and he settled in Caesarea, where he established what became a school. In a persecution in 250 he was imprisoned and tortured, and never really recovered. He wrote much, but because his teaching was later condemned, little survives in the original (there are some Latin translations). An imaginative biblical scholar, he produced a *Hexapla*, a work which set several versions of the Bible in parallel columns. His *De Principiis* is the first great systematic presentation of Christianity, in four books discussing God, the human and material world, free will and the Bible. He also wrote an apologetic work *Against* *Celsus. He interpreted the Bible as having three senses, literal, moral and allegorical, stressing the last, and divided Christians into two groups, the simple and the perfect. He believed that at a final restoration (*apokatastasis*), all creatures, even the devil, will be saved.

Orosius, Paulus
(early fifth century)
Spanish theologian. He fled from Spain in the Vandal invasions and came to *Augustine in Hippo, becoming his ally in his fight against *Origenists and *Priscillianists. He was then sent to *Jerome in Palestine to assist in an unsuccessful indictment against *Pelagius. He wrote a world history, *Against the Pagans*, in seven volumes, the turning points in which were adopted by other authors.

Orr, James (1844–1913)
Scottish theologian. Born in Glasgow, after parish ministry he returned to teach in colleges, becoming a professor. A defender of evangelical orthodoxy against the current views of *Darwin, *Ritschl and *Wellhausen, he wrote a good deal of apologetic, the most important of which is *The Christian View of God and the World* (1893).

Osiander, Andreas (1498–1552)
German Reformer. Born near Nuremberg, he studied at Ingolstadt and revised the Vulgate on the basis of the Hebrew text.

He became a Lutheran and was appointed professor at Königsberg. In Nuremberg he encouraged communion in both kinds; he sided with *Luther against *Zwingli over the eucharist, but engaged in controversy with Melanchthon over justification, arguing that in it believers partake of the divine nature. *Cranmer married his niece.

Otto, Rudolf (1869–1937)
German Protestant theologian. Born near Hanover, he studied at Erlangen and Göttingen, where he became professor and a colleague of *Husserl, subsequently moving to Breslau and Marburg. Influenced by *Schleiermacher and *Ritschl, he was interested in the essence and truth of religion. However, he reacted against ethical and rational liberalism in favour of 'feelings' as valid experiences of the transcendental; the concept in which he expressed what was experienced was 'the holy, the numinous'. His most famous book is *The Idea of the Holy* (1917); he applied his approach via the numinous to eschatology in the Gospels in *The Kingdom of God and the Son of Man* (1934). He also wrote on Hinduism.

Overbeck, Franz (1837–1905)
German Protestant theologian. Born in St Petersburg, he taught at Jena and Basle. An unbeliever and friend of *Nietzsche, his approach to Christianity was purely historical; he was particularly interested in the transition from earliest Christianity to the church, seeing the latter as an illegitimate development. He anticipated many of the insights of form criticism.

Ozanam, Antoine Frederic (1813–53)
French Roman Catholic scholar. He studied in Paris and became professor at the Sorbonne. As a student he founded the Society of St *Vincent de Paul, for work among the poor, and also as an instrument of social change. In his historical works he sought to vindicate the Roman Catholic church by a history of Christian civilization. Politically liberal, he was one of the leaders of the French nineteenth-century Catholic revival.

Pachomius (c.290–346)
Egyptian monk. Brought up a pagan, he was converted as a conscript soldier by Christian kindness. He went on after training as a solitary to establish a community in a deserted village, modelled on the primitive community in Jerusalem, and by the time of his death he was leader of communal monasticism, based on a simple rule. This rule, which combined strict discipline with recognition of individual differences and emphasized productive work as well as prayer, influenced *Basil, John *Cassian and *Benedict.

Paine, Thomas (1737–1809)
Political reformer. Born in Norfolk of a Quaker family, after a career as sailor, staymaker, excise officer and usher, he went to America, where he became an editor. He wrote a famous pamphlet, *Common Sense* (1776), in favour of American independence. Returning to England in 1787, he produced his best-known work *The Rights of Man* (1791–2), as a result of which he had to flee to Paris in 1792. Arrested the next year, he finished *The Age of Reason* (1794–5) in prison. This attacked traditional Christianity and reflected deist and Quaker views. He returned to America in 1802.

Paley, William (1743–1805)
English scholar. Educated at Cambridge, he taught mathematics, looked after a Westmorland parish and became archdeacon of Carlisle. A popular communicator, he wrote a standard textbook on ethics, *The Principles of Moral and Political Philosophy* (1785), and in *Pauline Hours* (1790) made a historical comparison of Acts with the letters of Paul. His fame rests on *A View of the Evidences of Christianity* (1794) and *Natural Theology* (1802), in which he saw creation in mechanistic terms and argued for the existence of God in terms of design. He produced the famous illustration of finding a watch on the seashore and inferring that it is the creation of an intelligent mind.

Pannenberg, Wolfhart (1928–   )
German Lutheran theologian. Born in Stettin, he studied philosophy in Berlin and Göttingen, turning to Christianity during his time there. He went on to Basle (to study with *Barth and *Jaspers) and Heidelberg and then became professor in Wuppertal, Mainz and eventually Munich. The first book in which he was involved, a symposium on *Revelation and History* (1961), challenged the dominant theology of the Word inspired by Barth and argued that revelation was mediated through history. His subsequent *Jesus – God and Man* (1964) was a reinterpretation of christology with a marked historical slant, taking apocalyptic seriously and centred on the resurrection as a historical and eschatological event. In his more recent theology he has shown an increasing concern to demonstrate that theology belongs with the other academic disciplines in universities and cannot exist in a ghetto. His *Theology and the Philosophy of Science* (1974) has been followed by a monumental *Anthropology* (1983) and the beginnings of a multi-volume systematic theology (Vol. 1, 1988).

Papias (c.60–130)
Bishop of Hierapolis. Nothing is known of his life, except that he was a companion of *Polycarp. Quotations from his book *On the Oracles of the Lord* survive in *Eusebius and form some of our earliest external information on the Gospels. He believed there would be a period of a thousand years between the resurrection and the kingdom of Christ.

Paracelsus (Theophrast Bombast von Hohenheim, 1493/4–1541)
Swiss physician. Educated in many universities, including Ferrara, he became city physician in Basle. He was opposed to the prevailing system of medicine based on the views of the second-century physician Claudius Galen and had to leave, thereafter moving from place to place. He advanced medicine by deriving his principles from nature study rather than from scholastic disputations and made important contributions to chemistry. He also developed a mysticism, claiming that as we know nature since we are nature, we know God since we are God. Knowledge of his thought is complicated by the attribution to him of much he did not write and his subsequent role as a cult figure.

Parker, Theodore (1810–60)
American Unitarian. Son of a New England farmer, he taught himself many oriental languages at Harvard, and then became a Unitarian pastor in Massachusetts. There he was denounced for what were considered extreme views and had to move to an independent congregation in Boston. His *Discourse of Matters pertaining to Religion* (1842) was also read in Europe; he argued that Christianity was the influence of Jesus and did not involve belief in miracles. He was very active in the cause of emancipation.

Pascal, Blaise (1623–62)
French mathematician and theologian. Born in Clermont-Ferrand of a distinguished father, he was educated privately, moving with his father to Paris and then Rouen. A mathematical prodigy, he experimented from an early age, discovering the principles of the barometer and hydraulics, devising a calculator and working out the theory of probability. At twenty-three he came into contact with the *Jansenists, visiting Port Royal regularly on his return to Paris after his father's death. His *Letters to a Provincial* (1657), attacking Jesuit theories of grace and morality, were highly controversial and officially condemned by Rome. After a miraculous vision, in a 'night of fire' in 1654 which brought him deep assurance, he began a defence of the Christian religion, but never finished it, leaving only his notes, published as *Pensées*. He believed God could only be known by faith, not reason. His 'wager' is famous, as is his phrase 'The heart has its reasons which reason does not know'.

Paschasius Radbertus (785–860)
French Benedictine theologian. Born in Soissons, he entered the abbey of Corbie, but later resigned to devote himself to study. A learned man, he wrote important commentaries on the Bible, but his best-known work is *On the Body and Blood of Christ*, which presented an early form of the doctrine of transubstantiation, arguing that Christ's crucified flesh is consumed in the eucharist.

Patrick (c.390–460)
Irish bishop. His dates and the details of his life cannot be determined with certainty. Born in Britain, he was captured by Irish pirates, and spent six years in their custody in Ireland. Having prayed God to rescue him, when he did get home he was a changed man. He trained for the ministry in Britain

and returned to Ireland where he spent the rest of his life as bishop, in work of reconciliation, education and establishing religious institutions. He and his church were independent of Rome. Sadly, he does not seem to have composed the hymn ('The Breastplate') attributed to him.

Paul of Samosata (third century)
Greek theologian. A wealthy man, after royal service to the queen of Palmyra he became bishop of Antioch. His theology was not thought sound either on God, whom he saw as a single person until creation, or on Jesus, whom he saw as a combination of two persons, human and divine, the human Jesus differing only in degree from the prophets. For this he was condemned and deposed, and subsequently seen as a major heretic.

Paulinus of Nola (353–431)
Christian poet. Son of a wealthy Bordeaux family, with the consent of his Spanish wife he gave up his wealth, was ordained in Barcelona on popular insistence and settled near the tomb of St Felix in Nola: he and his wife founded a home for monks and lived in great austerity. He later became bishop. He was particularly renowned for his Latin poems, combining old forms with new content.

Paulus, Heinrich Eberhard Gottlob (1761–1851)
German rationalist theologian. He was professor at Jena, Würzburg and Heidelberg. In his *Life of Jesus* (1828) he tried to reconcile belief in the accuracy of the Gospels with disbelief in miracles and championed Christianity for its spiritual worship and the loftiness of the personality of Jesus.

Peake, Arthur Samuel (1865–1929)
English biblical scholar. The son of a Primitive Methodist minister in Staffordshire, he remained a layman: he studied at Oxford and taught there before becoming tutor at the Primitive Methodist College in Manchester; he later became first professor of biblical criticism in Manchester. Writing for a wide audience, he produced many books on the Bible; his one-volume commentary still survives in revised form. He also worked hard towards Methodist reunion.

Pedersen, Johannes Peder Ejler (1883–1977)
Danish Old Testament scholar. He was professor in Copenhagen. His classic book *Israel. Its Life and Culture* (two vds, 1940, 1946), offered a strikingly different perspective on its subject, adopting a phenomenological and anthropological approach. He emphasized the role of cult and primitive psychology in the formation of Old Testament traditions, suggesting that Exodus 1–15 took shape as a passover liturgy.

Péguy, Charles (1873–1914)
French writer. Born of a poor and almost illiterate working-class family in Orleans, he went to the Sorbonne, but gave up his studies to run a bookshop. At first he was an ardent socialist and supporter of Dreyfus, the Jewish officer wrongly convicted of selling secrets to the Germans, defending Dreyfus in a journal of which he was co-founder. However, he later became a nationalist mystic with a love of mediaeval Catholicism and a deep eucharistic devotion, though he remained anti-clerical. He wrote a famous play, *The Mystery of the Charity of Joan of Arc* (1910, ET 1950), and a vast religious poem, *Eve* (1914). An immense influence on later Catholic writers, he was killed in battle at the beginning of the First World War.

Pelagius (died c.410)
British theologian. Trained in law, he was active in Rome at the end of the fourth century. Shocked by the moral laxity of his time, against dualistic views that human beings are intrinsically evil and therefore cannot be morally responsible he argued that they are free to choose good by nature. He subsequently moved to Africa and then Palestine, attracting followers. Though he does not seem to have denied the traditional Christian doctrine of original sin, a denial with which his name is associated, he was condemned for heresy. Initially he cleared himself, but was condemned again; *Orosius and *Augustine were vigorous opponents. Expelled from Palestine, he disappears from view; he may have died in Egypt. His influence continued and he has undergone a reassessment in modern times.

Pelikan, Jaroslav (1923–   )
American historian. Born in Akron, Ohio, he studied at Concordia Theological Seminary, where he taught after three years at Valparaiso university. In 1953 he became professor in the university of Chicago and in 1962 professor at Yale. As well as translating the works of Luther (1955–71), he has

written a large number of distinguished books on Luther and almost all aspects of Christian history, including a five-volume *The Christian Tradition* (1977ff.). His *Jesus through the Centuries* (1985) reached a particularly wide audience.

Penn, William (1644–1718)
Quaker and founder of Pennsylvania. Son of an admiral and born in London, he was expelled from Oxford for nonconformist views. After travel (during which he became a Quaker, as a result of a sermon he heard in Cork) and service in the navy he studied law in London. His writings on Quakerism brought him imprisonment in the Tower of London. While there, undeterred, he wrote *No Cross, No Crown* (1669), which became a Quaker classic. On his release, becoming increasingly interested in founding a colony for Quakers in America, he established Pennsylvania, of which he became governor. He then returned to London, but was again persecuted and deprived of his governorship. In this period he also wrote *Primitive Christianity* (1696), comparing Quakerism with the early church. Returning to Pennsylvania only for a brief period, he spent the rest of his life in or near London.

Perrin, Norman (1921–76)
American New Testament scholar. Born in Leicestershire, he studied in England and Germany under *Manson and *Jeremias. Not finding acceptance in England, he moved to America, and became professor at Emory and Chicago. His *Rediscovering the Teaching of Jesus* (1967) made much use of the 'criterion of dissimilarity': sayings of Jesus are more likely to be authentic if they differ from the trend of the Gospel tradition.

Peter Damian (1007–72)
Church reformer. Born at Ravenna of poor parents, he studied at Faenza and Parma and then entered a *Benedictine monastery at Fonte Avella, later becoming its prior. He founded new monasteries and gained fame as a preacher against clerical abuses. However, his horizons were limited and he was uninterested in the contemporary conflict between the Eastern and Western church. A devout man, in his sermons and letters he shows a tension between contemplation and an active life.

Peter Lombard (c.1095–1169)
Born in Lombardy, after study in Bologna he went to Reims and Paris, where he taught at the cathedral school and became bishop. He is known for his *Sentences*, a four-volume compilation of quotations, principally from the Latin church fathers *Augustine and *Hilary but also from some Greek fathers like *John of Damascus, previously unknown in the West. The resultant summary of doctrine covers the Trinity, creation and sin, the incarnation and virtue, the sacraments (first identified here as seven in number) and the last things. After initial hostility it became the standard mediaeval textbook, and though it was eclipsed by the *Summa* of *Thomas Aquinas, it was still influential in the time of *Luther and *Calvin.

Peter Martyr (Pietro Martire Vermigli, 1500–62)
Reformer. Born in Florence, the son of a follower of *Savanarola, he took his name from a famous thirteenth-century martyr. (Having lost several children, his father had dedicated him in this way.) After study at Fiesole he became a monk and was abbot at Spoleto and prior in Naples. Much impressed by reading *Bucer and *Zwingli, he developed Reformation sympathies and had to flee; after a time in Switzerland he became professor in Strasbourg, where he married. In 1547 he came to England and was made professor at Cambridge, but when Mary became queen he had to return to his chair at Strasbourg and, after differences there, ultimately to Zurich.

Pfleiderer, Otto (1839–1908)
German theologian. A pupil of *Baur at Tübingen, he also studied in Britain and later became professor in Jena and Berlin. He lectured in London and Oxford, his theology, midway between orthodoxy and the Tübingen school, proving congenial there. Major books are *Paulinism* (1893), *The Development of Theology since Kant* (1890) and *The Philosophy of Religion on the Basis of its History* (1886–8).

Philaret Drozdov (1782–1867)
Russian theologian. After studying in Moscow he taught at a church academy there; he became a monk in 1803. The same year he was made professor of philosophy in St Petersburg, and from there rose to become bishop of Jaroslav and archbishop (later metropolitan) of Moscow. A model bishop and ecclesiastical statesman, he produced a *Catechism* (1823) covering the Nicene Creed, Lord's Prayer and Ten Command-

ments, which became virtually a doctrinal standard before the Russian Revolution.

Philip Neri (1515–95)

Founder of the Oratory. Born in Florence, he led an ascetic life in Rome, earning his living as a tutor, while studying and working among the poor. He had a mystical experience there, and was led to found a confraternity to care for pilgrims. After ordination he went to live with a community of priests at San Girolamo, which under his influence grew to become the Congregation of the Oratory (probably after the room where they met). His optimistic and attractive spirituality made him one of the most popular figures in Rome, much sought after for spiritual counsel, and the Oratory later gained papal approval.

Philo (c.25 BCE–50 CE)

Jewish philosopher and exegete. He came from a prosperous priestly family; nothing is known of his life except that he went with a delegation to Rome to plead with Caligula for Jewish rights. A prolific author, he developed an allegorical interpretation of the Torah in terms of Platonic and Stoic philosophy, synthesizing Hebrew and Greek thought. His philosophy had a mystic dimension, moving towards the mystic vision of God in ecstasy. He was influential on Alexandrian Christian theologians like *Clement and *Origen, not least in his scriptural exegesis.

Photius (c.820–91)

Patriarch of Constantinople. From a noble family, he was a scholar and became a statesman. He taught at the university and became imperial secretary, then ambassador to Assyria. When palace intrigues led to the deposition of the current patriarch, though he was a layman, he was consecrated within a week and appointed. A controversy followed, at the end of which he was condemned by a Roman synod. This caused offence in Constantinople and the matter became political, complicated by the fact that there was a dispute as to whether newly-Christianized Bulgaria should depend on East or West. Photius in turn condemned the Roman addition of the *filioque* clause (the Holy Spirit proceeding from the Father *and the Son*) to the creed. A council in Constantinople excommunicated Pope *Nicholas I. On a change of emperor, harmony was temporarily restored between East and West at the expense of deposing Photius,

but he was later reinstated. On a further change of emperor he was deposed again and died in exile. The Photian schism, as it is called, was a forerunner of the final split between Eastern and Western churches. Photius' writings are important, not least for their bibliographical record of vanished works; he became a saint in the Eastern church.

Pico della Mirandola, Giovanni (1463–94)

Italian philosopher. He went to the universities of Bologna and Padua, at the latter studying *Averroism and the Kabbalah, and was also influenced by the Platonic Academy in Florence. As a result he looked for a unity which would underlie all these philosophical traditions and also Christianity. He later became a follower of *Savonarola. He put particular stress on human freedom and worth.

Pius IX *see Popes of Rome*

Plato (427 BCE–347 BCE)

Greek philosopher. Born in Athens, he became a pupil of Socrates, after whose death he travelled widely. On his return to Athens he set up a school on the outskirts of Athens, the Academy, where he spent the rest of his life, apart from his involvement in an abortive attempt to set up a liberal state in Sicily. His philosophy centred on a world of forms, above and separate from our changing world and related to it as model to imperfect copy. From this world of forms (ideas, hence idealism) eternal principles derive (the process is described in his famous parable of the cave). Happiness is knowledge of these forms, and this knowledge is sought by the soul, pre-existent and surviving bodily death. The soul is like a city state: both satisfy physical needs, resist attack from enemies, and guide the life of the individual. Through revivals of his doctrines from the first century BCE in a religious direction (Middle Platonism), he was influential on Christian thought, an influence which was further strengthened by the Neoplatonism developed by *Plotinus, and then *Porphyry and *Boethius. *Augustine helped to perpetuate his thinking. His *Republic*, setting out a blueprint for an ideal state, was also widely influential in Western social thought and the formation of social institutions.

Plotinus (205–70)

Greek Neoplatonist philosopher and mystic. Born in Lycopolis, Egypt, after travelling with the Emperor Gordian to Persia to acquaint himself with Eastern thought, he set up a school in Rome. His philosophy, rejecting dualism, sought to find a unifying principle behind the world and explain how the One, beyond the supreme mind and forms, gives rise to the Many. He attached great importance to contemplation as being the way by which the soul can gain knowledge and in so doing attain union with God by its own disciplined efforts, through asceticism and purity of heart. His works were edited in six groups of nine (*Enneads*) and published posthumously by *Porphyry. They proved important because of their stress on the immaterial world.

Polanyi, Michael (1891–1976)
Hungarian/British chemist and philosopher. Born in Budapest, he was first involved in chemical research in Berlin and then after the rise of Hitler became professor at Manchester university. Alongside his professional field, he became increasingly interested in philosophy and the nature of scientific knowledge. Critical of the view that scientific knowledge is detached, he emphasized the character of knowledge as personal (his best-known book is *Personal Knowledge*, 1958). In religion he particularly stressed the role of metaphor. His approach has been taken up by Christian philosophers of religion.

Polycarp (c.69–155)
Bishop of Smyrna and martyr. Little is known of his life; he is depicted as a champion of orthodoxy (against *Marcion) and a faithful pastor. He was a leading Christian in Asia Minor; his great age linked him with much earlier days of the church. He paid a visit to Rome at the end of his life to discuss the date of Easter, a controversial issue; on his return he was arrested and burnt to death.

Pomponazzi, Pietro (1462–1525)
Italian philosopher. He taught at Padua, Ferrara and Bologna, expounding *Aristotelianism in a different way from the scholastic tradition represented, say, by *Thomas Aquinas. Thus his *On the Immortality of the Soul* (1516) was an attack on immortality, questioning both the concept of the soul and the argument that immortality is necessary to ensure ethical conduct. In this way he prepared for a secular ethic independent of Christian thought. However, he himself also argued that divine revelation could go beyond human reason.

Popper, Karl (1902–   )
Austrian/British philosopher. Son of a Viennese lawyer, he studied in Vienna and then became a schoolteacher. In 1937 he went to New Zealand to teach philosophy, moving to the London School of Economics in 1946. Opposed to positivism, he argued that science is a matter of imaginative conjecture, tested by rigorous attempts at falsification. Nor is knowledge limited to science; falsifiable theses can also be produced by other disciplines. He has been highly critical of Marxism (*The Open Society and its Enemies*, 1945) and historicism, the idea that there are laws of historical development (*The Poverty of Historicism*, 1957); he has also challenged the view that the mental sphere can be reduced to physical dimensions. All this has made his work of interest to theologians.

Porphyry (232–304)
Neoplatonist philosopher. Born in Tyre, he travelled round Syria, Palestine and Egypt before studying philosophy in Athens. He met *Plotinus in Rome, subsequently editing his works. He moved to Sicily but returned to Rome at the end of his life. Sceptical of popular religion, he was especially hostile to Christianity, against which he wrote fifteen books: these are no longer extant because they were burned. He is important philosophically for the clarification he brings to Plotinus.

Priestley, Joseph (1733–1804)
English Presbyterian minister and scientist. Born in Yorkshire in a strict *Calvinist family, he was ordained and served as a minister in Suffolk before teaching at a dissenting academy in Warrington, distinguishing himself by his scholarship (he discovered oxygen). Moving to a ministry in Leeds, he became a Unitarian and found time to write as librarian to a nobleman. He then went to Birmingham, where his house was broken into and ransacked because of his support of the French Revolution. He moved to London, became one of the founders of the Unitarian society, but subsequently emigrated to America and lived in Pennsylvania. His writings were controversial; they include *Institutes of Natural and Revealed Religion* (1772–4) and *History of Early Opinions Concerning Jesus Christ* (1786).

Pringle-Pattison, Andrew Seth
(1856–1931)
Scottish philosopher of religion. He studied at Edinburgh, Berlin, Jena and Göttingen

(under *Lotze). After teaching at various places in Britain he became professor at Edinburgh. In the Idealist tradition following *Hegel, he argued that while God (the Absolute) could not be an individual, God could be the source of individuation, thus preserving the value of the individual. His distinctive work is contained e.g. in *Hegelianism and Personality* (1887) and *The Idea of Immortality* (1922); he also wrote an important survey *The Idea of God in Recent Philosophy* (1917).

Priscillian (d.386)
Spanish bishop. A nobleman with ascetic interests, he seems to have been influenced by Gnostic doctrines brought by an Egyptian called Marcus. He attracted many followers, particularly women, but including two bishops. Though condemned, he became bishop of Avila; he and his followers were then exiled, going to France and then Rome to appeal to the pope. Getting their exile annulled, Priscillian returned to Spain and his following grew. Not long after being tried for heresy by the emperor, he was executed for sorcery in Trier. His views seem to have been Manichaean: dualistic, anti-materialist, ascetic and astrological.

Procksch, Otto (1874–1949)
German Old Testament scholar. Professor of Old Testament at Greifswald and Erlangen, he was an influential figure, having among his pupils *Alt, *Eichrodt and *Von Rad. He wrote works on blood revenge among the pre-Islamic Arabs and the history of the Greek Old Testament, and several commentaries. His *magnum opus* was an Old Testament theology, published posthumously in 1950, which was perhaps the last of the old-style systematic works of biblical theology in which everything is centred on Christ.

Prosper of Aquitaine (390–463)
Christian theologian. He was probably a lay monk and lived in Marseilles. At first he was an ardent supporter of *Augustine's doctrines of predestination and grace, but as time went on he became less extreme, and excluded the possibility that anyone could be predestined to damnation. His views were influential on mediaeval theological thought.

Proudhon, Pierre Joseph (1809–65)
French socialist and political writer. The son of a poor family, he was self-educated and went to work for a printer, learning theology and Hebrew from his proofreading. This study enabled him to qualify for a grant to study at the Besançon academy. This grant was almost withdrawn when in an essay on property he made the famous remark 'property is theft', though he was put on trial (and acquitted) for a later pamphlet on the same subject. He became prominent in the 1848 revolution and was imprisoned; he led a quiet life under the second empire because his concerns were economic rather than political. However, his *Justice in the Revolution and the Church* (1858) incurred the wrath of the authorities and he had to escape to Brussels. His health broke, and he died in France after his return there. He had a brilliant and individual mind, and based his thought on the absolute truth of a few basic ideas – freedom, justice and equality. He was the first to use the term anarchy as for an ideal form of social organization.

Prudentius Aurelius Clemens (348–c.410)
Spanish poet. Trained in the law, he practised at the bar and was a successful administrator. He wrote many apologetic poems, often long and in classical metre. His *Psychomachia* (Battle of the Soul), an allegory of asceticism as spriitual warfare, was popular in the Middle Ages. He wrote the hymn 'Of the Father's Love Begotten'.

Przywara, Erich (1889–1972)
German philosopher of religion. Born in Kattowitz, he became professor at Munich. Basic to his theology was the analogy of being (i.e. the relation of God to his being is analogous to the relation of humans to their being); he expressed much of his thought in terms of polarities (grace–freedom, transcendence–immanence, faith–knowledge). His most important works are *Analogia Entis* (1932) and *Polarity* (1933). His view represented what *Barth found abhorrent in Catholicism.

Pusey, Edward Bouverie (1800–82)
English theologian. He studied at Oxford and then at Göttingen and Berlin, where he met many leading German biblical critics, going on to become professor of Hebrew at Oxford, a post he held for the rest of his life. He later withdrew an early work which was thought to favour German theology, and from 1833 was associated with *Keble and *Newman in the high-church Oxford Movement, writing tracts and giving it intellectual

backing. He was a gifted (and on occasion controversial) preacher; one of his sermons was instrumental in the reintroduction of private confession to a priest into the Anglican church. After his wife died in 1839 he became interested in the religious life. A conservative, he opposed university reform and

attempted to arraign *Jowett for unsound teaching. In the latter part of his life he was involved in discussion with Rome in the hope of reunion, and he fought for the retention of the *Athanasian creed in worship. His views are expressed in his many tracts, letters and sermons.

Quesnel, Pasquier
(1634–1719)
French scholar. After a Jesuit education he studied at the Sorbonne and entered the congregation of the Oratory in Paris, where he wrote spiritual books, including a New Testament with moral comments on every verse (*Moral Reflections*). His edition of the works of *Leo the Great was condemned because its notes had too much of a French nationalistic flavour (Gallicanism). Suspected of *Jansenism, he was then removed to Orleans; to avoid taking an anti-Jansenist oath he fled to Brussels but was imprisoned there. He escaped and went

to Holland, where he spent the rest of his life defending himself and his works against official condemnations.

Quiñones, Francisco de (died 1540)
Spanish liturgist. Of noble family, he became a Franciscan. He was in due course elected minister general, cardinal and then bishop of Coria. He defended Catherine of Aragon in her divorce by Henry VIII. His reformed edition of the breviary, commissioned by Pope Paul III, became highly popular, but was ultimately condemned for not being traditional enough. It had a great influence on *Cranmer.

Rabanus Maurus
(c.776–856)
German theologian. Born of a noble family in Mainz, he studied at Fulda and then at Tours under *Alcuin, who called him Maurus in honour of St Maur, a disciple of *Benedict, because of his scholarship. He became abbot of the monastery of Fulda and later archbishop of Mainz. He advanced the evangelization of Germany and was involved in controversy with *Gottschalk and *Paschasius Radbertus. A prolific writer but not an original thinker, he did much to compile and consolidate theological literature to educate the clergy of his day. A noted poet, he is said to have written the *Veni creator Spiritus* ('Come, Holy Ghost, our souls inspire').

Rad, Gerhard von, *see* Von Rad, Gerhard

Rade, Paul Martin (1857–1940)
German theologian. Son of a pastor, he studied at Leipzig, served as a pastor in Frankfurt and then taught systematic theology at Marburg. He became editor of the important journal *The Christian World*, concerned with social and political implications of Christianity, and was one of the few church supporters of the post-1918 democratic regime. Although he was a liberal, he did not get involved in the church struggle and thus became a marginal figure.

Ragaz, Leonhard (1868–1948)
Social reformer. Pastor at Basle cathedral, he became a professor in Zurich, but resigned in 1921 to devote himself to social work in industrial areas and peace work. He was influential on the development of the

Religious Socialist movement in Switzerland and an important influence on *Barth during and after the First World War. Influenced by *Tolstoy, *Kutter and the *Blumhardts, he saw signs of divine revelation in socialism.

Rahner, Karl (1904–84)
German Catholic theologian. Born in Swabia, he became a Jesuit and studied in Freiburg, where he was influenced by *Heidegger, and Innsbruck, where he subsequently became professor; from 1964 he was professor in Munich. He was also involved in the Second Vatican Council. His main concern was to present thinking in the tradition of *Thomas Aquinas (Thomistic theology) in such a way as to avoid the criticism of *Kant; he did this by means of the terminology of Heidegger. Under the influence of existentialism, he saw human experience as the key to all theological meaning; this is focussed on transcendental experience, which becomes conscious when we reflect on the conditions for knowing. His reinterpretation of the traditional dogmas of the church in the light of the modern world was usually done in essay form. The results are summed up in *The Foundations of Christian Faith* (1978), and the essays themselves are collected in his *Theological Investigations*, which extends to more than twenty volumes.

Ramsay, William Mitchell (1851–1939)
New Testament scholar. Born in Glasgow and educated in Aberdeen, Oxford and Göttingen, he taught in several Oxford colleges before becoming professor there and in Aberdeen. After much travelling in Asia Minor, he became an expert in its geography and history, which he applied to the New Testament. Among his books are *The Historical Geography of Asia Minor* (1890), and *St Paul. The Traveller and Roman Citizen* (1895).

Ramsey, Arthur Michael (1904–88)
English theologian and archbishop. Son of the president of Magdalene College, Cambridge, where he studied and was influenced by *Hoskyns, after pastoral work in Lincolnshire and a post at Lincoln Theological College he went on to become professor at Durham and Cambridge, bishop of Durham, archbishop of York and then of Canterbury. His patriarchal style earned him the reputation of being the last of the church fathers,

and the quintessentially Anglican character of his theology gained him a wide readership. His major books were *The Gospel and the Catholic Church* (1936), studies on the resurrection and transfiguration, and a social history of Anglicanism, *From Gore to Temple* (1960).

Ramsey, Ian Thomas (1915–72)
English philosopher. Born near Bolton, Lancashire, he studied science and theology at Cambridge. After a series of academic appointments he became professor of philosophy at Oxford and then bishop of Durham; the devoted way in which he served in this last post led to his premature death. In his philosophy he focussed on disclosure situations, in which we become aware of something which includes the visible elements of situations but goes beyond them. His best-known book is *Religious Language* (1957).

Ramus, Petrus (1515–72)
French humanist. Born of a noble family in Picardy which had seen better days, he studied in Paris and became a violent critic of *Aristotle, as a result of which he was banned from teaching. However, patronage secured him posts. He later became a Calvinist and spent three years in Germany escaping persecution. He was killed in the massacre of St Bartholomew, shortly after returning to Paris. His views (labelled Ramism) long proved a source of controversy in European universities. He believed that the validity of concepts and abstractions derives from God and that a method can be achieved of arriving at absolute truth from the analysis of human perception. As an educationalist, he sought to reform the curriculum by simplification, dividing subjects into components and arranging them in diagrams.

Rancé, Armand-Jean le Bouthillier de (1626–1700)
Monastic reformer. Son of a secretary of Marie de' Medici and godson of Cardinal Richelieu, from an early age he enjoyed the income from a number of benefices, including the monastery of La Trappe, of which he was lay abbot, and lived as a lay noble. After a distinguished career at the Sorbonne he frequented the Paris salons, but was then suddenly converted, following the death of close friends. Giving up everything but La Trappe and becoming a mon-

astic novice, he tightened up its discipline along the lines of the Cistercian reform. This involved him in controversy for the rest of his life, not least because he prohibited study, but he laid the foundations for the Trappist order. He wrote *On Sanctity and the Duties of Monastic Life* (1683).

Ranke, Leopold von (1795–1886)
German historian. Born in Saxony, he became professor of history in Berlin. He stressed the importance of studying original sources in an objective way, with the aim of discovering 'how it really was'. His most important work was on the history of the popes (1834–61) and England (1859–68). In his approach he was the founder of modern critical history.

Rashdall, Hastings (1858–1924)
English moral philosopher and theologian. After studying at Oxford he taught there, going on to hold cathedral posts in Hereford and Carlisle. First a distinguished historian of European universities, he wrote a utilitarian-type moral philosophy, *The Theory of Good and Evil* (1907), and then put forward an *Abelardian-type theory of the atonement in *The Idea of Atonement in Christian Theology* (1919). Fundamentally a rationalist, he was opposed to mysticism and sentiment.

Rauschenbusch, Walter (1861–1918)
American theologian. Born in Rochester, New York, the son of a German Lutheran turned Baptist seminary teacher, he studied there and in Germany, and after twelve years as pastor in the Second German Baptist Church in New York City was called back to Rochester to teach in his turn. The social problems he had encountered in New York made a deep impression on him and he attempted to find a theology which went some way towards meeting them. He combined social analysis, theological liberalism and biblical piety, stressing that Jesus preached social salvation and reiterating the kingdom of God as a dominant principle and unifying concept. His major work was *Christianity and the Social Crisis* (1907); it was followed by *Christianity and the Social Order* (1912) and *A Theology for the Social Gospel* (1917). Despite opposition because of his German ancestry he became known as the father of the social gospel in America. He was highly suspect to his church for his liberal views.

Raven, Charles Earle (1885–1964)
English theologian. After study at Cambridge he taught there until 1920, then becoming rector of an Anglican parish and canon of Liverpool Cathedral before returning to Cambridge as professor in 1950. He was particularly interested in the relationship between religion and science and used evolution as a background for interpreting theology. From 1951–55 he was president of the Botanical Society of the British Isles, and as well as books on war, Christian socialism and education he wrote on naturalism, including *Bird Haunts and Bird Behaviour* (1929). His two-volume *Natural Religion and Christian Theology* (1953) is perhaps the most important work relating to his central concern.

Reimarus, Hermann Samuel (1694–1768)
German deist and biblical critic. Born in Hamburg, after studying in Jena and teaching in Wittenberg he went to England, where he was influenced by the deists. From 1727 to his death he was professor in Hamburg. A thoroughgoing rationalist, he wrote a great deal, but it was only after his death, when *Lessing published fragments of his work, that his views became known and caused a sensation. He not only rejected miracles and the supernatural, but accused the biblical writers of fraud. *Schweitzer saw him as standing at the beginning of the quest for the historical Jesus.

Reitzenstein, Richard (1861–1931)
German philologist and historian of religions. He was professor of classics at Giessen, Strasbourg, Freiburg and Göttingen. An influence on *Bousset and *Bultmann, he thought that Hellenistic ideas were a great influence on the New Testament; he also encouraged the study of Gnosticism. He argued that New Testament language and ideas come largely from Hermetic sources and that early Christianity was directly dependent on Hellenistic and Iranian ideas. His major works were *Poimandres* (1904) and *Hellenistic Mystery Religions* (1910).

Renan, Joseph Ernest (1823–92)
French philosopher and theologian. Born in Brittany, he studied at a Paris seminary, but doubts caused him to leave. A work on *Averroes established him as a scholar, and the emperor sent him to do archaeological work in the Near East. In Palestine he wrote

his *Life of Jesus* (1863). This portrayed Jesus as a genial Galilean preacher and denied his divinity, causing a scandal. By now Renan was professor of Hebrew in the Collège de France, but as a result he was dismissed. Later in life he turned to scientific rationalism.

Reuchlin, Johannes (1455–1522)
German humanist. Born in Pforzheim, he studied law in Paris, Freiburg, Basle and Orleans, and served as legal adviser to the Duke of Württemberg. He was among the first to master Hebrew as well as Latin and Greek, thus opening up new horizons. His theology had a universalist vision in which Christianity, Judaism and Hellenism were essentially unified from the beginnings of time. Going against all late mediaeval notions, he demanded toleration of the Jews. He was eventually condemned by the pope.

Reuss, Edouard Guillaume Eugène (1804–91)
New Testament scholar. Born in Strasbourg, he spent most of his life there, becoming a Protestant professor. He established biblical criticism in French Protestantism, also being the first to argue a late date for Old Testament law, after the prophets. He edited *Calvin's works and produced a new French translation of and commentary on the Bible.

Ricci, Matteo (1552–1610)
Italian Jesuit. After training in the sciences at the Roman College, he was sent to Goa and Macao, where he studied Chinese. His first visit to China in 1583 ended in expulsion after six years, but he immediately made a second attempt and lived there for the rest of his life, latterly in Nanking and Peking. He gained converts by his scientific knowledge and his adaptation of Christianity to Chinese ideas. His methods proved controversial and after his death were condemned by the pope, but his *The True Doctrine of God* (1595), written in Chinese, became a standard missionary manual.

Richard of St Victor (died 1173)
Scholar and mystic. Born in Scotland, at an early age he entered the distinguished abbey of St Victor in Paris (he was less scholarly than *Andrew and less intellectual than *Hugh). There he spent his life, becoming prior. A mystic, he was attracted by the imagery of scripture; he also had a deep interest in architecture, which is reflected in his exegesis of the visions of Ezekiel and the tabernacle and temple. He also stressed the importance of demonstration and argument in theology; his main work was *On the Trinity*, an attempt to understand the personal nature of God.

Richardson, Alan (1905–75)
English biblical theologian. After a parish ministry he became professor of theology in Nottingham and dean of York. He was concerned to detach theology from positivism and empiricism and set it on a biblical basis through what he regarded as a proper understanding of history. A popular and prolific writer, his most substantial works were his very Anglican *An Introduction to the Theology of the New Testament* (1958) and his Bampton Lectures *History Sacred and Profane* (1964).

Ricoeur, Paul (1913–   )
French philosopher. Born in Valence and orphaned at an early age, he was brought up by grandparents in Brittany. He studied in Rennes and the Sorbonne (with *Marcel) and became a schoolteacher until the outbreak of war. During military service he was awarded the Croix de Guerre. He was then put in a prisoner of war camp, in which he created a 'university'. After a period of research he was made professor at Strasbourg and Nanterre, subsequently holding chairs in both Paris and Chicago. He initially became interested in phenomenology through *Husserl, whose work he translated into French while a prisoner. Because of the problem of evil he became interested in hermeneutics and symbolism. His first major work was his three-volume *Philosophy of the Will* (1950, ET 1980). His *Essays on Biblical Interpretation* (1980) explore the different ways in which religious texts point to a hidden God. He is concerned to demonstrate how different positions can be both 'less than' and 'more than' one another.

Ridley, Nicholas (c.1500–55)
English Reformer. Born in Northumberland, he studied at Cambridge, the Sorbonne and Louvain. He then taught in Cambridge, and after being *Cranmer's chaplain and a parish clergyman in Kent, he returned to Cambridge. Finally he became, successively, bishop of Rochester and of London. Study of *Ratramnus aroused his interest in eucharistic theology: he rejected the doctrine of a corporeal eucharistic presence. Increasingly involved with the Reformers, in the reign of Queen Mary he was deposed, ex-

communicated and finally burnt at the stake in Oxford.

Ritschl, Albrecht Benjamin (1822–89)
German Protestant theologian. Born in Berlin the son of a Lutheran bishop, after studying at Bonn, Halle, Heidelberg and Tübingen he became professor in Bonn and then Göttingen. Originally a disciple of *Baur, he moved to systematic theology, in which he became very influential. For him, faith was the main religious category, so philosophy was irrelevant. Christian revelation, he believed, is to a community, which makes the church important, but this has ethical consequences, so that religious doctrines are value judgments. His main work, *The Christian Doctrine of Justification and Reconciliation* (three volumes, 1870–84), covered what he believed to be the pivotal doctrine of Christianity. *Harnack, *Troeltsch and *Herrmann were among those whom he influenced.

Robinson, Henry Wheeler (1872–1945)
English Old Testament scholar. Born in Northampton, he studied in Edinburgh and Oxford and became a Baptist minister. After a brief period as a pastor he taught at Rawdon Baptist College and then became principal of Regent's Park Baptist College, London, which he moved to Oxford. He wrote many books, notably on the Old Testament and on the Holy Spirit; he is particularly known for his advocacy of 'corporate personality', the view that the portraits of individuals in the Old Testament (like the Servant in Deutero-Isaiah) refer to Israel as a whole. His major books are *The Religious Ideas of the Old Testament* (1913), *The Christian Idea of the Holy Spirit* (1928) and *Inspiration and Revelation in the Old Testament* (1946).

Robinson, James McConkey (1924–   )
American scholar. Son of a conservative Calvinist theologian, he studied at Princeton, and with *Barth and *Cullmann in Basle, before becoming professor at Emory and Claremont. He popularized the 'new quest of the historical Jesus' and *Bultmann's hermeneutics in America, but later turned from theology to work on Nag Hammadi literature of which he has edited a definitive edition (*The Nag Hammadi Library*, ²1984). He also wrote a study of *The Problem of History in Mark* (1957) and the chronicle of *A New Quest for the Historical Jesus* (1959).

Robinson, John Arthur Thomas (1919–83)
English New Testament scholar and theologian. Born in the cathedral close at Canterbury, he studied under *Dodd at Cambridge, where he taught before becoming bishop of Woolwich; he then returned to Cambridge for the rest of his life. A conservative New Testament scholar, he was initially in the Dodd mould but defied accepted opinions in his *Redating the New Testament* (1975), in which he argued that the bulk of the New Testament was composed before the fall of Jerusalem in 70 CE, and *The Priority of John* (1984), in which he argued that traditions in the Fourth Gospel antedate those of the Synoptics. He was interested in liturgical renewal long before that became the trend, and was much involved in the political and literary issues of the day. His *Honest to God* (1963), with its reflection of current radical thought in Germany and elsewhere, was an international sensation, but he never managed to develop its implications consistently.

Rolle of Hampole, Richard (1295–1349)
English mystic. Born in Yorkshire, he studied at Oxford and then went to live as a hermit. He spent his last years near a convent of Cistercian nuns. He wrote prolifically in Latin and English, composing lyric poems as well as scholarly works. His spiritual writing expresses simple ideas and stresses grace. Orthodox in belief, he attacked corruption in the church.

Roscelin (died c.1125)
Scholastic philosopher and theologian. Little is known of his life, but he seems to have been born at Compiègne, to have studied at Soissons or Reims, and then to have taught at a variety of places including Compiègne, Besançon and Tours. His most famous pupil was *Abelard. Abelard and *Anselm both attacked him, and his views are mainly known through them. It appears that he may have been the founder of the view known as nominalism, that universal concepts have no independent existence outside the mind.

Rousseau, Jean-Jacques (1712–78)
French writer and philosopher. Son of a French refugee family in Geneva, he was brought up a *Calvinist but became a Catholic in his teens under the influence of a benefactress who became his mistress.

Prompted by her, he read widely: *Descartes, *Leibniz, *Locke, *Pascal. In Paris he met *Diderot, for whose *Dictionary* he wrote articles on music, and had five children by another mistress, Thérèse Lavasseur. In 1754 he returned to Geneva and became a Calvinist again, soon settling in Montmorency, where he wrote the works that made him famous: *Julie, or the New Heloise* (1761), a love story defending natural religion; *Émile* (1762), on education to offer protection from the corruption of society; and *The Social Contract* (1762), his view of a just state. All were officially condemned, and he was forced to travel, eventually returning to Paris where he married his Thérèse and wrote his *Confessions* (1722). He was immensely influential after his death, not least because he seemed to offer an alternative religion.

Rowley, Harold Henry (1890–1969)
English Old Testament scholar. Educated at Bristol and Oxford, after serving as a minister in Somerset, he went out to China to become professor at Shantung Christian university. He returned to teach in Cardiff university, and then became professor in Bangor, North Wales, and Manchester. His works mainly took the form of judicious articles on a wide range of Old Testament subjects, characterized by vast bibliographies, on the basis of which he sought to arrive at balanced conclusions; many of them are collected in *From Moses to Qumran* (1963) and *Men of God* (1963). He also wrote *From Joseph to Joshua* (1948) and *The Faith of Israel* (1957). He was active after the Second World War seeking to restore international communication among Old Testament scholars.

Royce, Josiah (1855–1916)
American philosopher. Born in California, he studied at Berkeley and Johns Hopkins and at Leipzig and Göttingen under *Lotze. He then spent his whole career at Harvard. Influenced by *Hegelianism, he worked out his own form of idealism. Prompted not least by religious questions, he based his thought on the existence of an Absolute which gives value to all else, including personal selves. His quest also represented an attempt to find new philosophical foundations for American democracy. His works include *The Religious Aspect of Philosophy* (1885) and *The Concept of God* (1897).

Ruether, Rosemary Radford (1936–)
American theologian. Born in St Paul, she studied at Scripps College and Claremont Graduate school, going on to become professor at Howard University, Washington; in 1976 she became professor at Garrett Seminary, Evanston, Illinois. A leading Roman Catholic representative of feminist and liberation theology, she has written many books, most important of which are *Faith and Fratricide* (1974) and *Sexism and God-Talk* (1983).

Rufinus, Tyrannius (c.345–410)
Italian monk, historian and translator. Born in Aquileia, he became friendly with *Jerome in Rome and travelled first to Egypt, where he studied under *Didymus the Blind and became interested in the works of *Origen, and then to Jerusalem, where he founded a monastery on the Mount of Olives. He returned to Italy when Origen came under attack. Though he wrote works of his own, he is important for having translated the writings of the Greek fathers into Latin when knowledge of Greek was declining in the West. In many cases this ensured their survival.

Rutherford, Samuel (1600–61)
Scottish churchman. Born of a farming family in the Borders, he studied in Edinburgh and became professor of Latin. However, he resigned his post and after studying theology became a minister. Deposed for nonconformity, he was imprisoned in Aberdeen; after his release he went on to become professor at St Andrews and finally rector of the university. His most important work, *Lex Rex, or The Law and the Prince* (1644), on constitutional government, asserted the supremacy of the people, argued against tolerance and did not accept the existence of religious minorities. It was publicly burnt when Charles II was restored to the throne; his death spared him persecution.

Ruysbroeck, Jan van (1293–1381)
Flemish mystic. Born near Brussels, he was educated there and spent three years as a priest before retiring to a local valley, Groenendaal, where he founded a monastery, and attracted visitors from far and wide. His major work is *The Spiritual Espousals*, emphasizing a loving union with God (he was accused of pantheism), humility, charity and flight from the world. His prose helped to shape the Flemish language.

Sabatier, Louis Auguste (1839–1901)
French Protestant theologian. Born in Vallon, after schooling at Montpellier he studied at Basle, Tübingen and Heidelberg. He then taught dogmatics in the Protestant faculty at Strasbourg but resigned rather than work under the German government imposed after the Franco-Prussian war. He turned to journalistic work in Paris, but returned to the faculty when it was refounded there, finally teaching at the Sorbonne. Deeply religious, he was influenced by *Ritschl and *Schleiermacher. He was a pioneer in France in the historical criticism of the New Testament and sought to mediate between faith and science. Believing that all human beings were as religious as he was, he saw religion as a human attempt to reconcile what we are with what we want to be. The human quest proceeds through several stages, mythological, dogmatic and, most importantly, psychological, and theology has to strip away extraneous elements. Of interest to more than Protestants, he helped to prepare for the Modernist movement. His works include *The Religion of Authority and the Religion of Spirit* (1903).

Sabatier, Paul (1859–1928)
French Calvinist theologian. Born in Strasbourg, he studied in Besançon, Lille, and Paris under Auguste *Sabatier and *Renan. He went on to pastoral work, but ill-health compelled him to resign; after a period of study he became professor in Strasbourg. His main work was a *Life of St *Francis* (1893), which led to further research worldwide and the foundation of Franciscan studies; however, it was condemned by Rome. He sympathized with the Catholic Modernists like *Loisy and became involved in their cause.

Sabellius (third century)
Christian teacher. Little is known of his life; he may have come from Libya to Rome, where he was excommunicated by *Callistus. From the fragments of his teaching which remain it seems that he held that God is a monad who in the Father reveals himself as creator and lawgiver and through expansion projects himself in the Son as redeemer and in the Spirit as sanctifier. This form of belief, which became known as modalistic monarchianism, because it holds that the one God exists in different modes, was regarded as incompatible with Christian faith. However, it proved widely influential in circles which rejected any form of subordinationism of the person of Christ.

Saint-Cyran, Abbé de (Jean Duvergier de Hauranne, 1581–1643)
French *Jansenist leader. After studying at the Jesuit College at Louvain, and in Paris and Bayonne with Jansen, he was attracted to the works of *Augustine, which he preferred to scholasticism. Being made abbot of Saint-Cyran, from then on he lived mostly in Paris. He was concerned to reform Roman Catholicism by reviving the teachings of Augustine, opposing the Jesuits and scholasticism and criticizing Roman Catholic abuses. Having incurred the enmity of Cardinal Richelieu, he spent the last five years of his life in prison.

Saint Simon, Count de (Claude Henri de Rouvroy, 1760–1825)
French social philosopher. He was born in Paris and educated privately. Though from a noble family, he was convinced by the French Revolution that times had changed. From then on he became an apostle of positive science, industrialism, socialism and humanitarian lay religion. He called for a society in which individuals found their place according to their achievements and were rewarded according to their works. Since he believed that the one divine principle in Christianity is to be brothers to one another and to help the poor, he felt that Christianity endorsed his views. He was an influence on *Comte. He wrote many books; his religious views are expressed in *The New Christianity* (1825).

Sandmel, Samuel (1911–79)
Jewish biblical scholar. Born in Dayton, Ohio, he studied at Hebrew Union College and Yale before being ordained rabbi. After pastoral work in Atlanta, he became pro-

fessor first at Vanderbilt and then at Hebrew Union College. Espousing modern methods of biblical criticism, he played an important role in mediating between Judaism and Christianity in this area, and was notable for his sympathetic approach, in many ways ahead of its time. His books include *A Jewish Understanding of the New Testament* (1956), *We Jews and Jesus* (1965), *The First Christian Century in Judaism and Christianity* (1969) and *The Enjoyment of Scripture* (1972).

Sanday, William (1843–1920)
English New Testament scholar. After studying in Oxford, he went to be principal of a Durham college, but was recalled as professor to Oxford, where he spent the rest of his life. He communicated German critical theology to the Church of England and encouraged the acceptance of New Testament criticism. He wrote a good deal (including *Christologies. Ancient and Modern*, 1910), but he is most remembered for his commentary on Romans with *Headlam.

Sanders, Ed Parish (1937–   )
Born in Texas, after graduate work at Union Theological Seminary, New York, under W. D. *Davies, he went to Jerusalem to study rabbinic Judaism. He became a professor at McMaster and Oxford and is now professor at Duke University, North Carolina. His *Paul and Palestinian Judaism* (1977), based on a thorough study of the Jewish sources, prompted a reassessment of Judaism in the first century, demonstrating the degree to which it has been caricatured by Christian accounts of it, and was taken further in his *Jesus and Judaism* (1984). His *Jewish Law from Jesus to the Mishnah* (1990) among other things demonstrated that Jesus could hardly be said to have broken the Law; his *Judaism: Practice and Belief* (1991) is a definite study of Judaism at the time of Jesus.

Santayana, George (1863–1952)
American philosopher. Born in Madrid of a Spanish father and American mother, he was moved to Boston at an early age; he studied under William *James and became professor at Harvard. On the death of his father he had enough money to live independently, and in 1912 he returned to Europe; he spent his last years in a convent in Rome. His attachment to Catholicism was for historical and aesthetic, rather than religious, reasons. His basically materialist

philosophy saw rational processes as expressions of animal compulsion to believe. His philosophy was set out in *Scepticism and Animal Faith* (1923) and his four-volume *Realms of Being: The Realm of Essence* (1927), *The Realm of Matter* (1930), *The Realm of Truth* (1938) and *The Realm of Spirit* (1940).

Sartre, Jean-Paul (1905–80)
French existentialist philosopher. Born in Paris, the nephew of Albert *Schweitzer, at an early age he rebelled against the middle-class values of his surroundings. A year in Berlin led him to discover *Hegel, and also *Heidegger and *Husserl, whom he helped to introduce to France and whose method he developed. His thinking always remained influenced by German thought. During the Second World War he was a member of the Resistance and was then an advocate of existentialism, in novels and plays as well as academic works. An atheist, he stressed the burden of individual personal freedom. His major philosophical work was *Being and Nothingness* (1943, ET 1956), which essentially transposes Heidegger's *Being and Time* into a French setting.

Saussure, Ferdinand de (1857–1913)
Swiss linguist. Born in Geneva, he studied at Leipzig and Berlin and made his name at twenty-one with a work of comparative philology on Indo-European vowel systems. He taught in Paris and then returned as professor to Geneva, where he spent the rest of his life. His most famous work, *Course in General Linguistics* (1915, ET 1959), is not really a book at all but a transcription of lecture notes. He is regarded as the figure behind structuralism; he argued that language is a sign-system in which there is only an arbitrary link between the signifier and the signified (i.e. the word and what it denotes), and that the medium through which the sign-system is expressed is distinct from its form (i.e. the way in which the system is organized). Hence his well-known saying, 'in language there are only differences'. He was an influence on *Barthes, *Derrida and *Lévi-Strauss.

Savonarola, Girolamo (1452–98)
Italian Reformer. After studies in Ferrara he became a Dominican and led an ascetic life, being made prior of San Marco in Florence. He passionately denounced the immorality of nobility and clergy; his popularity led to a revolution in Florence which forced out the

ruling Medici family and created a theocracy. However, he made many enemies and was excommunicated by *Alexander VI. He retorted by calling for the deposition of the pope, but his support had dwindled and he was tortured and executed.

Scaliger, Joseph Justus (1520–1609)
French Protestant scholar. Son of a renowned Italian humanist, he was born in Agen and studied in Paris. For a long time he was a private tutor in France; he lectured in Geneva to escape persecution and finally became professor at Leiden, where he taught *Grotius. His knowledge of classical authors helped to set ancient chronology on a scientific basis.

Schaeffer, Francis August (1912–84)
American theologian. Born in the United States, he studied at Westminster Theological Seminary, Philadelphia and in 1948 moved to Switzerland, where he founded the community L'Abri, aimed at those disillusioned with humanism, relativism and existentialism. Markedly *Calvinist, he sought to restore the confidence of educated evangelicals in orthodox theology, to understand cultural trends and thus have a more positive view of the arts and culture. His books include *The God who is There* (1968) and *How Shall We Then Live?* (1980).

Schaff, Philip (1819–1913)
Theologian and church historian. Born in Switzerland, he studied in Tübingen, Halle and Berlin with the leading theologians of his time, including *Baur. In 1844 he was invited to become professor at the German Reformed church seminary in Mercersburg, Pennsylvania, and helped to develop Mercersburg theology. He went on to teach at Union Theological Seminary, New York. A gifted church historian, he was a leader in bringing German theology to America, and an advocate of church unity. He wrote a twelve-volume church history, and edited series of the Nicene and Post-Nicene Fathers.

Scheeben, Matthias Joseph (1835–88)
German Catholic theologian. After study in Rome he was professor in Cologne until his death. A pioneer of Neoscholasticism, in his works he combined patristic and scholastic learning; he was opposed to rationalism, a supporter of papal infallibility and an opponent of *Döllinger and the Old Catholics. His main work was his three-volume *Dogmatics* (1873–87).

Scheler, Max (1874–1928)
German phenomenologist. Born in Munich, he studied in Jena and taught there, later becoming professor in Cologne and Frankfurt. He was influenced by *Husserl and was originally a phenomenologist, but was later converted to Catholicism. Believing in the distinctive character of religious values, he advocated an evolutionary pantheism through which blind force and spirituality appear in history and human beings. His major work is *On the Eternal in Man* (1921), arguing that the human capacity for religion shows humankind to be more than a natural phenomenon. His stress on the person was taken up by existentialism.

Schelling, Friedrich Wilhelm Joseph von (1775–1854)
German philosopher. Son of a Württemberg pastor, he studied at Tübingen and became professor at Jena, at the time the centre of German Romanticism. He went on to teach in Würzburg, Erlangen, Munich and Berlin. His philosophy moved from Romantic idealism, through pantheism and a philosophy of nature, to a more Neoplatonist approach; he tried to reconcile his views with Christianity. Extremely influential on German thought and on the English Romantics through *Coleridge, he represented a stage in idealism on the way to *Hegel. His major work was *The System of Transcendental Idealism* (1800), which developed the views of *Kant and *Fichte, arguing that consciousness is the only immediate object of knowledge.

Schillebeeckx, Edward Cornelis Florentius Alfons (1914–   )
Belgian theologian. Born in Antwerp of a well-to-do family, he studied at the Jesuit College at Turnhout and then went on to the Dominican house in Ghent. After military service he studied theology at Louvain and taught there. Post-doctoral study in Paris broadened his horizons, and he met leading Dominicans. In 1958 he was called to be professor in Nijmegen, where he has been ever since. He was an adviser at the Second Vatican Council, but in subsequent years twice came under suspicion from the Vatican. His first major work was an existential interpretation of the sacraments, *Christ the Sacrament* (1959, ET 1963), but it was not until his *Jesus* (1974, ET 1979) that he attracted international attention. In the book, influenced by modern biblical scholarship, he saw Jesus as an eschatological prophet; the sequel, *Christ* (1980) relates early

Christian experience of salvation to contemporary Christian and non-Christian experience. A long interval separates these books from the last volume of his trilogy, *Church* (1990); two versions of a book he wrote on ministry during this period reflect his growing dissatisfaction with the move away from the ideas of Vatican II and the need for a revision of the Catholic theology of ministry. This dissatisfaction becomes even more evident in his latest work.

Schlatter, Adolf (1852–1939)
Swiss German New Testament scholar and theologian. Born in St Gall the son of a pharmacist, he taught at Berne, Greifswald, Berlin and Tübingen. He believed that biblical exegesis is the only foundation for systematic theology and was opposed to the idealistic theology of his time. In this way he anticipated the theology of *Barth, and he was respected by *Bultmann and *Hoskyns. Few of his works were translated into English. He wrote commentaries on the New Testament, a New Testament theology, a history of the earliest church and a major study of *Faith in the New Testament* (1885).

Schlegel, Friedrich von (1772–1829)
German Catholic apologist. A leader of the Romantic movement, he lived in Berlin, but lectured in Jena, Dresden and Paris. Most of his life was given to literary pursuits. He married a daughter of Moses *Mendelssohn and with her was converted to Catholicism. He then became opposed to the development of political and religious freedom in Germany and a vigorous defender of the Catholic mediaeval ideal against the rise of a German national state along Napoleonic lines.

Schleiermacher, Friedrich Daniel Ernst (11768–1834)
German theologian. Born in Breslau, the son of a Reformed army chaplain who was converted to the Herrnhutter Brethren, he had a pietist education. Finding this too narrow, he went to the university of Halle where he discovered *Aristotle and *Kant. After being a tutor he was ordained, and served as a pastor in Berlin. He then became professor at Halle and, after a further Berlin pastorate, professor in Berlin. A gifted preacher, against the background of the Napoleonic wars he supported German national and church unity. His first major work, *On Religion: Speeches to Its Cultured Despisers* (1799), was an apologia for religion as being a sense of the infinite without

which human life was incomplete, locating religion in intuition and feeling, not dogma. His major work was *The Christian Faith* (1821–22), with its famous definition of religion as 'the feeling of absolute dependence', in which he sought a middle course between orthodoxy and natural theology. It was related to the corporate piety of the Christian community as an alternative basis to Christian knowledge constructed by Kant. He also wrote a life of Jesus. Of enormous influence, his theology seemed to point a way forward after Kant's criticism of theology and became the epitome of liberal theology.

Schmidt, Karl-Ludwig (1891–1956)
German New Testament scholar. He was professor at Giessen, Jena and then Bonn, from where he was dismissed by the Nazis in 1933, after which he taught in Basle. A pioneer in form criticism, he wrote an influential book on the framework of the Synoptic Gospels; further works were on church and state and Jewish–Christian relations.

Schmucker, Samuel Simon (1799–1873)
American Lutheran theologian. His main concern was to Americanize the eastern American Lutheran churches, and he was founder of the Lutheran Theological Seminary in Gettysburg, where he taught. He believed that a genuinely American Lutheran theology was needed to combat rationalism. His *Elements of Popular Theology* (1834) was widely influential.

Schniewind, Julius (1883–1948)
German New Testament scholar. Born in Elberfeld, he was professor in Greifswald, Königsberg, Kiel and Halle, being dismissed by the Nazis in 1937. He was restored to office after the war. He wrote many works and commentaries on the Synoptic Gospels and New Testament theology.

Scholem, Gerhart Gershom (1897–1982)
German/Israeli historian of ideas. Born to a Jewish family in Berlin, he studied at Berlin, Jena and Berne. From an early age he was interested in Zionism, and through *Buber discovered the Kabbalah. He became an expert in it, and on finishing his doctoral study went to Israel, where after further research he became professor at the Hebrew university in Jerusalem. From then on he studied mysticism, examining experiences of the divine in the Jewish tradition. He was

a friend of Walter *Benjamin, about whom he wrote a memoir (1975). Important works are *Major Trends in Jewish Mysticism* (1954) and *On the Kabbalah and its Symbolism* (1965).

Schopenhauer, Arthur (1788–1860)
German philosopher. Son of a wealthy Danzig merchant, he studied in Göttingen and Berlin, where he heard *Fichte and *Schleiermacher and became an admirer of *Kant. He also drew on Buddhist sources. His main work was *The World as Will and Idea* (1819). Will (understood as striving) is the ultimate reality, extending beyond conscious life, and the evils of life are best remedied by subduing it: Schopenhauer claimed that his teaching paralleled that of the mystics. He saw art, poetry and music as a means to this end; he influenced the German composer Richard Wagner and the early *Nietzsche.

Schürer, Emil (1844–1910)
German Protestant New Testament scholar. Born in Augsburg, he was professor in Giessen, Kiel and Göttingen. He is best known for his pioneer five-volume study, *A History of the Jewish People in the Time of Jesus Christ* (1886, ET 1890), important enough to be revised and reissued in the 1970s–80s.

Schüssler Fiorenza, Elisabeth *see* **Fiorenza, Elisabeth Schüssler**

Schweitzer, Albert (1875–1965)
Theologian, physician and musician. Born in Alsace, he studied in Strasbourg, Berlin and Paris. His first book was *The Mystery of the Kingdom of God* (1901), which saw Jesus' teaching as centred on the imminent coming of the kingdom. Its publication led to his being made a lecturer and head of a theological college, and he went on to write his classic *The Quest of the Historical Jesus* (1906), criticizing the orthodox and liberal nineteenth-century lives of Jesus as being projections of their authors and putting forward his own eschatological interpretation. Meanwhile he was studying for a medical degree, and in 1913 he gave up his academic career to devote himself to mission and the care of the sick in Lambarene, in French Equatorial Africa. He had to return to France because of the First World War, during which his hospital was destroyed, but he rebuilt it afterwards. While still writing as a biblical scholar he produced an influential book on Paul, *The Mysticism of Paul the Apostle* (1931), but his views changed to a philosophy of 'reverence for life': all life must be cherished, including insects and plants. He was also a fine organist, and wrote a study of Bach.

Schweizer, Eduard (1913–   )
Swiss New Testament scholar. Son of a lawyer, he studied in Marburg and became involved in the work of the Confessing Church. He then moved back to Zurich and studied under *Brunner and *Otto, and finally in Basle under *Barth. After a pastorate in Switzerland, he was professor in Mainz, then returning to Zurich for the rest of his career. His main interest has been in the theological ideas of the New Testament, and particularly in christology; he has written two major books on Jesus (1971, 1988) as well as commentaries on the Gospels and a theology of the New Testament. His *Church Order in the New Testament* (1959, ET 1961) is an important study of the early church's ministry.

Schwenkfeld, Caspar (1489–1561)
Radical reformer. A German diplomat from Silesia, he became acquainted with the views of *Luther and other reformers, but had reservations over the eucharist, christology and church discipline which brought him into conflict with them. Opposed by both Catholics and Protestants, he had to leave Silesia for Strasbourg and south Germany. In 1540 the Lutherans branded him an outlaw and his followers formed a separate religious community which spread to Holland, England and America. A small group, with a life-style like the Quakers, still exists in the United States.

Seabury, Samuel (1729–96)
American Episcopalian bishop. Born in Connecticut, he studied at Yale and Edinburgh, before serving in parishes in Jamaica, Long Island and Westchester. After being consecrated bishop in Aberdeen (because he could not take the oath of allegiance to the English crown), the first American to hold this office, he served as rector in New London, Connecticut, until his death.

Segundo, Juan Luis (1925–   )
Uruguayan Catholic liberation theologian. He studied in Argentina, Louvain and Paris, and has taught at Harvard, Chicago, Toronto, Montreal, Birmingham and São Paulo universities. He now works in Montevideo. He is particularly concerned with the meth-

odology of liberation theology and has produced a five-volume systematic theology, *Jesus of Nazareth Yesterday and Today* (1982–8); he has also written *The Liberation of Theology* (1976).

Semler, Johann Salomo (1725–91)
German biblical critic. Born in Thuringia, from a Pietist background, he studied at Halle and was professor at Coburg and Altdorf before returning to Halle as professor in 1752. He was a pioneer in biblical criticism, to the point of falling foul of Lutheran orthodoxy. In textual criticism, he worked out a new classification of manuscripts which made further progress possible; in his distinction between Jewish Christianity and Pauline Christianity he anticipated *Baur. He also distinguished between theology and religion and between the Bible and the word of God. Though he was influenced by the deists, he remained a conservative in public religion, thus also endorsing the distinction between what is said in private and what is preached in public.

Servetus, Michael (1511–53)
Spanish physician and theologian. Born in Navarre, he studied at Saragossa and Toulouse and travelled in Italy and Germany, where he met *Bucer and *Melanchthon. A book on the Trinity putting forward an alternative view, aimed at helping to convert Muslims and Jews, shocked his friends. To avoid trouble he went to Paris to study medicine: he discovered the pulmonary circulation of the blood. A further book, *The Restoration of Christianity* (1553), published anonymously in answer to *Calvin's *Institutes*, led to his arrest and subsequent execution in Geneva, an action which led to a controversy in Protestantism over toleration.

Severus of Antioch (c.460–538)
Monastic theologian. After studying in Alexandria and Berytus, he became a monk and went to *Constantinople, where he secured imperial support for the monophysites (those who believed that Christ had only one, divine, nature) and was made patriarch of Antioch. The leading theologian of the moderates, he wrote many works, homilies and letters, which survive.

Shammai (died c.15 CE)
Jewish pharisaic scribe. He was a strict interpreter of law and therefore the opponent of *Hillel. Often in conflict with the Romans, his school had to yield to the Hillelites after the destruction of Jerusalem in 70 CE.

Siger of Brabant (1235–82)
Radical *Averroist philosopher. All that is known of him is that he taught at the university of Paris and was canon of St Paul's Church in Liège. He was attacked by *Bonaventure and *Thomas Aquinas. When he arrived in Paris, *Aristotle had recently been put on the curriculum and Siger wrote commentaries on his works. These brought out the conflict between Aristotle and orthodox Christianity, since Aristotle taught, for example, that the world was eternal and that there was no future life. Siger had to flee to escape charges of heresy because he was alleged to have taught a double truth, and is reported to have been killed in Orvieto by a mad cleric.

Silesius, Angelus (Johannes Scheffler, 1624–77)
Polish poet. Son of a Lutheran nobleman, he studied medicine and became physician to the Duke of Württemberg. His interest in mysticism, prompted by followers of *Boehme, caused difficulty with Lutheran leaders and he went to Breslau where he became a Roman Catholic and later a monk. He wrote hymns, mostly during his Lutheran days, and, later, mystical poems.

Simeon, Charles (1759–1836)
Evangelical Anglican. After studies at Cambridge he became an Evangelical, and on ordination was appointed to a Cambridge church, where he spent the rest of his life. He became immensely influential in the Evangelical revival, particularly in missionary work; his sermons were published in twenty-one volumes.

Simeon Stylites (390–459)
Born on the Cilician border, after time in a monastery he became a hermit and then spent his life on a pillar, the height of which was steadily increased. He produced no written works, but was a great influence on the religious and political life of his time, and an advocate of the orthodox Christian doctrine of the Council of Chalcedon.

Simon, Richard (1638–1712)
French biblical scholar. A member of the French Oratory, he was expelled for his *Critical History of the Old Testament* (1678), which denied that Moses wrote the Penta-

teuch. However, his work was in fact written to defend orthodoxy against *Spinoza. He moved to Rouen and then Dieppe, where he wrote several books about the New Testament.

Smart, Roderick Ninian (1926–   )
After studies at Oxford, he learned Chinese on military service and went to Ceylon. Subsequently he became professor in Birmingham, Lancaster and Santa Barbara. A pioneer in developing religious studies in Britain, he writes on phenomenology and the history of religions. Among his many works are *The Religious Experience of Mankind* (1969) and *The Phenomenon of Christianity* (1979).

Smith, George Adam (1856–1942)
Scottish Old Testament scholar. Born in Calcutta, after studies in Edinburgh, Tübingen and Leipzig, he was a minister in Aberdeen and then became Old Testament professor at the Free Church College in Glasgow. He finally became principal of Aberdeen university. He wrote a number of biblical commentaries, but is best known for his *The Book of the Twelve Prophets*, and his *Historical Geography of the Holy Land* (1894), still available, based on his extensive travelling in the Near East. In his works he tried to reconcile criticism with reverence.

Smith, John Edwin (1921–   )
American philosopher of religion. Born in Brooklyn, he studied at Columbia University and Union Theological Seminary, New York, and went on to teach at Barnard College, becoming professor of philosophy at Yale. His books include *Reason and God* (1961), *The Philosophy of Religion* (1965) and *The Analogy of Experience: An Approach to Understanding Religious Truth* (1973).

Smith, Joseph (1805–44)
Founder of the Church of Jesus Christ of Latter Day Saints (Mormons). Born into a frontier family in Vermont, he moved to Palmyra, New York, where he had a religious conversion. Claiming to have been shown by God golden plates covered with mysterious writing, he produced a translation of them as the *Book of Mormon*. This was followed by *Doctrine and Covenants* (1835), the basis of Mormon teaching. He formed a community and founded the city of Nauvoo, Illinois, but was killed by a mob angry at his financial failures and polygamy.

Smith, Morton (1915–   )
American scholar. Born in Philadelphia, he studied at Harvard and the Hebrew University of Jerusalem, going on to the American School of Classical Studies in Athens. He then taught at Brown university before being appointed professor at Columbia, where he spent the rest of his career. Of great learning, he has regularly questioned accepted ideas, in relation to the Old Testament in his *Palestinian Parties and Politics that Shaped the Old Testament* (1971) and to the New in *Jesus the Magician* (1978), which demonstrated the way in which magical practices shed light on the ministry of Jesus.

Smith, William Robertson (1846–1894)
Scottish Old Testament scholar. Son of a clergyman, he studied in Aberdeen, Edinburgh, Bonn and Göttingen before becoming professor at the Free Church College in Aberdeen. Seven years later he was expelled for articles in the *Encyclopedia Britannica* alleged to undermine belief in scriptural inspiration. He subsequently became editor-in-chief of the *Encyclopedia* and professor of Arabic at Cambridge. His most important book is *The Religion of the Semites* (1889), which saw sacrifice as communion, not propitiation.

Smith, Wilfred Cantwell (1916–   )
After studying in Canada, the United States, Britain and Europe he taught in India, and then returned to his native land to found and direct the Institute of Islamic Studies at McGill university. He later became professor at Harvard, where he also directed the Center for the Study of World Religions, returning again to Canada to become professor at Dalhousie university, Nova Scotia. He has written many books on Islam and on world religions; his major works in this area are *The Meaning and End of Religion* (1963), which distinguishes faith from religion, and *Toward a World Theology* (1981).

Sobrino, Jon (1938–   )
Spanish Catholic theologian. Working in El Salvador, he tries to reconcile orthodox belief with work among the poor; in his theology 'from below' he sees parallels between Latin America and the time of Jesus. His main works are *Christology at the Crossroads* (1978) and *The True Church and the Poor* (1984).

Socrates Scholasticus (c.380–450)
Greek church historian. He was born in Constantinople, where he became a lawyer. He

wrote a church history which he intended to be a continuation of that of *Eusebius. After reading the works of *Athanasius he discovered it had mistakes in it and revised it; though clearly written, it is more of a second-hand chronicle.

Söderblom, Nathan (1866–1931)
Swedish Lutheran theologian. Born in Trönö, he studied in Uppsala, and wrote a book on *The Religion of *Luther* (1893), whom he admired greatly, published in the year of his ordination. In Paris, where he was chaplain to the Swedish legation, he lectured on comparative religion, as he did subsequently in Leipzig. though by then he was professor at Uppsala. In 1914 he became archbishop, against some opposition from conservatives. He was prominent in the reunion movement and Life and Work, organizing a famous conference in Stockholm in 1927; he sought to bring about the practical co-operation of all Christian churches, especially in social problems. irrespective of doctrine. In his theological works, he defended biblical criticism, and argued that God's revelation is not limited to Bible or church. His *The Living God* (1933) is the one book which appeared in English.

Sölle, Dorothee (1929–   )
Radical German theologian. She studied in Cologne, Freiburg and Göttingen, and became professor of systematic theology at Union Theological Seminary, New York. She also has been much involved as a freelance writer, journalist and in television work. Influenced by Marxism, she rejects traditional theism, believing that it puts people in a position of dependence: God is loving solidarity. She also rejects existential and private forms of religion in favour of a political hermeneutic. Major books are *To Work and to Love* (1984) and *Thinking about God* (1990).

Sohm, Rudolf (1841–1917)
German Lutheran lawyer and historian. After teaching law in Göttingen he became professor in Freiburg, Strasbourg and Leipzig. He developed the view that the church is spiritual but the law is secular; thus canon law is incompatible with the true nature of the church, which is basically charismatic. Among his books is *The Relationship of Church and State* (1873).

Solovyov, Vladimir Sergyevich (1853–1900)
Russian philosopher and theologian. The son of the rector of Moscow university, he studied and taught there. After extensive travel, and lecturing in philosophy in Moscow to an audience which included *Dostoievsky and *Tolstoy, he worked at the ministry of education in St Petersburg, but resigned after a controversial lecture against capital punishment. He then devoted himself to writing. Mystical experiences led him to frame a cosmic theology centred on the incarnation, death and resurrection of Christ and the need to realize unity by integration into the unity of the world. Though initially hostile to the Roman Catholic Church, he was increasingly drawn to church union. This approach led to a ban on his religious writings from the Holy Synod, so he turned to politics. In 1896 he seems to have become a Roman Catholic, a move also hinted at in his *Russia and the Universal Church* (1889).

Song, Choan-Seng (1929–   )
Taiwanese theologian. His interest is in the indigenization of theology in Asia, and the way in which Asian symbols from non-Christian religions can help communication. His theology begins from everyday life, and he is against 'Christianization'; his main works are *Third-Eye Theology* (1980), *The Compassionate God* (1982), and *Theology from the Womb of Asia* (1988).

Sozomen (Salaminius Herminias Sozomenus, fifth century)
Palestinian church historian. Little is known of his life except that he lived near Gaza, was educated by monks, travelled widely, and settled in Constantinople. Like his older contemporary *Socrates, he planned a continuation of *Eusebius' church history, and drew widely on Socrates, though improving his style.

Sozzini, Fausto (1539–1604)
Founder of Socinianism. His uncle Lelio (1525–62), a lawyer from Siena, had denounced Roman 'idolatry', as a result of which he had to spend his life wandering through Europe. Influenced by Lelio's views, he left Italy for Basle and later Poland, where he built up a church at Racov, near Cracow, which produced a famous catechism. Strongly rationalistic, he rejected the doctrine of the Trinity, seeing Jesus as a man, and taught only a selective resurrection. In-

fluential beyond their number, his followers were scattered at the Counter-Reformation but continued to influence radical thought for some time to come, especially in England.

Spencer, Herbert (1820–1903)
English philosopher. Born in Derby, son of a schoolmaster, he was virtually self-taught. He became a railway construction designer before devoting himself to writing. He was deeply influenced by *Darwin and coined the phrase 'survival of the fittest'. He was the chief nineteenth-century exponent of agnosticism, dividing reality into the knowable and the unknowable, but acknowledging that the unknowable could still be reality. His books were all very individualistic: a series of 'Principles' includes *Principles of Philosophy* (1872), *Sociology* (1877), and *Ethics* (1893).

Spener, Philipp Jakob (1635–1703)
German pietist. Born of devout parents in Alsace, he studied history and philosophy at Strasbourg. In subsequent travels he encountered Reformed Christianity, which made him want to change the Lutheranism he knew. A minister in Strasbourg and Frankfurt, he held devotional meetings in private homes, and in Frankfurt wrote his best known work *Pious Desires* (1675), which set out the essence of his pietism. He gained followers but, encountering opposition, moved to Dresden as court preacher. After more opposition there he went to Berlin, where the Elector of Brandenburg supported him. He was influential in founding the university of Halle but, more importantly, his views left a permanent mark on German Lutheranism.

Spinoza, Benedict de (1632–77)
Dutch Jewish philosopher. Born in Amsterdam of Portuguese parents, he read widely and developed unorthodox views, as a result of which he was expelled from the synagogue. He travelled around, earning his living by grinding lenses, and ended up in The Hague. His views were pantheistic: there is one reality which can be called God or nature and all other things are modifications of this. God only loves and hates in us. Religions like Judaism and Christianity do not express philosophical truth but convey moral truths to those incapable of seeing them by reason. However, he is perhaps most important in that his *Tractatus Theologico-politicus* (1670) shows him as a forerunner of biblical criticism.

Spitta, Friedrich (1852–1924)
German Protestant theologian. Born near Hanover, he taught in Bonn, Strasbourg and Göttingen. He was particularly interested in church music and liturgy, but also wrote a history of early Christianity.

Spurgeon, Charles Haddon (1834–92)
English Baptist preacher. Born in Essex into a family of Independent ministers, he became a Baptist minister; in South London his preaching drew such crowds that a new church had to be built for him. He also founded a college which still exists today under his name, and other evangelical organizations. A strict *Calvinist, his views estranged him even from the Baptist Union. Books of his sermons spread round the world, and his devotional books are still used.

Stein, Edith (1891–1942)
Carmelite nun. Born of a Jewish family in Breslau, she studied at Göttingen and Freiburg under *Husserl and became a significant phenomenologist. She was converted to Roman Catholicism in 1922 and sought to interpret phenomenology in a *Thomistic way. She became a Carmelite in Holland in 1934 and during the German occupation was deported by the Germans and killed in a concentration camp.

Steiner, George (1929–   )
American critic. Born in Paris, he studied there and in Chicago, Harvard and Oxford. He then joined the staff of *The Economist*: after a period at Princeton he came to teach at Cambridge in 1961; he still combines work there with being professor of English in Geneva university. He became known for a series of essays (*Language and Silence*, 1971) analysing a crisis arising from the pressures of modern culture on language. His long-standing concerns with language, culture, art and Jewishness and his opposition to many current secular trends make him an important figure for theology. His many books include *After Babel* (1975), *Real Presences* (1989) and *Grammars of Creation* (1990).

Steiner, Rudolf (1861–1925)
Founder of Anthroposophy. Son of a stationmaster at Kraljevec, in what is now Yugoslavia, he was brought up as a Catholic, studied science in Vienna and worked on Goethe. He tried to develop a scientific way of studying spirituality, and after reject-

ing theosophy because of its Eastern connections, founded his own Anthroposophy, aimed at developing spiritual potential by which men and women could regain contact with an estranged spiritual world. His views are contained in *Philosophy of Freedom* (1894, ET 1916) and his life is recorded in an autobiography (1924, ET 1928).

Stendahl, Krister (1921–)
Swedish/American New Testament scholar. Professor at Uppsala and Harvard, he became bishop of Stockholm in 1980. In his major work *The School of Matthew* (1954), he used Qumran to illuminate New Testament interpretation. In a famous article 'Paul and the Introspective Conscience of the West', he sought to rescue Paul from Lutheran interpretation. He has been particularly concerned with Jewish-Christian relations.

Strauss, David Friedrich (1808–74)
German theologian. Born near Stuttgart, he studied under *Baur at Tübingen and in Berlin but lost any prospect of an academic career by writing his controversial *The Life of Jesus Critically Examined* (1835–36). This argued consistently that the Gospels were myths developed from the Old Testament and elsewhere, with minimal historical foundation. The true significance of Christianity was to be seen in *Hegelian philosophy. He later turned to biography before returning to theology and a second *Life* of Jesus, but never achieved the impact of his first work. That proved immensely influential in subsequent theology, and remains so to the present day.

Streeter, Burnett Hillmann (1874–1937)
English New Testament scholar. He studied and taught at Queen's College, Oxford, finally becoming Provost. His best-known work, *The Four Gospels* (1924), became the standard text on the Synoptic problem, in which he persuaded English readers of the priority of Mark and the existence of another source, Q, underlying Matthew and Mark. With wide theological interests, in his *Reality* (1926) he sought to relate theology to science. He was influenced by *Buchman's Oxford Group and also by Buddhism. He was one of the first theologians to be killed in a plane crash.

Strong, Josiah (1847–1916)
American theologian. A Congregational clergyman, he was a vigorous exponent of the Social Gospel movement. His *Our Country* (1885) was a pioneer sociological treatise, challenging the churches to become the conscience of society, reconciling socialism and individualism, social responsibility and property rights. He formed the American and British Institutes of Social Service and was involved in the formation of the US Federal Council of Churches.

Suarez, Francisco (1548–1617)
Spanish theologian. Born in Granada, he studied canon law at Salamanca before joining the Jesuits and turning to theology and philosophy. After ordination he taught in many Spanish universities. He wrote important and original works on political theory and the philosophy of law, rejecting e.g. the divine right of kings; in theology he was much influenced by *Thomas Aquinas, on whose theology he made an extensive commentary. However, he had sufficient individuality to create his own system, combining Aristotle and Thomas Aquinas with Duns Scotus.

Suso, Heinrich (1295–1366)
Swabian mystic. Of noble family, he entered a Dominican friary at Constance as a boy. Later he had a deep conversion and finished his studies at Cologne under Meister *Eckhart. Back at Constance, a book in defence of Eckhardt was condemned and he was banned from teaching. He travelled as a director of women's convents and finally lived in Ulm, never far from criticism. His *Little Book of Eternal Wisdom* (1328), a practical book of meditation, is a spiritual classic, and was admired by *Thomas à Kempis.

Swedenborg (Svedberg), Emanuel (1688–1772)
Swedish philosopher. Son of a distinguished theologian, he studied at Uppsala and in England (where he was influenced by *Locke and *Newton). A gifted scientist and inventor (he was the founder of crystallography), he was appointed to the Swedish Board of Mines. He already felt that the universe had a spiritual basis, and in 1734 wrote *On the Infinite and Final Cause of Creation* to demonstrate this. Ten years later he had a mystical conversion, in which he became conscious of direct contact with the supernatural, and felt a call to be God's prophet and disseminate the doctrines of a 'new church', as a spiritual brotherhood. He resigned his government post and spent the rest of his life in Sweden, Holland and England. He died in London.

Swete, Henry Barclay (1835–1917)
English biblical scholar. After studying at King's College, London, and Cambridge, he returned to both successively as professor. He was involved in founding the *Journal of Theological Studies* and the *Patristic Greek Lexicon* (finished 1968[!] under Geoffrey *Lampe) along with other scholarly initiatives. His own best-known work is his edition of the Septuagint, but he also wrote a history of the doctrine of the Holy Spirit and two New Testament commentaries.

Symmachus (second century)
Biblical translator. He seems to have been an Ebionite (one who believed that Jesus was a mere man), but virtually nothing is known of his life. He gave his name to a free translation of the Old Testament into Greek.

Tatian (active c.160)
Christian apologist. Born in Assyria, he was trained in Greek rhetoric and philosophy. He became a Christian in Rome and was a pupil of *Justin Martyr. He is best known for his compilation, the *Diatessaron*, a harmony of the life of Christ based on the four Gospels. He wrote a defence of Christianity entitled *Oration to the Greeks*, a polemic against Greek culture, which he contrasted with the great age and purity of Christianity. He returned to Syria to found an ascetic sect, the Encratites.

Tauler, John (1300–61)
German mystic. He became a Dominican at Strasbourg and seems to have been influenced by *Eckhart and *Suso. He gained a reputation as a preacher and spiritual director, and cared for the sick during the Black Death. He travelled widely and in his sermons was concerned to commend a balance between active concern for everyday life and the inner quest. His only surviving works are transcripts of these sermons: they had a great influence on Luther.

Taylor, Jeremy (1613–67)
Anglican devotional writer. He lived, studied and taught in Cambridge, but after being noticed by Archbishop Laud, he was given a fellowship at All Souls', Oxford and was made chaplain to Charles I. After a parish in Uppingham, he served as chaplain to a member of the nobility before going to Ireland, where he became bishop of Down and Connor and vice-chancellor of Dublin university. His best-known books are his *Holy Living* (1650) and *Holy Dying* (1651), which have become devotional classics, being clear, balanced and powerful. He was less balanced theologically, engaging in violent polemic against both Roman Catholics and Presbyterians. He was influential on the thought of John *Wesley during his early development.

Taylor, Nathaniel William (1786–1858)
American theologian. Born in Connecticut, he studied at Yale, and after a pastorate in New Haven became the first professor of theology at Yale Divinity School. The last champion of New England theology, he sought to reconcile *Calvinistic theology to revivalism, stressing that while sin was inevitable, each individual was responsible for his or her own moral choice. His *Practical Sermons*, *Lectures on the Moral Government of God* and *Essays and Lectures upon Select Topics in Revealed Religion* were published posthumously in 1859.

Teilhard de Chardin, Pierre (1881–1955)
French Catholic theologian and scientist. Born near Clermont-Ferrand, he trained as a Jesuit at Aix-en-Provence. He was particularly interested in geology and palaeontology, and after serving in the First World War worked in China, where he became a distinguished palaeontologist. Returning to France after the Second World War, he was forbidden to accept a professorship at the Collège de France because of his views, or to publish what became his best-known book, *The Phenomenon of Man* (1959). He then went to the United States. His books appeared only after his death and increased his reputation greatly. He saw the universe in evolutionary terms: God is part of the process, which has a Christic centre and

moves towards the Omega Point; human beings form the noosphere, a spiritual area between the biosphere and the Omega point. His view, which saw the universe as Christ's body, was overly optimistic, but his concern to relate theology to science was important. His other major book is his devotional *Le milieu divin* (1960).

Temple, William (1881–1944)
English theologian and philosopher. Son of an archbishop of Canterbury, after studying and teaching at Oxford, he became headmaster of Repton School, rector of St James', Piccadilly, canon of Westminster, bishop of Manchester and successively archbishop of York and Canterbury. Prominent in national life, he was concerned for social and economic justice; he was instrumental in founding the British Council of Churches and then developing the World Council of Churches. Remarkably, he found time to write significant books. Trained as a philosopher in the idealist tradition, he produced *Mens Creatrix* (1917) and *Nature, Man and God* (1934); his devotional commentary, *Readings in St John's Gospel* (1939), became a classic; however, perhaps his most-read book was *Christianity and the Social Order* (1942).

Teresa of Avila (Teresa de Cepeda y Ahumada, 1515–82)
Spanish mystic. Descended from an old Spanish family, she became a Carmelite nun in Avila. After a lax beginning, at forty she began her mystic life, founding a house where the rule could be more strictly observed. There she wrote for her nuns *The Way of Perfection*; her other major work is *The Interior Castle*. She went on to found other houses and press for reform in the face of opposition, receiving support for her 'discalced' (without sandals, i.e. stricter) Carmelites from *John of the Cross. Her religious life deepened to the point of what she called 'spiritual marriage'. She is important for her descriptions of the whole life of prayer.

Tertullian, Quintus Septimius Florens (160–220)
African theologian. Brought up in Carthage as a pagan, he was converted to Christianity and later joined the ascetic and apocalyptic sect of the *Montanists. He wrote a large number of works and forms a bridge between the early Greek and Latin church fathers. Most of his writings are polemical:

against the heretics, against *Marcion, against a Praxeas who sees the Trinity simply as modes of God's being. A brilliant but difficult writer, he uses every rhetorical trick in the trade to demolish his opponents' views. His own views were rigorist, and his theology basically scriptural: he is well characterized by his two most famous sayings: *credo quia impossibile* (I believe because it is impossible) and 'What has Athens to do with Jerusalem?'

Theissen, Gerd (1944–   )
German New Testament scholar. Successively New Testament professor at Göttingen, Copenhagen and Heidelberg, he has pioneered the sociological and psychological interpretation of the New Testament, producing some of the most significant recent works on the Bible. His sociological interpretation of the New Testament, begun in *The First Followers of Jesus* (1978), has been continued in articles; he wrote a major psychological account of Paul. Perhaps his best-known books are a brilliant account of Jesus in narrative form, *The Shadow of the Galilean* (1987), and *Biblical Faith* (1984), an account of Christian theology from an evolutionary perspective.

Theodore of Mopsuestia (350–427)
Theologian and biblical exegete. He studied rhetoric at Antioch, but then entered a monastery there with John *Chrysostom and studied under *Diodore. After ten years there he became bishop of Mopsuestia. In the Antiochene tradition, he rejected allegorical interpretation of the Bible. In his view of the person of Christ he explained the incarnation as a moral union brought about by the initiative of divine grace, talking of the 'assumed man': God dwells in Jesus as in the prophets and apostles, but is different in that God dwells in him as a Son. His views were later condemned – from a modern perspective, probably unjustly.

Theodoret of Cyrrhus (393–466)
Theologian and bishop. Born and educated in Antioch, he gave up his possessions and entered a monastery. Becoming bishop of Antioch, he was a model pastor and administrator, but was caught up in the controversy between *Cyril and *Nestorius, whose friend he was. His support for the latter earned him deposition and exile, and he was only restored to his see after anathematizing Nestorius, after which he was left in peace. He is thought to have changed his views on

christology during his life, the Council of Chalcedon being a watershed; he wrote on the Bible, and composed a church history and an apologia for Christianity.

Theodosius I ('The Great', c.346–95)
Roman emperor. Taking *Constantine's approval of Christianity one stage further, he made it the sole official religion of the Roman empire, forbidding assemblies of Christian heretics and ordering pagan temples to be destroyed. In 390, having ordered a massacre in Thessalonica after a riot, he publicly acknowledged his guilt to *Ambrose.

Theophilus of Antioch (died c.180)
Christian apologist. Little is known of his life except that he became bishop of Antioch. He is known as author of three books *To Autolycus*, showing the superiority of the Christian God and the doctrine of creation to pagan deities and Greek myths. He developed the doctrine of the Logos, contrasting the Logos in the Godhead (*endiathetos*) with the Logos brought forth to create (*prophorikos*).

Theophylact (eleventh century)
Byzantine theologian. A native of Euboea, he was made archbishop of Achrida in Bulgaria. He wrote a commentary on the New Testament (except Revelation) and most of the Old, and stressed practical morality.

Thérèse of Lisieux (Thérèse Martin, 1873–97)
French Carmelite nun. Youngest daughter of a watchmaker in Alençon, and devout from a very early age, she entered the convent at Lisieux when fifteen and there spent the rest of her life. She wrote her autobiography (in English it appears under different titles, e.g. *Autobiography of a Saint, The Story of a Soul*) on the orders of her superiors; it was circulated to all Carmelite houses on her death and secured her fame. Her *Little Way*, which she described as 'spiritual childhood, confidence and abandonment in God', became a popular spiritual classic.

Thielicke, Helmut (1908–85)
German Protestant theologian and preacher. Born in Barmen, he taught at Heidelberg until dismissed by the Nazis; after a brief period in the army he served as a Lutheran pastor. However, he still had a large following, above all for his preaching; this continued when after the war he became

professor in Tübingen and then moved to be rector in Hamburg. His sermons had a prophetic character, presenting Christianity as a belief for a time of crisis. His main work was a three-volume *Theological Ethics* (1955ff.), moving through ethical problems of the present world to the underlying theological truths. He also wrote a three-volume systematic theology, *The Evangelical Faith* (1968–78), presenting Christianity as the answer to alienation.

Tholuck, Friedrich August Gottreu (1799–1877)
German Protestant theologian. After studying oriental languages in Breslau and Berlin he turned to theology, under the influence of *Neander and Pietist friends. He taught in Berlin and became professor in Halle. His *Doctrine of Sin and the Reconciler* (1823) was influential as opposition to rationalism; he also wrote some New Testament commentaries of a moral kind. A friend of *Pusey, he was more concerned with personal piety than dogmatic orthodoxy.

Thomas à Kempis (Thomas Hemerken, c.1380–1471)
German monk and devotional writer. Born at Kempen, near Cologne, of poor parents, he became a monk and spent his life in a monastery near Zwolle, writing, copying manuscripts and acting as a spiritual adviser. He is known solely through his *The Imitation of Christ* (1418), which with its clarity and perceptive insights is still one of the most popular of spiritual classics.

Thomas Aquinas (1225–74)
Dominican theologian. Born in Italy of a noble family, he was educated at the Benedictine abbey of Monte Cassino and then at the university of Naples. Against the wishes of his family, who imprisoned him at home for more than a year, he became a Dominican, going to Paris. He studied with *Albertus Magnus, who introduced him to the works of *Aristotle, then went to Cologne. Much of his teaching life was subsequently spent in Paris, though he also taught for a decade in Italy and spent the last two years of his life setting up a Dominican school in Naples. He died on his way to the Council of Lyons. The greatest mediaeval theologian, his main achievement was to produce a system of Christian doctrine that reconciled it with the philosophy of *Aristotle, newly rediscovered through the work of Arab philosophers, which had seemed a great threat to

Christian belief. Among other teachings he is well known for having established five 'ways to God', demonstrations of God's existence. His first great work was the *Summa contra Gentiles*, intended as a textbook for missionaries and defending natural theology. His *magnum opus* is the *Summa Theologica*, the supreme mediaeval theological system.

Thoreau, Henry David (1817–62)
American naturalist and transcendalist. Born at Concord, Massachusetts, from an early age he had a deep love of nature. He studied at Harvard and briefly became a teacher, but decided to give that up to lecture and write. He earned his living as a surveyor. Resolving on a return to nature, he lived at Walden Pond from 1845 to 1847, a period recorded in his classic *Walden* (1854). He was then arrested for non-payment of the poll tax. This resulted in a famous essay on civil disobedience. He became increasingly critical of commercialism, urbanism and industrialization, always with his idiosyncratic and unconventional approach.

Thurneysen, Eduard (1888–1974)
Swiss Protestant theologian. Born in Wallenstadt, after youth work in Zurich he became pastor at Leutwil, a neighbouring parish to that of Karl *Barth; he proved a kindred spirit and it was with him that Barth worked out his dialectical theology (as recorded in their *Revolutionary Theology in the Making*, ET 1964). He subsequently moved to Basle cathedral and was then made professor in Zurich. His sermons were published as *Come, Creator Spirit* (1924, ET 1934).

Tillich, Paul Johannes (1886–1965)
Philosopher and theologian. Son of a Lutheran pastor, he studied at Berlin, Tübingen, Halle and Breslau and served as an army chaplain in the First World War. He was then professor in Dresden, Marburg, Leipzig and Frankfurt, where he became a Religious Socialist. As a result he had to leave Germany when Hitler came to power in 1933, teaching at Union Theological Seminary, New York, Harvard and Chicago Divinity School. He wrote a great deal, but his most important work was his three-volume *Systematic Theology* (1951–64). In it he used a method of correlation between an analysis of the human situation and the symbols used in the Christian message: reason and revelation, being and God; human existence and Christ; life in ambiguities and the Spirit; the

meaning of history and the kingdom of God. He understood God as the ground of Being, who is known through ultimate concern, and Jesus Christ as the New Being, points which he brought out in shorter books. In addition to *The Courage to Be* (1952) he published two influential volumes of sermons: *The Shaking of the Foundations* (1948) and *The New Being* (1956).

Tillotson, John (1630–94)
Anglican preacher. Born near Halifax, Yorkshire, of a Presbyterian family, he studied at Cambridge and became an Anglican. He was ordained, and in due course was appointed dean of St Paul's and then archbishop of Canterbury. Hostile to the Roman Catholic church, he tried to bring all Protestant dissenters within the Church of England. He was a famous preacher, and his sermons, regarded as models, were read for well over a century.

Tindal, Matthew (1655–1733)
English deist. He studied and taught at Oxford; for a while he became a Roman Catholic but returned to the Church of England. He wrote two books making a rationalist criticism of the church, one of which was burned by order of Parliament. His best-known book, written towards the end of his life, was *Christianity as Old as the Creation* (1730), arguing that the gospel reinforces the immutable laws of nature and reason. It became a kind of deists' Bible.

Tischendorf, Lobegott Friedrich Konstantin von (1815–74)
German New Testament textual critic. An inveterate traveller, after studying at Leipzig, where he later became professor, he visited many libraries in Europe and the Near East in search of manuscripts, and discovered two of the most important, Codex Sinaiticus and Codex Vaticanus. He was professor at Leipzig from 1860 and published several editions of the Greek New Testament.

Tocqueville, Alexis Charles Clérel de (1805–1859)
French Catholic statesman and writer. His main work was *La démocratie en Amérique* (1835–40), which was influenced by Montesquieu's belief that Christianity was a great moral force. He believed that democracy needs a moral support in religion, and religion must accommodate itself to demo-

cracy. He was hostile to Roman Catholicism and advocated reform.

Toland, John (1670–1722)

Deist. An Irish Roman Catholic by birth, he became a Protestant at sixteen and studied at Glasgow and Leiden universities. He then went to Oxford, where he finished his *Christianity not Mysterious* (1696), arguing that God and his revelation can be understood by human reason and that the so-called mysteries of Christianity were the tricks of priests. In Ireland, to which he had returned, his book was condemned and burned by Parliament. He fled to England and over subsequent years travelled widely on the continent, being welcomed at the Prussian court. He wrote other books and pamphlets, in his *Nazarenus* (1718) anticipating *Baur in distinguishing between Jewish and Gentile Christianity. He seems to have been the first to use the word pantheist, to describe the views of philosophers like *Spinoza.

Tolstoy, Leo (1828–1910)

Russian social critic and writer. He studied at the university of Kazan, but did not get a degree. The influence of *Rousseau made him interested in social reform; he first joined the army and then travelled widely. In 1862 he married and wrote his famous novels *War and Peace* (1864–9) and *Anna Karenina* (1873–7) but later turned to books on moral and religious topics. He fell under the influence of *Schopenhauer and became critical of the Orthodox Church, by which he was eventually excommunicated. His was literally a gospel faith, but one shorn of the miraculous. He saw the key to religion in the Sermon on the Mount, which led to pacifism, chastity, rejection of oaths, refusal to serve as magistrate and love of enemies.

Torrance, Thomas Forsyth (1913–   )

Scottish theologian. Born in China the son of a minister, he studied at Edinburgh, Oxford and Basle and then served as a chaplain during the war. After a pastorate he became professor in Edinburgh. He had been influential in writing on theological method and the relationship between theology and science. Opposed to analytical and dualistic thought, he believes modern science is similar to theology in that it is developed in terms of relation and integration. Science and theology are fully rational, each with its own distinctive method. His best known book is *Theological Science* (1969).

Torrey, Charles Cutler (1863–1956)

American biblical scholar. Professor at Andover from 1892 and at Yale from 1900–1932, he was a founder-member and director of the American School of Oriental Research in Jerusalem and made important archaeological finds. His work, particularly on the Old Testament prophets (whose books he dated very late) and the 'exile' and 'restoration' (which he felt needed to be rethought), always proved controversial, but much that seemed far-fetched is now being given more serious consideration. He also wrote a number of books on the New Testament and argued that original Aramaic underlay the Gospels.

Tracy, David (1939–   )

American theologian. Born in Yonkers, he studied at the Gregorian university, Rome, at the time of the Second Vatican Council, specializing in the work of *Lonergan, and then taught at the Catholic University in America in Washington, DC, before becoming professor in Chicago. His interest lies in discussion between the disciplines of fundamental, practical and systematic theology. His books deal mainly with the relationship of Christianity to modern pluralistic culture and its place within that culture, developing the idea of the religious classic. The best known are *Blessed Rage for Order* (1975) and *The Analogical Imagination* (1980).

Traherne, Thomas (1636–74)

English poet. Born in Hereford, after studying at Oxford he returned there and after a decade moved to London, where he was chaplain to a government official as well as having a parish. Only one work appeared during his lifetime, *Roman Forgeries* (1673), a criticism of the Roman Catholic Church; his *Christian Ethics* appeared the year after he died. His poems, for which he is best known, were not published until the beginning of this century, as *Centuries of Meditation*. They are in the tradition of the metaphysical poets like George *Herbert.

Troeltsch, Ernst (1865–1923)

German philosopher and theologian. Born in Augsburg, he was professor in Göttingen, Bonn, Heidelberg and Berlin. He was influenced by *Dilthey and *Ritschl, and a friend of *Bousset and *Weber, and may be regarded as the systematic theologian in the history of religions school. He is particularly important for having stressed the omnipresence of history and the consequent relativity of knowledge and institutions. A famous article 'On Historical and Dogmatic Method' crystallizes his views, which led him to write *The Absoluteness of Christianity* (1902), seeking to establish the status of Christianity from this perspective. His best-known work is *The Social Teaching of the Christian Churches* (1912), a sociological study in which he made a classic distinction between church and sect.

Tyconius (died c.400)
Donatist theologian. A member of the schismatic Donatist church in Africa, he got into trouble there for expressing too much sympathy for the Catholics in a work, now lost, which argued that the church must contain good and bad. His main work was a *Book of Rules*, seven in number, for interpreting scripture; this influenced St Augustine and the Middle Ages. He also wrote a commentary on Revelation.

Tylor, Edward Burnett (1832–1917)
Born in London the son of a Quaker brassfounder, on leaving school he travelled to the United States for health reason. Here he began research which led to *Researches into the Early History of Mankind* (1865), which made his name. This was followed by *Primitive Culture* (1871). He became keeper of the university museum at Oxford and in 1896 was appointed its first professor of anthropology. He assumed that human culture has laws which can be studied scientifically and that there is an evolutionary development in them. So he saw higher religion as having developed out of an original animism, the primitive belief that natural objects have their own spirits.

Tyndale, William (c.1494–1536)
English Bible translator and reformer. Born in Gloucester, he studied in Oxford and Cambridge. Around 1522 he planned to translate the Bible, and when the church would not support him, settled in Hamburg. His translation of the New Testament, after a chequered printing history, was published in Worms, Germany, and was attacked when it arrived in England. He then lived in Antwerp, beginning to translate the Old Testament and writing tracts against the church and defending the authority of scripture. Having been harried and pursued by secret agents all his life, he was eventually arrested and burned.

Tyrrell, George (1861–1909)
Irish Modernist theologian. Born an Evangelical in Dublin, he became a Roman Catholic and entered the Jesuit college. After lecturing at Stonyhurst he was moved to the Jesuit church in Farm Street, London, where he became a sought-after confessor. He published meditations and lectures and became a friend of *von Hügel. From 1899 he began to depart from traditional doctrine, particularly that of eternal punishment. He moved to Yorkshire and continued to write, but his works were now suspect and he was expelled from the Jesuits, was later excommunicated and refused Catholic burial. His later work was highly critical of the Roman Catholic church, contrasting living faith with dead theology, and his last book *Christianity at the Crossroads*, published posthumously, explored the possibility of a higher religion beyond Christianity.

Unamuno y Jugo, Miguel de (1864–1936)
Spanish philosopher. Born in Bilbao, he studied in Madrid and became professor at Salamanca; in the 1920s he was exiled for his political views. An advocate of doubt and distrust, yet longing to find some assurance of a personal future life beyond this world, in his work he demonstrated the inadequacy of the closed systems of dogmatic theology which Protestants and Roman Catholics developed after the Reformation. For him faith comes through anguish and trial rather than through rationality. However, the hope that death is not the end remains, and the tension between this and reason is agonizing. His main works were *The Tragic Sense of Life* (1913) the *The Agony of Christianity* (1921).

Underhill, Evelyn (1875–1941)
Anglo-Catholic writer on mysticism. The daughter of a barrister, she was educated

at King's College, London, and travelled on the European continent. After a conversion experience in 1907, she became interested in mysticism and in relating personal spiritual experience to the formal theology of the church. Her *Mysticism* (1911) became a standard work. She met and was much influenced by *von Hugel and became a much sought after spiritual director. She wrote many other books on mysticism, the most important of which is *Worship* (1936) which relates mysticism to Eastern Orthodox Christianity.

Ussher, James (1581–1656)
Irish archbishop and scholar. Born and educated in Dublin, he became professor there, and chancellor of St Patrick's cathedral, and subsequently bishop of Meath and archbishop of Armagh. He was an ardent Calvinist, but is best known for producing a scheme of biblical chronology, published posthumously (*Sacred Chronology*, 1660), which concluded that the world was created in 4004 BCE. His dates were printed in many editions of the King James Version of the Bible.

Vahanian, Gabriel (1927–   )
American theologian. Born in Marseilles, France, he studied at the Sorbonne and at Princeton, and in 1956 became a permanent US resident, teaching at Syracuse university. Like *Altizer, he was a leading member of the 1960s 'death of God' school, interpreting the term to denote the death of a sense of God as a cultural phenomenon. His major books were *The Death of God: The Culture of our Post-Christian Era* (1961), *Wait without Idols* (1964) and *No Other God* (1966).

Valdes, Juan de (1500–41)
Spanish humanist and religious writer. Born in Castile, he moved to Italy and lived in Naples, in the service of a cardinal. Here he became the focal point of a group anxious for reform. Though he remained a Catholic, his stress on feeling and disregard for church authority anticipated Protestantism and many of his followers became Protestants after his death. He wrote devotional books and translated some of the Bible into Spanish.

Valentinus (second century)
Gnostic theologian. Little is known of his life: he is said to have lived in Rome, hoped to have become a bishop, been passed over, and to have left the church, perhaps going to Cyprus. Only fragments of his work remain, unless he can be associated with some of the new material discovered at Nag Hammadi. The most influential of the Gnostics, he had a large following and seems to have developed a systematic theology of a dual-istic kind, based on a hierarchy of personifications of divine attributes, paired as male and female and making up the pleroma or spiritual world.

Valla, Lorenzo (1405–57)
Italian humanist. Ordained priest, having accepted a chair in Pavia he had to leave after quarrels with the university lawyers. After years of wandering he came under the protection of the king of Naples, and went to Rome, where he later became apostolic secretary and a professor at the university. One of the first to practise historical criticism, he demonstrated the inauthenticity of a number of works and even questioned the apostolic authorship of the Apostles' Creed. He demonstrated the Donation of Constantine, a document in which Constantine was shown to have given the pope great secular power, to be a forgery. In this way he made a major contribution to future developments.

Van der Leeuw, Gerhardus (1890–1950)
Dutch phenomenologist. Born to a Dutch Reformed Church family, he studied theology at Leiden and became professor at Groningen. In his work there he sought to introduce understanding into the study of religions, rather than simply describing religious activities. In his *Religion in Essence and Manifestation* (1933, ET 1938), he argued that the study of religion must be necessarily subjective, and claims the involvement of the person studying it, though questions of truth and falsehood must be held in suspense. He classified religions by

types: remoteness, struggle, repose, form, infinity, nothingness, will, majesty and love. Christianity, in the last category, is the central form.

Vatke, Johann Karl Wilhelm (1806–82)
German Old Testament scholar. A professor in Berlin, he had a *Hegelian perspective on the Old Testament. He wrote the first Old Testament theology from the perspective of historical criticism, seeing the Priestly Source (P) as the last Pentateuchal writer.

Vaughan, Henry (1621–95)
English poet. From a Welsh family, he studied at Oxford, fought in the Civil War and spent the rest of his life as a country doctor. The author of religious poems, collected in *Silex Scintillans* (1650), he was influenced by *Herbert, but his work is more mystical. He also wrote a collection of meditations, *The Mount of Olives* (1652). His poems influenced Wordsworth.

Vaux, Roland Guérin de see De Vaux, Roland Guérin

Venn, Henry (1724–1797)
Anglican Evangelical. From a long line of clergymen, he was born in London and studied and taught in Cambridge. After various curacies he became vicar of Huddersfield in Yorkshire for twelve years until health reasons compelled him to go to a country parish in Huntingdonshire. A gifted letter writer, he is best known for his book *The Complete Duty of Man* (1763). He was one of the founders of the evangelical Clapham Group, of which his son John became a leading member.

Vianney, Jean-Baptiste-Marie (1786–1850)
The Curé d'Ars. Born near Lyons, he had little formal education because of the Revolution and conscription. He wanted to become a priest, but was dismissed from two seminaries; he was finally ordained after private tuition. On ordination, he went to Ars-en-Dombes, a small country parish near Lyons of which he was priest for forty years. Thousands of penitents came each year to make their confessions to him and he was canonized as the patron saint of parish priests. He wrote no books, but led a deeply spiritual and ascetic life centred on the mass, and put great stress on the love of God.

Vico, Giovanni Battista (1668–1744)
Italian jurist and philosopher. The son of a bookseller in Naples, he was educated at the Jesuit school and university there, and became professor of rhetoric. His main work was his *Principles of a New Science about the Common Nature of Nations* (1725), one of the first modern attempts at a philosophy of history. Responding to *Descartes' attack on history, he distinguished between scientific and historical method: scientific method is mathematical, applying man-made rules; history relates to human understanding. Accordingly he distinguished between knowledge and understanding. His work became particularly important from the end of the nineteenth century on.

Victorinus of Pettau (died c.304)
Bishop and biblical commentator. Little is known of his life, and all his works are lost, perhaps because he was a millenarian. However, he is important for introducing Greek exegesis to the Latin church, a discipline which it had not possessed earlier.

Victorinus Afer, Caius Marius (fourth century)
Rhetorician and theologian. Born in Africa, hence his name, he taught in Rome where he became famous. His resignation as a rhetorician to become a Christian caused a great stir and influenced *Augustine. Taking up the Neoplatonists *Plotinus and *Porphyry, but developing their thought in a different direction, he wrote systematic theology against the *Arians, often anticipating Augustine.

Vilmar, August Friedrich Christian (1800–68)
German Lutheran theologian. Born in Kurhessen, he studied in Marburg and became a rationalist, but when he returned as professor there after holding pastoral and administrative posts, he became a confessionalist. He defended *Lutheranism against growing rationalism. He stressed the authority and autonomy of the church, sacramentalism and the divine right of the clergy.

Vincent de Paul (c.1580–1660)
French Catholic pastor. Born of a peasant family in south-west France, he studied at Dax and Toulouse. He spent two years as a slave in Tunisia after being captured by pirates, and having come under the influence of *Bérulle in Paris, decided to devote his life to serving the poor. He worked

among prisoners in the household of the general of the galleys, and founded charities for men and women. These culminated in the Lazarists, who trained clergy and carried on missions among country people, and the Sisters of Charity, the first non-enclosed women's mission, devoted to the care of the sick and the poor. He was a firm opponent of *Jansenism.

Vincent of Lérins (died before c.450)
Presbyter. Little is known of his life, except that he lived in a monastery on the French island of Lérins (off Cannes). He was the author of two *Commonitoria*, the first of which contains what is known as the Vincentian canon: 'What has been believed everywhere, always, by all.' This he intended to be a yardstick for true doctrine.

Vitoria, Francisco de (1485–1546)
Spanish theologian. Born in Vitoria in the Basque country, he became a Dominican and studied in Paris. He lectured in Valladolid and was then professor in Salamanca, where he replaced *Peter Lombard's *Sentences* with *Thomas Aquinas' *Summa*. He wrote pioneering works on law, arguing that natural law applies to nations as well as individuals; on this basis he became a champion of the political rights of the Indians in America. He himself published no works, and his views are to be found in summaries of his lectures.

Vives, Juan Luis (1492–1540)
He was born in Valencia, but was brought to England from Bruges by Henry VIII to be tutor to Princess Mary. He fell foul of Henry by opposing his divorce. After imprisonment he returned to Bruges. His prayers were used by both Catholics and Protestants, in England and Germany, for at least a century.

Voillaume, René (1905–   )
Inspired by the writings of Charles *de Foucauld, with four companions in 1933 he settled on the edge of the Sahara according to de Foucauld's rule. The community was scattered during the Second World War but returned afterwards and spread over the world as 'Little Brothers of Jesus'. He has written many books, including *Seeds of the Desert* (1955) and *Brothers of Men* (1966).

Voltaire (François Marie Arouet, 1694–1778)
French philosopher and writer. Educated by the Jesuits in Paris, he was a lifelong enemy of the Catholic church (he made a famous remark that it should be destroyed, *écrasez l'infame*). He was exiled to England after a dispute; there he encountered deism and the philosophy of *Locke, and his *Letters on the English* (1734) idealized the country as a land of enlightenment. As a postscript he added an attack on *Pascal. The book was burnt and he fled to Lorraine, where he lived on a country estate for sixteen years. In 1750 he went to the court of Frederick II of Prussia and in 1758 bought a country house at Ferney, on the Swiss border, and established a model village around it. Theologically he was concerned with the problem of theodicy, justifying the alleged actions of God, and though considering *Leibniz's solution, rejected it violently in his brilliant satire *Candide* (1759). He was in his element in this kind of work, and wrote more than twenty plays.

Von Hügel, Friedrich (1852–1925)
English Roman Catholic. Son of an Austrian diplomat, and inheriting the title Baron of the Holy Roman Empire, he grew up in Tuscany and Belgium before settling in England and having a private education. Immensely learned, and of wide interests, in science, philosophy and history, he became convinced of the validity of biblical criticism and was friendly with Modernists like *Loisy and *Tyrrell. His major work was *The Mystical Element of Religion* (1908), focussed on *Catherine of Genoa. For all his liberal views he did not clash with the church; his openness and attractive personality comes out clearly in his published letters. He was more influential outside the Roman Catholic Church than within it.

Von Rad, Gerhard (1901–1971)
German Old Testament scholar. Son of an upper-class Nuremberg psychiatrist, he studied at Erlangen and Tübingen and then under *Alt in Leipzig, becoming his assistant. He served as a pastor before becoming professor at Jena, Göttingen and Heidelberg, having been attracted to Old Testament studies by the antisemitism of his fellow-countrymen. He was particularly active defending the Old Testament in the Nazi period. Conscripted for military service during the war, he became a US prisoner. Making use of form criticism he argued that the Sinai tradition and the tradition of the Exodus and conquest were originally separate, brought together as a piece of creative theology. He wrote influential studies on the

origin of Deuteronomy, seeing it as the core of history writing in Israel, and went on to produce a two-volume *Old Testament Theology* (1957–60) which struggled to reconcile the biblical record to historical research. His last work was on the wisdom literature (*Wisdom in Israel*, 1972). He was a gifted violinist.

Warfield, Benjamin Breckinridge (1851–1921)
American theologian. Born near Lexington, Kentucky, into an old American family, after private education he studied at Princeton and in Europe, becoming a minister in Baltimore and subsequently teaching New Testament at Westminster Theological Seminary, Philadelphia. He finally became professor at Princeton, succeeding *Hodge. A committed *Calvinist, he held dogmatically to the inerrancy of scripture and sought to define the inspiration and total truthfulness of scripture in the face of biblical criticism, writing polemically against scholars like *Briggs. He continues to be influential in evangelical circles. His books include *The Lord of Glory* (1907) and *Counterfeit Miracles* (1918).

Watts, Isaac (1674–1748)
Anglican hymn writer. Born in Southampton and educated in London, after a period as tutor he became pastor of a church near the Tower of London until he had to resign through ill-health. He is known as the first great British hymn writer, composing among others, 'O God, our help in ages past', 'When I survey the wondrous cross', 'Jesus shall reign where'er the sun'. He also wrote on prayer and had marked theological views, opposing the imposition of the doctrine of the Trinity on dissenters and leaning towards Unitarianism.

Weatherhead, Leslie Dixon (1893–1975)
Pastor and cousellor. He was minister of the City Temple, London, for thirty years and a broadcaster for forty, also pioneering the use of psychiatry in pastoral work. He began in the liberal tradition, but the Second World War brought home the dimension of suffering, and as he grew older, he became more aware of current doubts and questionings,

as evidenced in his *The Christian Agnostic* (1965).

Webb, Clement Charles Julian (1865–1954)
English religious philosopher. He spent all his academic life at Oxford, where he produced important studies in the history of philosophy and also major works of philosophy in the idealist tradition, seeking to reconcile the importance of personality in the face of the idea of God as Absolute. His books include *Problems in the Relation of God and Man* (1911), *God and Personality* (1918) and *Divine Personality and Human Life* (1920).

Weber, Karl Emil Maximilian (Max) (1864–1920)
German sociologist. Born in Erfurt, he became professor of political economy at Freiburg and Heidelberg, suffering a breakdown between 1898 and 1903. A legacy enabled him to continue work privately. For a while he lived in the same house as *Troeltsch, who influenced him. His main work, *The Protestant Ethic and the Spirit of Capitalism* (1904–5), argues that Calvinist asceticism arising out of the doctrine of predestination was an important factor in the formation of capitalist society. In his posthumously published writings on the sociology of religion he produced a system for classifying different types of religious leader, introducing the subsequently popular term 'charismatic'.

Weber, Otto (1902–66)
German Protestant theologian. Professor of Reformed Theology at Göttingen, he was the author of several books including an introductory study of Karl Barth's *Church Dogmatics* (1953) and a magisterial two-volume *Foundations of Dogmatics* (ET 1981), a critical reappraisal and

explication of the basic components of Christian theology with a view towards maintaining them in a fruitful inter-relationship.

Weil, Simone (1909–43)
French philosopher. Born in Paris to a secularized Jewish family, she studied philosophy along with Simone de Beauvoir. After graduation, she taught for a while and then worked as a labourer in order to identify with the working class. She also served in the International Brigade against Franco in the Spanish Civil War. Profound religious experiences made her deeply interested in Roman Catholicism, though she was never baptized nor joined any church. In 1942 she escaped with her family to the United States, but returned to London to work for the Free French. She died of starvation and tuberculosis, refusing to eat to show solidarity with the French under German occupation. Her posthumously published books like *Gravity and Grace* (ET 1949) and *Waiting on God* (ET 1950) revealed her serious and deeply personal religion, and she has been an influence on both religious thinkers and social activists.

Weiss, Johannes (1863–1914)
German New Testament scholar. Son of a famous conservative Protestant scholar Johannes, he studied at Marburg, Berlin, Göttingen and Breslau and taught in Göttingen, Marburg and Heidelberg. With *Bousset, *Gunkel and *Reitzenstein he was a representative of the history of religions school. His best-known book, *Jesus' Proclamation of the Kingdom of God* (1892), stressed the eschatological nature of Jesus' preaching and marked the end of the old liberal approach. He also did some pioneer work in form criticism and wrote an unfinished history of early Christianity. He was a teacher of *Bultmann.

Weiss, Paul (1901–   )
American philosopher. Born in New York City, he studied at City College and Harvard, then taught at Bryn Mawr and Yale. After his retirement he continued to teach at the Catholic University of America. He founded the Metaphysical Society of America and had a distinctive metaphysics of his own. He saw reality as consisting of four modes of being: actuality, ideality, existence and God. However, instead of putting these modes over or under one another, as happened in the past, he saw them as independent and to be explored separately. He expressed his views in *Modes of Being* (1958) and *The God We Seek* (1964).

Welch, Claude (1922–   )
American theologian. Born in Geona City, Wisconsin, he studied at Upper Iowa University and Garrett Theological Seminary and Yale before being ordained a Methodist minister. After teaching at Princeton he became professor first at Yale Divinity School and then at the University of Pennsylvania in Philadelphia, before moving to Berkeley in 1971 to be successively professor, dean and president of the Graduate Theological Union. He is the author of a two-volume study of *Protestant Thought in the Nineteenth Century* (1972).

Wellhausen, Julius (1844–1918)
German biblical critic. Born in Hamelin the son of a Lutheran pastor, he studied in Göttingen and after teaching there became professor of Old Testament at Greifswald. He resigned his chair after ten years, claiming that his teaching was not helping his pupils to do what they were training for, namely to be church ministers. He then became professor of philosophy in Halle and later professor of Semitic studies at Marburg and Göttingen. Working along the lines developed by *Graf, he developed the classic theory of the sources of the Pentateuch which bears both their names (the Pentateuch consists of the famous four sources J, E, D, P); his dating of these sources transformed the history of Israel, putting the prophets before the law. In later years he turned to the New Testament, but his studies there did not have such influence and lasting effect. The classic expression of his views on the Old Testament is to be found in the *Prolegomena to the History of Ancient Israel* (1883).

Wesley, Charles (1707–88)
Anglican hymn writer and preacher. Eighteenth child of Samuel and Susanna Wesley and brother of John *Wesley, he was born at Epworth and studied at Oxford. After ordination, he went with John to Georgia, where he was secretary to the governor. On his return he was converted as the result of an encounter with a group of Moravians. After an itinerant ministry he lived first in Bristol and then in London and was involved in

preaching at City Road Chapel. However, he never left the Church of England. He was a gifted hymn writer, composing more than 7,000, including 'Love divine, all loves excelling', 'Lo, he comes with clouds descending' and 'Jesus, lover of my soul'.

Wesley, John (1703–91)
Founder of Methodism. Brother of Charles *Wesley, he studied at Oxford and subsequently taught there. He formed a 'Holy Club', including his brother and *Whitefield, who became known as Methodists (for reasons which have yet to be explained satisfactorily). He went with Charles on mission to Georgia, but fell foul of the colonists and returned home. An encounter with Moravians influenced him, and he went to their community at Herrnhut; in May 1738 he had a famous conversion experience. Taking up field preaching, he covered the whole of the British Isles in amazing journeys on horseback; he wrote countless letters and sermons (forty-four of which were selected as a kind of canon) and kept a journal. He started a conference of lay preachers which became annual, and the basis of the future Methodist constitution. From 1760 Methodism spread throughout America, and Wesley was persuaded to ordain *Asbury and *Coke as ministers there. Though he wanted his movement to remain within the Church of England it became increasingly independent.

Westcott, Brooke Foss (1825–1901)
Anglican bishop. He went to school in Birmingham with J. B. *Lightfoot, his lifelong friend, and then to Cambridge. He taught first at Harrow school and went on to become professor at Cambridge. Here, with *Hort, he prepared a famous edition of the Greek text of the New Testament and wrote three commentaries for a planned series with Lightfoot and Hort. In 1889 he became president of Scott *Holland's Christian Social Union and in 1890 bishop of Durham, where he showed a deep concern for social issues, mediating in a coal miners' strike.

Wette, Wilhelm Martin Leberecht de *see* **De Wette, Wilhelm Martin Leberecht**

Wettstein, Johann Jakob (1693–1754)
Swiss biblical scholar. Born in Basle, he became pastor there and was twice removed from office on charge of Socinianism (*see* **Sozzini**). He had a lifelong interest in textual criticism, and in 1733 went to be professor in Amsterdam, where he produced an important edition of the Greek New Testament.

Whitefield, George (1714–70)
English evangelist. Born in Gloucester, he met the *Wesleys at Oxford and joined the 'Holy Club', where he experienced an evangelical conversion. After ordination he proved a powerful preacher. He went with the Wesleys to Georgia and remained for some time after they left. When back in England he was a pioneer in open-air preaching, and covered vast distances, including fourteen visits to Scotland and seven to America, where he died. Since he was more *Calvinistic than the Wesleys, differences arose, and he became associated with the Countess of *Huntingdon, working within her Connexion.

Whitehead, Alfred North (1861–1947)
English philosopher and mathematician. He taught at Cambridge and London universities, and became professor at Harvard in 1924. Originally associated with Bertrand Russell, he broke away in search of a new comprehensive synthesis of knowledge, which among other things would integrate science and religion. He saw the world in dynamic terms as process; God is such that all the happenings in the world become part of his nature. His views led to the formation of schools of 'process philosophy' and 'process theology', including figures like *Hartshorne. A major work is *Process and Reality* (1929).

Wieman, Henry Nelson (1884–1975)
American philosopher. He studied at Park College, San Francisco Theological Seminary, Heidelberg, Jena and Harvard, then taught at Occidental College, Chicago, and Southern Illinois University. His philosophy emphasized creativity, but he did not see creation as an act of God; rather, he identified it with God. He saw his theology as being a contemporary interpretation of the Christian faith and of moments of 'creative interchange' which bore revelatory value. His leading interest was in the character of God as established in saving experience. He united an empirical, scientific approach with the importance of a faith commitment and interpreted God as the supreme value and the integrating force in the universe. His writings include *Religious Experience and Scientific Method* (1926) and *Methods of Private Religious Living* (1929).

Wilder, Amos Niven (1895–)
American literary critic. A Congregationalist, he studied at Yale, Brussels and Oxford and served in the Great War. Afterwards he became professor at Chicago Theological Seminary and Harvard. Much of his work was in secular literary criticism and poetry, but he also pioneered the literary criticism of the New Testament, notably in *Early Christian Rhetoric* (1964).

Wiles, Maurice Frank (1923–)
After ordination and a parish curacy, he returned to teach at Cambridge, where he had studied, and subsequently worked in Ibadan, Nigeria. He returned to Cambridge and was then professor at King's College, London, and Oxford. First writing books on the patristic interpretation of Paul and John, he turned to doctrinal criticism, the application to Christian doctrine of the approach used for a century on the Bible. His *The Making of Christian Doctrine* (1967) and *The Remaking of Christian Doctrine* (1974) proved controversial, as did his contribution to *The Myth of God Incarnate* (1977).

William of Ockham (1280–1349)
Scholastic theologian and philosopher. Born in Surrey, he studied at Oxford, where his views earned him a summons to Avignon to answer charges of heresy before *John XXII. After being excommunicated, he went from there to Bavaria, under the protection of its ruler, Louis. He is most famous for his principle of economy ('Ockham's razor': entities are not to be multiplied unnecessarily). Refusing to follow the current line of positing the existence of universals, he argued that these are mental constructs: only individuals exist, and awareness of them is the basis of knowledge (a view generally described as nominalism). Metaphysical analysis was replaced by logical analysis, destroying the foundation of earlier scholasticism. This was to be of importance in the future development of scientific exploration because of the way in which it destroyed the old idea of causality. Knowledge was limited to experience. He also differed from previous thought in arguing that the existence of God cannot be proved rationally; it is necessary to be content with faith and revelation, but this could be relied on, since it is God's world.

Williams, Charles Walter Stansby (1886–1945)
English writer. Born in London, after studying at University College there, he spent most of his life at Oxford University Press. He was influenced by Evelyn *Underhill and wrote a wide range of literature: Arthurian legend, drama, criticism and theology as well as the novels for which he is best known. His *The Descent of the Dove* (1939) is a history of the work of the Spirit; his novels, which he called 'metaphysical thrillers', explore a theology of romantic love.

Williams, Daniel Day (1910–73)
American theologian. Born in Denver, he studied there and in Chicago, and became professor at Chicago Theological Seminary and Union Theological Seminary, New York. His books include *What Present-Day Theologians are Thinking* (1952), *The Minister and the Cure of Souls* (1961) and *The Spirit and the Forms of Love* (1968).

Windisch, Hans (1881–1935)
German New Testament scholar. Born in Leipzig, he first taught as a private tutor, but subsequently became professor at Leiden, Kiel and Halle. A member of the history of religions school, he wrote commentaries and studies of early Christian thought. His books include *Baptism and Sin in Primitive Christianity* (1908) and *The Making of the Sermon on the Mount* (1929).

Wittgenstein, Ludwig Josef Johann (1889–1951)
Austrian/English philosopher. Born in Vienna, he studied engineering in Berlin and Manchester and ultimately settled in England. He worked with Bertrand Russell in 1912–13 and served in the Austrian army during the First World War, during which he had a mystical experience. This led to his *Tractatus Logico-Philosophicus* (1921), the only book to appear during his lifetime, on the limits of meaningful language (at this stage his philosophy was prescriptive, stating what must be true for language to work as it does); it contains his famous statement 'Whereof one cannot speak, thereon one must remain silent'. Also as a result of his experience he gave away a fortune he had inherited and worked as an elementary schoolteacher in Austria. However, in 1929 he returned to Cambridge, where in 1939 he became professor of philosophy. His posthumously published *Philosophical Investigations* indicates a major move in his thought. By then he was talking in terms of 'language games', the different ways in which language is used. The important thing was now to discover the rules of the game.

The latter approach, especially, has been of particular influence in religious discussion.

Wobbermin, Georg (1869–1943)
German religious philosopher. After lecturing in Berlin he became professor in Marburg, Breslau, Heidelberg and Göttingen, then returning to Berlin. He was particularly interested in the transcendental foundations of religion and sought to relate psychological and historical aspects in religion.

Wolff, Christian (1679–1754)
German philosopher. Born in Breslau, he studied in Jena and Leipzig. He was influenced by *Leibniz and aimed at following his principles. He taught at Halle, but came under attack from pietists for his stress on reason and was expelled by the king, Frederick William. He then moved to Marburg until 1740, when Frederick the Great summoned him back to Halle university, of which he became chancellor. He had a considerable reputation in Europe, and was much admired by *Kant. His classification of philosophy into various divisions influenced the way in which it was studied and taught in universities, and he introduced various terms into philosophical discussion, which have been prominent ever since: monism, dualism, teleology, cosmology and ontology. He wrote many books which were in fact textbooks, including a *Natural Theology* (1736–7).

Wrede, William (1859–1906)
German New Testament scholar. He spent his career as professor at Breslau and was a founder-member of the history of religions school. His best-known work was *The Messianic Secret in the Gospels* (1901), in which he challenged the view that the Gospel of Mark was a historical account, and pointed to the role played by the messianic secret which, he argued, was read back into the Gospel record. Perhaps even more important, however, was his study of the nature of New Testament theology, raising questions which have still not been answered today.

Wyclif, John (1325–84)
English reformer. Born in Yorkshire, he studied in Oxford, where he held many posts, also being in charge of parishes *in absentia*. In a sceptical age which separated natural knowledge from supernatural knowledge, he argued that human beings had their origin in God, and he resorted to the Bible and the fathers rather than scholastic discussions. This led him to distinguish an ideal church from the actual church, so that, for example, he questioned the ownership of property by monasteries. He also saw the eucharistic doctrine of transubstantiation as popular superstition. This last view brought to breaking point tensions with the university: he was condemned and forced to retire to Lutterworth, one of his parishes. After his death he was condemned at the Council of Constance. He was a major influence on *Hus. Among many works, he wrote a *Summa Theologica* and initiated a translation of the Bible into English.

Ximenez de Cisneros, Francisco (1436–1517)
Spanish cardinal. Born in Castile, he studied at Alcala and Salamanca and then in Rome. After the beginnings of a distinguished career in the Spanish church he suddenly became a friar, leading a life of great austerity. In 1492 he was appointed confessor to Queen Isabella and under her influence became Franciscan provincial in Castile, doing much to reform the order. He was finally made archbishop of Toledo, the most influential post in Spain, but he continued his austere life and was concerned for the conversion of the Moors. On Isabella's death, for a while he virtually ruled Castile; he was later made a cardinal. A patron of learning, he founded the university of Alcala (Latin name Complutum) and sponsored a multilingual Bible, the Complutensian Polyglot, with the Hebrew, Latin and Greek texts printed in parallel.

Young, Brigham (1801–77)
Second president of the Church of Jesus Christ of the Latter Day Saints. Born in Vermont, and with little education, he joined the Mormons in 1832 and in 1847 led them from Nauvoo, Illinois to Utah after the death of Joseph *Smith. His gifts of leadership were instrumental in making Smith's system a successful social organization; he became governor of Utah territory, planned the Mormon Temple at Salt Lake City and founded the university of Utah.

Zahn, Theodor von (1838–1933)
German Lutheran New Testament and patristic scholar. He was professor at Göttingen, Kiel, Erlangen and Leipzig. His approach was conservative, and he defended the authenticity of the Bible and early church tradition at a time of radical views, though his own exegesis was often eccentric. He is best known for his history of the New Testament canon; he also edited a commentary series on the New Testament to which he contributed, and wrote a number of patristic studies.

Zimmerli, Walther (1907–83)
Swiss Old Testament scholar. Born into the large pietistic family of the director of a Protestant school, he studied in Zurich, Berlin and Göttingen. After a pastorate, he became professor in Zurich. A vigorous opponent of the Nazis, during the war he worked with the Red Cross, and then moved as professor to Göttingen. He wrote a magisterial commentary on Ezekiel and much in article form.

Zinzendorf, Nicholas Ludwig, Count von (1700–60)
Moravian pietist leader. Born in Dresden of noble family, and deeply religious, he wanted to be a missionary, but his family wanted him to go into government. He studied law in Wittenberg and entered the civil service, at the same time sponsoring religious gatherings at his home in Dresden. He then purchased an estate at Berthelsdorf where in 1722 he founded a Christian community with a group of Bohemian refugees, which he called Herrnhut. Five years later he retired, to devote himself full time to the community. He stressed a religion of the heart and his piety was focussed on Christ; he also had visions of ecumenical reunion. In 1737 he was ordained and his movement was eventually recognized, but circumstances forced it to become a separate organization, the Moravian church. He travelled round Europe founding communities, and also went abroad on mission to the West Indies and the United States.

Zwingli, Huldrych (1484–1531)
Swiss Reformer. Son of a village magistrate, he studied in Berne, Vienna and Basle, and after a pastorate became chaplain to Swiss mercenaries in Italy. He then became priest at the Great Church in Zurich. His views of reformation were far more radical than those of *Luther: he established a different style of discipline and organization, and his views differed on baptism, preaching and the eucharist. Much of his life was spent in political activity, though he never held political office; he was killed in battle. In his theology, baptism is a sign but cannot provide cleansing, and the eucharistic elements have no power without the believer's faith.

Appendix: The Popes of Rome

(Dates of birth, where known, are in square brackets; antipopes are named in italic)

Peter (died c.64)   Disciple of Jesus: see the New Testament. By a third-century tradition he was the first bishop of Rome. He was probably active there and was martyred there, but more than this cannot be established. At this stage the later office of bishop had not been established.

Linus (c.66–78)   According to all the early lists of bishops, he followed Peter, but nothing else is known of him.

Anacletus (c.79–91)   Another shadowy figure, known only from lists.

Clement I (c.91–101)   Known from a letter which bears his name, written on behalf of the church of Rome to deal with disputes going on in the church in Corinth (I Clement). The letter achieved almost-scriptural status and is the first instance of intervention by Rome in the affairs of another church.

Evaristus (c.100–109)   Nothing certain is known of him.

Alexander I (c.109–116)   Another shadowy figure.

Sixtus I (c.116–25)   Another shadowy figure.

Telesphorus (c.125–c.36)   The only second-century bishop whose martyrdom is well attested.

Hyginus (c.136–40)   The tradition that he was a Greek from Athens may be correct, but nothing more is known.

Pius I (c.140–54)   He is said to have been brother of Hermas, author of the *Shepherd*, an early doctrinal work.

Anicetus (c.154–66)   By tradition a Syrian, he is another shadowy figure.

Soter (c.166–75)   He probably presided over the introduction of Easter in Rome as an annual festival.

Eleutherius (175–89)   By tradition a Greek; nothing else is known.

Victor I (189–98)   Apparently an African by birth, he made vigorous attempts to settle the Quartodeciman controversy, seeking to stop churches keeping Easter on 14 Nisan instead of the next Sunday. His calling of synods throughout the church was an important step in papal superiority.

Zephyrinus (198–217)   Said to have been a simple and uneducated man, and accused of being lax and not sufficiently authoritarian.

Callistus I (217–22)   Apparently originally a slave

who had been sent to the mines for fraud, he is said to have been lax and to have tolerated heresy. Because of this,

Hippolytus (217–c.235)   supposedly set himself up as an antipope. He was the most important Roman theologian of the third-century church and his extant writings are valuable evidence of church life, theology and worship at the time. At the end of his life he may have been exiled to Sardinia. The evidence is difficult to interpret.

Urban I (222–30)   A shadowy figure, still probably eclipsed by Hippolytus.

Pontian (230–5)   He was threatened with deportation to Sardinia in a time of persecution; since this amounted to a death sentence, he abdicated.

Anterus (235–6)   Nothing is known of his brief reign.

Fabian (236–50)   A much-respected figure, he was first to suffer martyrdom when the Decian persecution broke out. By tradition he divided the city of Rome into seven church regions, each under a deacon.

Cornelius (251–3)   He became bishop of Rome after an interregnum caused by persecution and was vigorously opposed, because of his tolerance to those who had lapsed in persecution, by the group led by

Novatian (251–8)   Consecrated a rival bishop of Rome, he adopted an uncompromisingly rigorist attitude to those who had lapsed; he himself was martyred in 257 and his followers excommunicated.

Lucius I (253–4)   There is no reliable information about him.

Stephen I (254–7)   A nobleman. He upheld the validity of baptism by heretics, leading to a split between Rome and North Africa/Asia Minor. He seems to have been the first pope to appeal to Matthew 16.18 for his authority.

Sixtus II (257–8)   He mended the split under his predecessor; he was martyred under the Emperor Valerian.

Dionysius (260–68)   He was active in reorganizing the Roman church after persecution and in offering help to other Christians in trouble.

Felix I (269–74)   A completely obscure figure.

Eutychian (275–83)   There is no reliable information about him.

Caius (283–96)   Another bishop who is just a name.

Marcellinus (296–304)   Also an unknown figure.

Marcellus I (308–9)   So shadowy that he is even sometimes identified with Marcellinus.

Eusebius (310)   By tradition a Greek physician.

Miltiades (311–14)   Bishop of Rome when Constantine defeated Maxentius and issued the Edict of Milan, he was the first to enjoy the favour of the government.

Sylvester I (314–35)   Legend has it that he baptized Constantine (cleansing him from leprosy), but he seems to have been an insignificant figure. The (forged) Donation of Constantine, giving the pope wide rights over the church, was addressed to him.

Mark (336)   Another unknown figure.

Julius I (337–52)   A firm supporter of orthodoxy in the *Arian dispute, he sheltered those condemned by Arian councils (including *Athanasius, whom he had declared rightful bishop of Alexandria by calling the Council of Sardica). He was a considerable statesman.

Liberius (352–66)   He was ordered by the Arian emperor Constantius to condemn *Athanasius, refused, and was banished in 356. The next year, in misery, he submitted, signed an Arian formula, and was allowed to reoccupy his see. Meanwhile,

> *Felix II* (355–65) was appointed by the government, but this caused an uproar, and on Liberius's return, Rome had two bishops. Felix's inclusion in the papal list caused confusion in subsequent numbering.

On the death of Liberius, there was a dispute between the two rival parties and Liberius's followers elected *Ursinus* (366–7; he died in 385), one of his deacons, bishop. However, the vast majority of the clergy and people supported

Damasus I (366–84)   Riots followed the choice of him as pope, and the emperor had to intervene. Ursinus was banished, but troubles continued for some time. Damasus was very active against heresy and did much to strengthen the see of Rome; it was in his papacy that the emperor *Theodosius made Christianity (in Roman form) the official religion. He created a proper papal archive, and commissioned the famous scholar *Jerome to revise the biblical text.

Siricius (384–99)   Though overshadowed by the famous *Ambrose, bishop of Milan, he maintained the status of Rome. His letter to a Spanish bishop about the treatment of public penitents is the first papal decretal.

Anastasius I (399–401)   The main event of his time of office was a synod which he called to condemn the works of *Origen.

Innocent I (402–17)   Son of *Anastasius I. He so stressed the primacy of Rome that he is sometimes known as the first pope. He insisted that major cases under dispute should be tried by Rome and exercised authority in the East as well as the West. He wrote many peremptory letters, one of which reserved confirmation to bishops.

Zosimus (417–18)   A Greek who was unsuccessful because of high-handed attempts to establish his authority and his ignorance of the West. On his death,

> *Eulalius* (418–19), another Greek, was consecrated on the same day as

Boniface I (418–22)   Elderly and frail, he did not get possession of the see for a year, until the emperor intervened. But he did much to restore the authority of the papacy after the blunders and unpopularity of *Zosimus.

Celestine I (422–32)   A firm supporter of orthodoxy, he continued the policies of Boniface and was intent on condemning heresy wherever it might appear; he became involved in the dispute over *Nestorius in the East.

Sixtus III (432–40)   He founded the earliest recorded monastery in Rome.

Leo I ([400]440–61)   He was born in Tuscany; little is known of his life. A courageous man, he prevented the destruction of Rome when Attila the Hun attacked; at a time of general disorder, including the sack of Rome, he did much to strengthen the church by energetic central government, using Roman law in church order and believing that his position was based on divine and scriptural authority. At the Council of Chalcedon his *Tome* (a letter to Flavian, Patriarch of Constantinople) was accepted as a statement of orthodox belief in the person of Christ, but he was no great theologian and knew no Greek.

Hilarus (461–8)   In difficult circumstances, he struggled hard to maintain order in the church.

Simplicius (468–83)   As power in the Mediterranean spread eastwards, he had to fight off the claims of Constantinople that it was on a par with Rome and the dominance of monophysitism (the belief, contrary to Chalcedon, that Jesus had only one, divine, nature).

Felix III (II) (483–92)   An authoritarian figure, his involvement in a dispute in the Eastern church over monophysitism led to the alienation of Rome and Constantinople and the first division (the Acacian schism).

Gelasius I (492–6)   Possibly an African, though revered as a humble man he continued the policy of Felix III, upholding the claims of Rome against Constantinople in a high-handed way. He is the first pope to have been called 'vicar of Christ', and he set out a theory of two powers governing the world: the emperor and the pope. However, he did much to improve the difficult situation of Rome as a result of the barbarian wars. He is not author of either the decree or the sacramentary which bear his name.

Anastasius II (496–8) His appointment was a reaction to the hard line taken by Rome against Constantinople and he made moves towards restoring church unity, thwarted by his sudden death. Thereupon his supporters elected as pope the archpriest *Laurentius* (498). However,

Symmachus (498–514) was elected by the majority, who wanted the hard line maintained. Though his election was confirmed by the Gothic king, supporters of Laurentius accused him of misdemeanours and irregularities and occupied most of the churches. By refusing to appear before a council called by the king, Symmachus gave rise to ongoing conflict, worsened by the temporary official return of *Laurentius* (501–5). The latter part of his papacy was more peaceful. He introduced the singing of the *Gloria* in the mass on Sundays.

Hormisdas (514–23) He mended the Acacian schism on the basis of a reaffirmation of the Tome of Leo and the Chalcedonian Definition; he was also an able diplomat with the Arian Goths. He further developed the authority of the Roman see, among other things on the basis of Matthew 16.18.

John I (523–6) He was the first pope to visit Constantinople, but this was on a mission prompted by the Gothic king of Italy, the failure of which led to his imprisonment and death in Gothic captivity. He introduced the Eastern way of calculating Easter to Rome.

Felix IV (III) (526–30) Chosen as a supporter of the Goths, on his deathbed he attempted to nominate *Boniface his successor; this led to a ruling that there should be no discussion of a pope's successor during his lifetime. Indignant at the attempt, most influential people supported

Dioscorus (530) A pro-Byzantine, he died three weeks after consecration.

Boniface II (530–2) Consecrated by a minority on the same day as Dioscorus, he was the first Germanic pope, though born in Rome. After harsh reprisals on his opponents, he worked hard for reconciliation, but then in turn tried to influence the succession; however, he had to retreat.

John II (Mercury, 533–5) A compromise candidate after much intrigue, he was the first pope to take a new name on consecration – because he had that of a pagan god. He seems to have been a good diplomat.

Agapetus I (535–6) A strong defender of orthodoxy, he made a visit to Constantinople aimed at strengthening discipline; he died there.

Silverius (536–7) Son of Hormisdas, he was forced on the church by the king of Italy to be a pro-Gothic pope. However, he was deposed under pressure from the East and died in exile.

Vigilius (537–55) Of noble family, he had been Boniface II's chosen successor; he went with Agapetus I to Constantinople and was urged back to Rome as a potential ally of monophysitism. However, open support for this position was impossible in the orthodox West, and he soon came out as a supporter of the Council of Chalcedon. This led to a summons back to Constantinople, where he was forced to toe the line; as a result he was excommunicated in Rome. His death released him from a political tangle.

Pelagius I (556–61) A Roman living in Constantinople, as the imperial nominee for the papacy he received a hostile reception in Rome; though a good administrator and pastor, he faced constant opposition.

John III (561–74) Pope at a time of great political crisis, caused by an invasion of Italy from the north, very little is known of him.

Benedict I (575–9) In his time the crisis intensified; again little is known of him.

Pelagius II (579–90) He appealed to the East for help but was ignored; a truce mid-way through his reign allowed him more scope for activity.

Gregory I (590–604) Born in Rome, he became a law student and was so gifted that he was a city prefect of Rome by the age of thirty. He then sold his vast property for the relief of the poor and founded seven monasteries, in one of which he became a monk. He was brought back to public life by Benedict I as a deacon of Rome and then became papal representative in Constantinople (though he never learned Greek). Returning to Rome he became abbot (making his famous remark *Non Angli sed angeli*, 'Not English, but angels'). Made pope, he worked hard to improve a ravaged Italy, secured the conversion of England through Augustine of Canterbury, promoted monasticism, helped to develop liturgical music (the Gregorian chant is named after him, if not his), revised the liturgy, developed the doctrine of purgatory and wrote what was to be the textbook for the mediaeval episcopate.

Sabinianus (604–6) He was elected in reaction to Gregory, who was unpopular when he died; he preferred assistance from secular clergy rather than monks. Little is known of his reign, but his handling of famine relief was so unpopular that there were demonstrations at his funeral.

Boniface III (607) Gregory's protégé, he showed signs of being a capable diplomat. A synod he called banned all discussion of potential successors during the lifetime of popes and bishops.

Boniface IV (608–15) Another protégé of Gregory, he greatly encouraged monasticism; he turned the Roman Pantheon into a church, the first such take-over of a pagan temple.

Adeodatus I (Deusdedit, 615–18) He was a priest; little is known of his reign except that he reversed the trend of appointing monks to high office.

Boniface V (619–25) He continued the policy of favouring secular clergy; he gave away much of his personal fortune to the poor.

Honorius I (625–38) Son of a consul, he took Gregory as a model, and like him was interested in the Christianizing of the Anglo-Saxons. He favoured monks, turning his mansion into a monastery; he was a good financial administrator and in his activity generally strengthened the papacy. However, he was unwise enough to use the term 'one will' of Christ in a letter to the patriarch of Constantinople, unwittingly giving support to the heresy of monothelitism (the view that Christ had only one, divine, will). As a result, later he was formally anathematized at the 681 council of Constantinople, though subsequently this fact was conveniently forgotten in the West.

Severinus (640) An elderly Roman, pope for only three months, his death was probably hastened by pressure from the emperor in Constantinople to subscribe to monothelitism.

John IV (640–2) From Dalmatia, he opposed the theological views of Constantinople effectively and did much to relieve conditions in his homeland.

Theodore I (642–9) A Greek refugee from Jerusalem and implacably orthodox, he maintained opposition to monothelitism.

Martin I (649–55) From Umbria, he was vigorous and independent, and continued the policy of his predecessor. However, this resulted in much suffering for him, ending in abduction to Constantinople, imprisonment, flogging and banishment on imperial orders. He died in exile.

Eugenius I (654–7) An elderly Roman presbyter, elected under pressure from Constantinople before the death of his predecessor, he did his best to be conciliatory, but the Roman clergy and people refused to accept a compromise theological formula. Death probably saved him from Martin's fate.

Vitalian (657–72) In a period of continuing strained relations over the monothelite controversy, he did his best to keep on good terms with the East. However, the emperor snubbed him by doing much to raise the status of Ravenna as a place of religious authority. He was much concerned with reorganization of the English church after the synod of Whitby (664).

Adeodatus II (672–6) An elderly Roman monk, he is an obscure figure, but revived vigorous opposition to monothelitism.

Donus (676–8) Another elderly Roman, his reign is even more obscure than that of his predecessor.

Agatho (678–81) A Sicilian, he was fortunate to experience the end of the Byzantine policy of pressing for monothelitism and made an important contribution to the 681 Council of Constantinople (Trullan), during which he died. He regained supremacy over Ravenna and also maintained an active interest in the English church, not least in its liturgy.

Leo II (682–3) A Sicilian, he was an able diplomat and handled the situation arising after the Council of Constantinople (including its condemnation of a former pope, *Honorius) with skill. He was also a singer and interested in church music.

Benedict II (684–5) A Roman, he continued the work of his predecessor.

John V (685–6) A Syrian, he was seriously ill for most of his reign. On his death there were two rival candidates, Peter, supported by the clergy, and Theodore, supported by the militia. When an impasse was reached which involved the use of force, the clergy put forward an alternative candidate, son of a general:

Conon (686–7) Another constantly ill man, he was also inept; on his death, *Theodore* was again put forward, with the archdeacon *Paschal* as his rival (687). Each was elected by his supporters (Theodore later submitted; Paschal continued to intrigue and was ultimately deposed and imprisoned); however, the same year yet another compromise candidate was elected and received imperial approval:

Sergius I (687–701) He was born in Antioch and educated in Palermo. He proved capable and vigorous. He was actively interested in English affairs and resisted pressure from the emperor Justinian II to support a further council in Constantinople which would have given that city status second only to Rome. He introduced the singing of the *Agnus Dei* in the Mass.

John VI (701–5) He was Greek by birth; little is known of his reign.

John VII (705–7) Another Greek, he was the first pope to be son of a Byzantine official. He was very much under the thumb of Constantinople; he was also a patron of the arts.

Sisinnius (708) A Syrian, he was ill and old when appointed and was pope only a month.

Constantine (708–15) Another Syrian, he paid a triumphant year-long visit to the East, but his success with Justinian II was ruined when the emperor was murdered and a rabid monothelite appointed.

Gregory II ([669] 715–31) A wealthy Roman, he had accompanied Constantine to the East. His problems lay to the north, dealing successfully with the Lombards. In his reign the prohibition of images (iconoclasm) had developed in the East and Gregory had to cope with imperial pressure to implement it. He supported the missionary work of Wynfrith (whom he renamed Boniface) among the pagan German tribes.

Gregory III (731–41) A Syrian, he was elected pope by acclaim at his predecessor's funeral; he was the last pope to seek imperial approval. After appeals to the East to abandon iconoclasm, he held a synod banning it; this earned him imperial reprisals. He also had to cope with the hostility of the Lombards, against whom he appealed for help in vain from the Frankish ruler Charles Martel. He saw the future importance of the north and supported the church in Germany and England. He also did much to beautify Rome.

Zacharias (741–52) Last of the Greek popes, he was a good diplomat. He made peace with the Lombards, but through the influence of Boniface he strengthened ties with the Franks. Although opposed to iconoclasm, he was able to keep the controversy over it in the background.

Stephen II (752) An elderly presbyter, he died four days after his election and was never consecrated. Hence a dual numbering of subsequent popes named Stephen.

Stephen II (III) (752–7) A wealthy Roman aristocrat, he detached the papacy from Byzantine power and allied it with the Franks, through negotiations with their king Pepin. He was also first to preside over a papal state, territory including Ravenna and former Byzantine cities, donated to him by the king.

Paul I (757–67) Brother of Stephen II. He was much preoccupied with defending his state; at the same time he had to cope with attempts by Constantinople to woo both the Lombards and the Franks. He made further attempts to end iconoclasm. He was, however, a harsh administrator relying on strong ecclesiastical bureaucracy. On his death this led to a move by the lay aristocracy to elect as pope a layman, *Constantine* (767–9), who was ordained and consecrated under military pressure. Appeals were made to the Lombards by the clerical party in Rome and during a coup the Lombards attempted to install their own pope, *Philip* (768). However, he was rejected; Constantine was later mobbed, blinded in a gang attack, and subsequently deposed and sentenced to lifelong penance in a monastery.

Stephen III (IV) (768–72) A Sicilian, elected with the support of the Franks, he began by holding a Frankish-backed synod to regularize the situation caused by the irregular election of Constantine. However, he later became suspicious of the Franks and entered into an ill-fated alliance with the Lombards.

Hadrian I (772–95) A Roman of noble birth, he restored close relations with Charlemagne, who invaded and conquered Lombardy. Subsequently Charlemagne re-established the papal state. He

also asked the king's help to suppress adoptianism, a heresy which had arisen in Spain claiming that Jesus was only the adopted son of God. The price of all this, however, was to limit church freedom. Hadrian differed with Charlemagne over iconoclasm, which the latter supported. A good administrator, he did much to restore and fortify Rome.

Leo III (795–816) A Roman priest of humble birth and a difficult character, he clashed with ambitious aristocratic relatives of Hadrian I, was attacked and imprisoned. He escaped to Charlemagne, and, when Charlemagne accompanied him back to Rome, crowned him emperor there. At the prompting of the emperor, he took severe measures against the adoptianists, but refused to alienate the Greeks by including the *filioque* (the addition that in the Godhead the Spirit proceeds from the Son as well as the Father) in the creed. He also intervened in differences between archbishops of Canterbury and the Anglo-Saxon kings.

Stephen IV (V) (816–17) A Roman aristocrat, he tried to heal divisions in Rome caused by his predecessor. He crowned and anointed Charlemagne's successor, the first pope to anoint an emperor.

Paschal I (817–24) A Roman priest and abbot, he enjoyed good relations with the Frankish emperor and received confirmation of the papal state. He protested against the revival of iconoclasm in the East. However, he was so unpopular because of his stubbornness and harshness that it proved impossible to bury him in St Peter's as planned.

Eugenius II (824–7) A Frankish candidate, he swore loyalty to the emperor and restored order in Rome with Frankish support: this strictly limited his independence. However, he did go against the Franks in his stubborn opposition to iconoclasm.

Valentine (827) A Roman aristocrat, he died forty days after his consecration.

Gregory IV (827–44) Another Roman aristocrat, he was much caught up in disputes over succession among the Franks; he also had to face a growing Saracen threat to Italy. On his death, a Roman deacon *John* was elected pope by popular acclaim (844). However, the aristocracy elected

Sergius II (844–7) An elderly Roman aristocrat, he was consecrated without Frankish approval and had to face an invasion and thorough investigation of his status. An ambitious builder, in a situation where bribery and simony were rife, he was involved in some shady dealings. An attack on Rome by Muslim pirates who plundered the treasures of St Peter's was seen as a divine response.

Leo IV (847–55) A Benedictine monk, he did much to restore and refortify Rome after the damage done by Muslim pirates. He also stood up to the Franks and sought to bring church dissidents under his control. These included

Anastasius Bibliothecarius (855) A Greek

scholar with associations with Greek monks; he was proclaimed antipope by an imperialist group, but proved too rash for the office and was disowned by his followers within a month.

Benedict III (855–8) A pious Roman scholar and the choice of clergy and people, he remains an obscure figure.

Nicholas I ([c.820] 858–67) Of noble royal family, he was a close adviser to *Benedict III. He had high ideas about the role of the pope, whom he saw as God's representative on earth and not subject to imperial interference. He also asserted his authority over other bishops, clashing vigorously with them. In asserting papal claims in the East, he was involved in the beginnings of a schism which arose from the appointment of Photius, a layman, to the see of Constantinople, a dispute complicated by Nicholas's interference in Bulgaria, which Constantinople claimed as its sphere. His vigour won him much respect.

Hadrian II ([792] 867–72) Having twice declined an invitation to be pope, he accepted as a compromise candidate. An elderly churchman and weak-willed, he was not a successful diplomat and also had to retreat over Rome's claim to Bulgaria.

John VIII (872–82) Another elderly man, he tried hard to provide leadership but had great problems. Though active in fortifying Italy against continuing Muslim raids, he had to pay tribute; he also ran into trouble in the north, where he had great difficulty in finding support. Driven to look to the East for help, he accepted the decisions of a council which reinstated Photius and paved the way for military aid from Constantinople. He seems to have been the first pope to be assassinated.

Marinus I (882–4) Son of a Tuscan priest; little is known of his reign.

Hadrian III (884–5) Another obscure figure, who may not have died a natural death.

Stephen V (VI) (885–91) A Roman aristocrat, he had to face disputes in Rome and further raids from the Muslims.

Formosus ([c.815] 891–6) Skilled and well educated, he sought to strengthen the church in England and northern Germany and to make peace with the East, particularly by clarifying the validity of ordinations carried out by Photius. He faced political turmoil in Italy. Though he was an honest man and an ascetic, he had bitter enemies, including his successor *Stephen VI (VII); after his death they charged him with having usurped the Holy See, and a synod exhumed, stripped and mutilated his body. This decision was later reversed.

Boniface VI (896) Elected in a riot on the death of Formosus, he reigned only fifteen days.

Stephen VI (VII) (896–7) A Roman, he presided over the macabre treatment of *Formosus; the next year he was deposed in a popular reaction, imprisoned and strangled.

Romanus (897) Little is known of him except that he supported *Formosus.

Theodore II (897) Another obscure figure.

John IX (898–900) In 898 *Sergius*, bishop of Cerveteri, was appointed pope, but supporters of *Formosus deposed him and substituted John. John sought to restore peace and harmony after the conflicts in which his predecessors were involved.

Benedict IV (900–3) An upper-class Roman, he was still faced with the turmoil in the wake of the *Formosus affair; he also had to cope with a political void in the empire.

Leo V (903) A country parish priest, he was overthrown within a month of being made pope by *Christopher* (903–4), a Roman parish priest, who put him in gaol. Christopher was deposed by an armed force led by Sergius, who had him imprisoned also. Both he and Leo were killed in prison.

Sergius III (904–11) Nominated in 898, he had been in exile and took advantage of the confusion in Rome to re-establish himself. A supporter of Stephen VI (VII), he set out to undo the work of his predecessors by force, causing incredible confusion.

Anastasius III (911–3) A Roman, he had an obscure reign. At this point the papacy was dominated by the powerful Roman family of Theophylact and Theodora.

Lando (913–14) An obscure figure, probably a pawn of Theophylact.

John X (914–28) Another Theophylact candidate, he was appointed not least to put an end to the Muslim menace, and took a personal part in the fighting. He worked hard to establish the prestige of the papacy more widely in the church, but was deposed by the next generation of the Theophylact family, who feared his independence, and was imprisoned and murdered.

Leo VI (928) An elderly aristocratic Roman priest, he was a stop-gap appointment.

Stephen VII (VIII) (928–31) An obscure figure, another stop-gap appointment.

John XI (931–5) The illegitimate son of Pope Sergius III by Theophylact's daughter, Marozia, he was appointed in his early twenties and intended to enhance her power. However, she fell in a coup and he was deposed.

Leo VII (936–9) An obscure figure, he was appointed by Alberic II, prince of Rome, who toppled Marozia, and was allowed only to perform restricted functions.

Stephen VIII (IX) (939–42)   Another appointee of Alberic with a limited role.

Marinus II (942–6)   Yet a third tamed pope.

Agapetus II (946–55)   Again appointed by Alberic, he was a more energetic figure and was involved in monastic reform.

John XII (Octavian, 955–64)   The bastard son of Alberic, he was appointed at the age of eighteen to fulfil a promise made to his father on the latter's deathbed. His dissolute life caused great offence, but he was a vigorous administrator. Having failed to extend the papal territory, he had to reverse previous policy by calling to Otto I of Germany to help him, in return having to concede the emperor's right to involve himself in papal elections. He then changed sides, and the inevitable conflicts which followed left the papacy much weakened. At one time he was deposed and replaced by a layman, Leo; he fought back to power, but the return of Otto with an army proved too much; he fled, and died soon afterwards.

Leo VIII (963–5)   The emperor Otto's replacement for *John XII: a layman, he received all the religious orders in two days. On John's death the Romans did not want Leo back as pope, but chose a deacon, Benedict; however, Otto intervened on Leo's behalf. Little is known of his reign.

Benedict V (964–6)   Made pope by the Romans on the death of *John XII as he was a reformer, he was opposed by the emperor Otto, who had him deposed within a month and exiled to Hamburg.

John XIII (965–72)   A Roman brought up in the papal court and later bishop, he was nevertheless faced with a revolt on his appointment, and banished for a year. The revolt was put down by the emperor Otto, who protected him for the rest of his reign by residing in Italy.

Benedict VI (973–4)   Another Roman, he was a reforming pope, but also an imperial appointment, and on the death of emperor Otto was deposed and put in prison, where his successor had him murdered.

Boniface VII (Franco, 974 and 984–5)   A deacon, he had been the choice of Rome rather than the emperor on the death of *John XIII and became pope after the revolt which toppled *Benedict VI. However, popular horror at his subsequent murder of Benedict led to an uprising against him and he had to flee, being then excommunicated by the new pope, Benedict VII. He struck back in a coup, establishing himself again in Rome for a while. Driven out to Constantinople, he returned yet again on the death of emperor Otto II, seized power, and murdered the then pope *John XIV before dying a sudden death.

Benedict VII (974–83)   A Roman aristocrat, he was appointed pope as a compromise candidate

with imperial approval. Extremely dependent on the emperor for his position, he was nevertheless a deeply religious man and did much to promote monastic reform.

John XIV (Peter Campenova, 983–4)   Another imperial candidate, imposed without consultation, he was overthrown by the antipope *Boniface VII on emperor Otto II's sudden death and was murdered by him.

John XV (985–96)   A candidate of the Roman aristocracy, who asserted themselves in the face of an infant emperor, he alienated the clergy by his greed. Caught up in many political issues, he eventually found himself in an untenable position and had to appeal to the emperor, at fifteen now managing his own affairs. However, he died before Otto III could arrive to help.

Gregory V (Bruno, 996–9)   Son of Duke Otto of Carinthia and a young well-educated priest, he was the first German pope. He crowned Otto III, but then came increasingly to differ from him. When Otto returned to Germany, Gregory was deposed by the Romans, only being restored a year later on the emperor's return.

John XVI (John Philagathos, 997–8)   A Greek, formerly an imperial tutor and a bishop, he was pressurized into becoming pope in the revolt against *Gregory V; when Gregory was restored to the papacy he was mutilated and imprisoned.

Sylvester II (Gerbert, [c.945] 999–1003)   An imperial tutor, bishop of Reims and archbishop of Ravenna, he was the first Frenchman to become pope. He was a brilliant teacher, scientist and theologian, and may have been one of the first to use *Aristotle in Christian education. Originally hostile to the papacy as having no moral credibility, on being made pope he worked hard for reform, denouncing nepotism, enforcing celibacy and reorganizing the church.

John XVII (John Sicco, 1003)   A Roman, and an obscure figure, appointed by the leading family of Rome, the Crescentii, in protest against so much foreign rule.

John XVIII (John Fasanus, 1003–9)   Like his predecessor appointed by the Crescentii, he was active in church affairs and seems to have achieved temporary reconciliation with the Eastern church.

Sergius IV (Peter, 1009–12)   Son of a shoemaker and nicknamed 'Pig's Snout', he was bishop of Albano. Another obscure nominee of Crescentius, he died within a week of his patron.

Gregory (1012)   The new nominee of the Crescentii, he was never able to exercise office because power in Rome had now passed to another noble family, the Tusculans. They appointed

Benedict VIII (Theophylact, 1012–24)   He was

second son of Count Gregory of Tusculum, and a layman. He restored good relations with the German royal house and under him Rome came to follow the practice of including the *filioque* (the Spirit proceeding from the Son as well as the Father in the Godhead) in the creed at mass. He acted more like a baron than a pope, but did much to improve the reputation of his office.

John XIX (Romanus, 1024–32) Younger brother of *Benedict VIII, he was said to have become pope by bribery; he was raised from layman to pope in one day. Generally thought ineffective, he was mainly active in the political sphere.

Benedict IX (Theophylact, 1032–44) Nephew of his two predecessors, and appointed pope through bribery, he was a profligate young man and like his uncles was more involved in politics. He had to leave Rome during a rebellion in 1045 sparked off by disgust at his conduct and the domination of his family in city affairs and was replaced briefly by **Sylvester III** (John of Sabina, 1045), a candidate from the former dominant family of the Crescentii. However, he made a comeback, though only for two months, after which he abdicated.

Gregory VI (John Gratian, 1045–6) An elderly priest, godfather of Benedict IX, he had been pope only a year when he was summoned before King Henry III of Germany at a synod near Rome, convicted of simony, and deposed.

Clement II (1046–7, Suidger) Bishop of Bamberg, he was appointed by King Henry III to rescue the papacy from feuding Roman families. However, he died before he could begin on his reforms. Thereupon the papacy was again taken over by **Benedict IX** (1047–8), supported by a combination of bribery and popular acclaim against the Germans. A year later he was ejected on the orders of King Henry.

Damasus II (Poppo, 1048) Another German appointment, from Bavaria, and bishop in the Tyrol, he died of malaria less than a month after becoming pope.

Leo IX (Bruno, 1048–54) Son of a count from Alsace, he was a supporter of the monastic reform arising from Cluny and on becoming pope sought also to reform the church. He enforced celibacy, acted against simony and was a humble and good pastor. A feature of his rule was a series of journeys through major cities in Europe. However, in his last years he came up against the Normans, who were gaining power, and was captured in a military expedition. It was during his imprisonment that the final schism between the Eastern and Western churches took place. He died a month after his release.

Victor II (Gebhard of Dollstein-Hirschberg [c.1018] 1055–7) Son of a Swabian count and bishop of Eichstätt, he was a good administrator and politician. He was also concerned for church reform.

Stephen IX (X) (Frederick of Lorraine, 1057–8) Abbot of Monte Cassino, he was consulted about a new pope, gave five names, but found that he himself was the chosen one. Remaining abbot, he worked hard to continue reform.

Benedict X (John Mincius, 1058–9) Cardinal archbishop of Velletri and a member of the influential Tusculan family, he was hastily appointed, through bribery, by a coalition of Roman nobles when the main reforming party was disorganized. However, a synod deposed him and he was replaced by

Nicholas II (Gerard [c.1010] 1059–61) Born in Lorraine, he was a leading reformer. He promulgated a decree regularizing the means by which a pope was legitimately appointed, legislated against clerical marriage and prohibited clergy from acquiring churches from lay persons. He also reversed previous policy and entered into an alliance with the Normans. This aroused the hostility of the German royal family.

Alexander II (Anselm of Lucca, 1061–73) Born near Milan, he studied under *Lanfranc at Bec and became bishop of Lucca. He tried to continue a reform programme, particularly fighting against simony and enforcing clerical celibacy; he also insisted that archbishops had to come personally to Rome to receive the pallium, the sign of their authority. He blessed the invasion of England by William the Conqueror. He also tried to negotiate with the East. However, because he had been elected pope without the support of the German emperor, he had to contend with an antipope.

Honorius II (Peter Cadalus, [c.1009] 1061–72) Of a wealthy German family living in Verona, he was nominated pope by the German court. Because of superior French backing, Alexander II came to hold office, but Honorius contested him throughout his reign.

Gregory VII (Hildebrand, [c.1010] 1073–85) Born in Tuscany of a humble family, he was a papal chaplain and administrator, archdeacon and chancellor, and a leading light in the reforming party. On being elected he sought to promote reform, centralize church authority and make alliances with secular rulers. However, his prohibition of lay investiture (the appointment of clergy by the laity) provoked vigorous opposition in Germany, France and England. After a heated controversy, in 1077 the emperor Henry IV was ultimately forced to do penance to Gregory at Canossa, but later retaliated by setting up *Clement III as antipope. After a battle over Rome, Gregory had to flee, dying soon afterwards. Nevertheless, by his efforts, in both ideology and action he had so exalted the reputation of the papacy that it became a dominant force throughout Western Christendom.

Clement III (Guibert, [c.1025] 1080, 1084–1100) Born in Parma, he went to the German court and in 1072 was nominated archbishop of

Ravenna by Henry IV. He personally clashed with *Gregory VII, and in the course of Gregory's dispute with the emperor was made pope. An able and honest man, he too was intent on reform and enjoyed support among the clergy, not least because of his devolution of authority to the college of cardinals.

Victor III (Daufer or Desiderius, [1027] 1086–7) While abbot of Monte Cassino he rebuilt the abbey and encouraged literature and the arts. He was a great mediator during the conflicts under Gregory VII. Rioting before his consecration forced him to leave Rome and even after he was made pope a year later he spent most of his time at Monte Cassino because of the unrest caused by Clement III's troops; ill-health and an ongoing concern for his abbey meant that he achieved little.

Urban II (Odo of Lagery, [1035] 1088–99) A Frenchman, and former prior of the monastery of Cluny, he was called to Rome by *Gregory VII, who made him cardinal bishop of Ostia. On appointment to the papacy he sought to follow in Gregory's footsteps, though more diplomatically, and had to cope with *Clement III, the interference of secular authorities and the immorality of the clergy. He was unable to enter Rome because of the presence of the antipope, but once there he summoned councils at Piacenza and Clermont to reform the church. At the latter the 'truce of God', a pause in fighting on days ordered by the church, was pronounced a church law. He proclaimed the First Crusade and thus began the crusading movement; he also tried to heal the schism with the East through synods at the Lateran and at Bari.

Paschal II (Ranierus, 1099–1118) An Italian monk and abbot, as pope he renewed the decrees against lay investiture but could not settle the issue. This led to much political controversy, including Paschal's imprisonment and subsequent capitulation to King Henry V of Germany, which was a setback to the cause of reform. Jerusalem was recaptured around the time of his enthronement, and he warmly endorsed crusades. His support of violence set dangerous precedents.

Theoderic (1100–2) Cardinal archbishop of Albano, he was made pope by the supporters of antipope *Clement III on the latter's death, but was soon arrested and imprisoned by *Paschal II. The same supporters then appointed *Albert* (1100), cardinal bishop of Silva Candida, to succeed him; he too was imprisoned. Five years later yet another attempt was made to appoint a rival pope to *Paschal II, *Sylvester IV* (Maginulf, 1105–11), this time by the Roman aristocracy. An obscure figure, a Roman archpriest, he caused problems until his money ran out, after which he faded into obscurity.

Gelasius II (1118–19) A former monk of Monte Cassino and papal chancellor, he was old when made pope and had a troubled reign, not least

because of a clash with the emperor Henry V. He was the victim of physical attacks during a series of disturbances and eventually had to flee to France, where he died.

Gregory VIII (Maurice Burdinus ['ass'], 1118–21) He was born in France and educated in Spain, where he became archbishop of Braga. An imperial supporter, he had crowned Henry V, for which he was excommunicated by Paschal II; he was rewarded when Gelasius II clashed with the emperor. However, Gelasius and his successor Callistus destroyed any credibility Gregory had with the church and he was later publicly ridiculed and imprisoned.

Callistus II (Guido of Burgundy, 1119–24) Closely connected with almost all the royal families of Europe, and archbishop of Vienne, he was a vigorous reformer; a synod over which he presided denounced lay investiture and excommunicated king Henry, whom it did not recognize as emperor. Made pope in Vienne because of the troubles in Rome, he sought reconciliation with the empire and this was achieved in the Concordat of Worms, which ended lay investiture which allowing privileges to the emperor. At the First Lateran Council, which ratified the concordat, Callistus also issued decrees against simony and the marriage of priests.

Celestine II (Teobaldo Boccapecci, 1124–5) On the death of Callistus several candidates were put forward as future pope. While Celestine II, an elderly cardinal deacon from a leading Roman family, was being installed after unanimous acclamation, a rival family broke in and at sword point proclaimed another cardinal pope. Celestine II resigned.

Honorius II (Lamberto Scannabecchi, 1124–30) Of humble origins, and cardinal bishop of Ostia, he was appointed with the backing of force in a move endorsed by the reforming group. He continued the diplomacy of his predecessor, very much under the thumb of his chancellor Aimeric, and was particularly supportive of the newer religious orders. His work was cut short by illness and death; Aimeric arranged a temporary clandestine burial as part of an attempt to influence the succession.

Anacletus II (1130–8) Cardinal Pietro, a member of one of Rome's most prominent families, was elected publicly with the support of the more traditional majority in opposition to the reforming minority; however, although he had the power and influence, he lost the propaganda battle, in which the reformers had *Bernard of Clairvaux as their champion. They had chosen

Innocent II (1130–43) Clandestinely elected, he had widespread recognition but no power as pope until the death of *Anacletus. Thereupon the latter's supporters appointed Gregorio Conti, but he ruled as *Victor IV* (1138) for only three months before resigning. The Second Lateran Council which Innocent held in 1139 rigorously put right irregularities which had arisen over the schism; he also called the Council of Sens, which confirmed the condemnation of *Abelard.

Celestine II (Guido of Città di Castello, 1143–4) Son of an aristocrat and pupil of *Abelard, he was a scholar. An old man when appointed, his reign was only brief.

Lucius II (Gherardo Caccianemici, 1144–5) A leading member of the Curia, who served under many popes, he had to face a revolution in Rome against the papacy and was killed fighting in an attempt to end it.

Eugenius III (Bernardo Pignatelli, 1145–53) A Cistercian monk and abbot, he had come under the influence of *Bernard of Clairvaux. Because of the revolution in Rome, which had set up an independent senate and was later backed by *Arnold of Brescia, he never established himself securely there. He commissioned Bernard to preach the Second Crusade and held several reforming synods; he put forward the claim that the pope had supreme authority in secular as well as spiritual matters.

Anastasius IV (1153–4) A very old man when appointed, he was chosen to bring about some agreement between the papacy and the popular Roman senate; he was an able conciliator.

Hadrian IV (Nicholas Breakspear, [c.1100] 1154–9) The only English pope, he was born in St Albans and studied in France, where he became abbot of a monastery near Avignon. After being made cardinal bishop of Albano he was sent by Eugenius III to reorganize the churches in Scandinavia. As pope he secured the expulsion and execution of *Arnold of Brescia from Rome (though he did not suppress the revolutionaries) and extracted homage from the emperor Frederick I Barbarossa, but then quarrelled with him again. Consequently, on his death, there was imperial support for an antipope (who was followed by three others before the schism ended):

> *Victor IV* (1159–64; the earlier Victor IV was ignored) Cardinal Ottaviano of Monticelli was appointed by a minority of cardinals supporting the emperor, but despite continued backing from Frederick and the Roman populace he could not gain the recognition of the whole church.

Alexander III (Orlando Bandinelli, [c.1100] 1159–81) A former professor of canon law and an influence on *Hadrian IV, he was never established in Rome because of the antipopes. He had hesitantly supported Thomas à Becket against Henry II of England, but the opposition of emperor Frederick limited his capacity to take a stand as pope. On the death of Victor IV he was faced with the antipope

Paschal III (Guido of Crema, 1164–8), who was succeeded by *Callistus III* (1168–78), an abbot of whom little is known, and *Innocent III* (1179–80), but opposition was crumbling, and the schism was effectively ended in 1179 at the Third Lateran Council, which established that in future a pope was to be elected by a two-thirds majority of the college of cardinals (a rule which has lasted virtually unchanged until today), over which Alexander presided. The Italian city of Alessandria is named after him.

Lucius III (Ubaldo Allucingoli, [c.1110] 1181–5) A Cistercian monk influenced by Bernard of Clairvaux and adviser to *Alexander III, he was old, honest and weak. Though he tried to come to an understanding with the emperor, circumstances were too much for him. One of his decretals in effect laid down the pattern for the Inquisition, and he tried fruitlessly to launch another crusade.

Urban III (Umberto Crivelli, 1185–7) From an aristocratic Milan family, he was a vigorous opponent of emperor Frederick I, but the emperor proved too strong for him and only sudden death saved him from crisis.

Gregory VIII (Alberto de Morra, [c.1110] 1187) An elderly man, who had been involved in reconciling Henry II after the murder of Thomas à Becket, he was chosen to restore good relations with the emperor. However, the capture of Jerusalem by the Saracens that year meant that his two months as pope were spent promoting a new crusade.

Clement III (Paolo Scolari, 1187–91) A wealthy Roman, he settled the long-standing dispute between the popes and the citizens of Rome (at a cost). He also continued to promote the Third Crusade which *Gregory VIII had launched.

Celestine III (Giacinto Bobo, [c.1105] 1191–8) He was made pope at the age of eighty-five. He had defended *Abelard at the Council of Sens which condemned him for heresy, and as a cardinal had urged moderation on Becket and on emperor Frederick Barbarossa. His reign was dominated by the imperialistic efforts of the German king Henry VI (who imprisoned King Richard Coeur de Lion on his return from the Third Crusade) to expand his rule as far as Sicily.

Innocent III (Lotario de' Conti di Sengi, [1160] 1198–1216) Of noble family, he studied at Paris and Bologna and rose rapidly to become pope at thirty-eight, before even being ordained priest. A born ruler, who introduced the title 'Vicar of Christ' for the pope, with an ideal of ruling the world as well as the church, in Rome he surrounded himself with his own men and purged corrupt practices at the papal court; he then used his status to dominate European rulers. A keen reformer, he also preached crusades against Islam and the Albigensians in France, commissioning *Dominic Guzman to dispute with the latter. The Fourth Lateran Council of 1215 set the seal on his efforts, among other things banning new religious orders, requiring an annual confession from Catholics, ordering distinctive dress for Jews and Muslims, condemning heresies, defining transubstantiation as eucharistic doctrine, and calling for a new crusade. A fever brought his life to a sudden end.

Honorius III (Cencio Savelli, 1216–17) Old and frail, from an aristocratic Roman family, he was much involved in promoting the ultimately unsuccessful Fifth Crusade. In 1220 he crowned emperor Frederick II of Germany in Rome as the preliminary to a Sixth Crusade, subsequently threatening excommunication if Frederick did not fulfil his promise to go on it. He did much to improve administration and produced a first book of canon law. He gave official approval to the Dominicans, Franciscans and Carmelites, and his sanctions against heretics contributed further to the development of the Inquisition.

Gregory IX (Ugolino of Segni, [c.1155] 1227–41) Son of a count and nephew of Innocent III, he too studied at Paris and Bologna. After diplomatic missions in Germany he was commissioned to preach a crusade in Italy; he was a friend of *Dominic and *Francis of Assisi. As pope he soon clashed with emperor Frederick II, who had broken his promise to *Honorius III to go on crusade and was excommunicated, and though an uneasy truce was established, his reign ended in military action and he died during an imperial siege of Rome. He established a papal Inquisition under Dominicans and imposed the death penalty on heretics; he sought union with the Eastern church; he gave a new constitution to the university of Paris, and by commissioning a translation of *Aristotle into Latin furthered the study of Aristotle's works.

Celestine IV (Goffredo da Castiglione, 1241) Elected in Rome under imperial siege by cardinals under pressure from the virtual dictator of Rome and imprisoned in vile conditions, he was a frail old man, probably chosen because his expected early death would make possible a freer election.

Innocent IV (Sinibaldo Fieschi, 1243–54) Son of a Genoese count and a brilliant canon lawyer, he was an unscrupulous operator, using his spiritual prestige and any other means at hand to further his ends. At the Council of Lyons which he called in 1245, emperor Frederick was officially deposed, and Innocent thenceforward constantly interfered in imperial affairs. He established a permanent Inquisition in Italy, allowing it the use of torture, and encouraged Louis IX to set out on the unsuccessful Seventh Crusade.

Alexander IV (Rinaldo, Count of Segni, 1254–61) A former cardinal protector of the Franciscans, he was weak and ineffective. His reign was overshadowed by the political problems arising from the activities of his predecessor. However, he did much to support the mendicant orders.

Urban IV (Jacques Pantaleon, [c.1200] 1261–4)

Elected pope by a reduced conclave when he was visiting Rome as patriarch of Jerusalem, he had been born in Troyes the son of a shoemaker and studied in Paris. An able diplomat, unhampered by Italian politics, he tried unsuccessfully to break free from the domination of the German emperors; in so doing he laid the foundation for French domination of Italy. Though never resident in Rome because of the political situation, he did much to revive the papacy, strengthening the curia with able Frenchmen and restoring papal territories and finances. When he died he was engaged in attempts to restore relations with the Eastern church.

Clement IV (Guy Foulques, [c.1195] 1265–8) Son of a successful judge, he had studied law and been legal consultant to King Louis IX of France before his ordination and rapid advancement in the church. Urban IV sent him to England to support King Henry III against the barons. With his encouragement and financial support, Charles Count of Anjou became the most powerful figure in Italy and Sicily, and was in a position to dominate the papacy. A papal bull giving the pope certain rights to appointments in benefices was a major step towards the centralization of the Western church on Rome.

Gregory X (Teobaldo Visconti, [c.1210] 1271–6) Born in Piacenza of noble family, he studied in Paris under *Thomas Aquinas and *Bonaventura, was adviser to the French and English royal families, and became archdeacon of Liège. He was elected pope after a three-year vacancy, being summoned back from a pilgrimage to the Holy Land, and a new crusade was his central concern. With this in view he tried to reconcile European disputes, and also sought union with the Eastern church. This union lasted for a time after the 1274 Council of Lyons. In view of the delay preceding his appointment, among many reforms he laid down strict rules governing the conclave at the election of a pope (which successors kept revoking). He died prematurely of fever.

Innocent V ([c.1224] 1276) The first Dominican pope, he studied and taught in Paris and worked with *Albertus Magnus and *Thomas Aquinas to draft a rule of studies for Dominicans; his important commentary on the *Sentences* of *Peter Lombard was a major influence in the development of a post-*Augustinian theology. A pious and learned man but no politician, he died after only five months in office.

Hadrian V (Ottobono Fieschi, ([c.1205] 1276) From a family of Genoese counts and a nephew of *Innocent IV, he had undertaken a successful crusading mission in Henry III's England. Appointed under pressure from Charles of Anjou, he died before he could be crowned or consecrated.

John XXI (Pedro Juliao, 1276–7; there was no John XX) A Portuguese doctor's son, he studied in Paris and taught medicine in Siena before rising to become archbishop of Braga in his native land.

He wrote logical and medical textbooks and other works. On becoming pope he continued his scholarly interests (he in fact died prematurely, crushed when his study ceiling collapsed), leaving curial business to the influential Cardinal Orsini. The cardinal resorted to the policies of *Gregory X, seeking to bring Europe together for a crusade and achieve further reconciliation with the Eastern church.

Nicholas III (Giovanni Gaetano Orsini, [1210] 1277 –80) Of a noble Roman family and already the power behind *John XXI, he sought to make the papacy independent of the dominant Anjou rule over Italy; he continued efforts for peace in Europe preparatory to a crusade, but got no further in negotiations with the Eastern church because of the severity of his demands. He was the first pope to live in the Vatican.

Martin IV (Simon de Brie, 1210 [1281–85]) A candidate of Charles of Anjou, chancellor of Rouen and then royal chancellor to Louis IX, he was very much Charles's man and reversed his predecessor's policies; no politician, he even refused the offer of papal rule over Sicily when offered it after the famous rebellion against Charles ('the Sicilian Vespers'). His excommunication of Emperor Michael VIII Palaeologus of Constantinople ended the fragile union with the East agreed under *Gregory X. His favouring of the mendicant orders over parochial clergy led to major disputes.

Honorius IV (Giacomo Savelli, [1210] 1285–7) From a noble Roman family, he was a nephew of *Honorius III. Though he was old and ill when appointed, his Italian origins helped him with his work of restoring order in Rome and its surroundings. With Europe in upheaval after the death of several rulers including Charles of Anjou, he was involved in much political activity; he continued support for the activities of Dominicans and Franciscans.

Nicholas IV (Girolamo Masci, 1288–92) The first Franciscan pope, and successor to *Bonaventure as general of the order, he was a reluctant compromise candidate after a long and divided conclave. As support for the papacy he favoured the Colonna family in Rome and this landed him in constant disturbances; he was also caught up in the complexities of European politics. New appeals for another crusade fell on deaf ears because of these disputes; however, missionaries he sent out to the fabled emperor Kubla Khan led to the establishment of the Catholic church in China.

Celestine V (Pietro del Morrone, [1209] 1294) An aged hermit, he became pope after a more than two-year vacancy caused by constant disputes. He came to the notice of the conclave as a prophet of disaster for the church if they did not appoint a head quickly; they chose him. A Benedictine at seventeen, he had sought solitude in the Abruzzi, gathering around him disciples who later became the heart of the Celestine Order, and was a noted ascetic. A puppet pope manipulated by Charles

II of Anjou, and utterly incompetent, he had a disastrous five months before resigning, alienating all his supporters.

Boniface VIII (Benedetto Gaetani, [1235] 1294–1303) Canon lawyer and papal notary, he was instrumental in achieving the abdication of *Celestine V. A domineering, cruel and impulsive man, he tried to pacify Europe and liberate the Holy Land. He failed in both, getting the worst of a conflict with Philip the Fair of France and falling foul of the leading Roman Colonna family in the process. This not only prevented his crusading attempts but ended in his imprisonment and subsequent death. He promulgated a famous bull, *Unam sanctam*, stressing that the church wielded both the temporal and the spiritual sword, but failed to recognize how times had changed and papal political influence had diminished.

Benedict XI (Nicola Boccasino, [1240] 1303–4) A Dominican scholar and master general, he attempted to resolve the crises left by Boniface's death through negotiation, but only made things worse. Then he died.

Clement V (Bertrand de Got, [c.1260] 1305–14) From an influential French family, he was crowned in Lyons in the presence of Philip the Fair and remained under his thumb. He made his residence in Avignon; the following seventy years this arrangement continued and came to be known as the 'Babylonian captivity'. Continuing his vendetta, King Philip sought a formal condemnation of *Boniface VIII, but this was dropped – at a cost; he also forced Clement to suppress the Knights Templar, who had much valuable property. Among Clement's more independent actions was the excommunication of Robert the Bruce of Scotland for murder. He founded chairs of oriental languages at several universities to further missionary work and centralized church government further. He was a great nepotist and died an embarrassingly rich man.

John XXII (Jacques Duese, [c.1244] 1316–34) A compromise candidate from a rich bourgeois family in Cahors, after study in Paris and other French universities he became bishop of Avignon and was made pope there. Though old and physically feeble, he was a sound administrator, and did much to rebuild and reform the church. However, harsh action against Franciscan spirituals for their doctrine that Christ and the apostles had owned no property, which the Inquisition had called heresy, brought him up against that order. The dispute had political dimensions, ultimately drawing in *Marsilius of Padua against the pope. Marsilius accompanied the emperor to Rome, where an antipope was installed. However, Nicholas V (Pietro Rainalducci, 1328–30), a Franciscan and born of a lowly family in the Abruzzi, never had a significant following and abdicated after two years, humbling himself to John in Avignon. John promoted mission, founded a university at Cahors and condemned Meister *Eckhart, but himself fell into official heresy over his views of the nature of the vision of God and had to recant on his deathbed.

Benedict XII (Jacques Fournier, [c.1280], 1334–42) Born of lowly parents near Toulouse, a Cistercian and a learned theologian, as bishop in two dioceses he proved a vigorous inquisitor. On being made pope he was a reformer, fighting pluralism of church posts and encouraging study. French domination and the curia thwarted his plans to return to Rome; he started the building of the papal palace at Avignon.

Clement VI (Pierre Roger, [1291] 1342–52) Educated as a Benedictine he rose rapidly, becoming abbot of Fécamp and eventually archbishop of Rouen. A good diplomat and ardent supporter of France, he relaxed the discipline of his predecessor and was more like a secular prince. However, he helped the poor during the Black Death and protected the Jews when they were accused of causing it.

Innocent VI (Etienne Aubert, [1282] 1352–62) A former professor of law and chief judge in Toulouse, he became a bishop and administrator of Avignon. Though another old and frail pope, he returned to the reforming spirit of *Benedict XII. Seeking a return of the papacy to Rome, he became involved in Italian politics, but here as in his other political initiatives he failed.

Urban V (Guillaume de Grimoard, 1362–70) Born of a noble family, he became a Benedictine and taught canon law and rose to be an abbot. A spiritual man and always a Benedictine, he worked hard at reform and in 1367 managed to re-establish the papacy in Rome as a prelude to his vision of a crusade and reunion with the East. However, circumstances were against him, and three years later he had to return to Avignon, dying soon afterwards.

Gregory XI (Pierre Roger de Beaufort, [1329] 1370–8) The last French pope, he was trained as a canon lawyer, having been made a cardinal at the age of eighteen. Sharing the ideals of his predecessor, he too tried to re-establish the papacy in Rome but was faced with a revolt of the papal state centred on Florence; he put a ban on the city, quelled the rebellion and went to Rome, but hostilities broke out again and he had to return to Avignon. There he died, bitterly blamed by *Catherine of Siena. He also turned his attention to heretics, supporting the Inquisition and publicly condemned the teaching of *Wyclif in England. His death led to a period of major disturbances in the papacy, known as the 'great schism'.

Urban VI (Bartolomeo Prignano, [1318] 1378–89) Born in Naples, archbishop of Bari, and noted for his austerity and acumen, he was elected pope in Rome, amidst popular clamour for an Italian. As pope, however, he was arrogant, obstinate and violent – some thought the appointment had turned his mind. The French cardinals therefore chose a new pope, Robert of Geneva, who became Clement VII. Urban still had his supporters, including *Catherine of Siena, and the two popes existed side by side. Obsessed with conquering the kingdom of Naples, Urban was constantly caught up in politics and military campaigns and he died leaving the papal state in ruins.

Clement VII (Robert of Geneva, [1342] 1378–94) Son of a count, a bishop in northern France and leader of troops fighting against a rebellious Florence, he was appointed pope by a group convinced that *Urban was deranged. When Italy proved untenable, he went to Avignon and established a splendid court and large-scale administration, but never stopped trying to get back to Rome. A good politician, he was hampered by lack of money.

Boniface IX (Pietro Tomacelli, [c.1350] 1389–1404) Born to an aristocratic Naples family, he is an obscure figure before being made pope; though inexperienced, he was a natural manipulator who had no scruples over money and was quite prepared to sell futures in benefices and indulgences; he made no effort to end the schism.

Benedict XIII (Pedro de Luna, [c.1328] 1394–1423) A Spaniard, born in Aragon, and a learned canon lawyer, he became antipope because he promised to put an end to the schism, even if it meant abdicating. However, once elected he was so stubborn and skilful in maintaining his legitimacy that he made the schism even worse; attempts were made to depose him but he took refuge in an impregnable castle in Spain, intractable to the last and abandoned by all his supporters.

Innocent VII (Cosimo Gentile de' Migliorati, [c.1336] 1404–6) Born of middle-class parents in the Abruzzi, he became a professor of canon law at Perugia and Padua and then spent ten years collecting papal taxes in England before being elevated to archbishop and cardinal. Lax and ineffective, he could do little to end the schism; he did, however, reorganize the university of Rome.

Gregory XII (Angelo Correr, [c.1325] 1406–15) Born to a noble family, he had been Latin patriarch of Constantinople. Having promised to abdicate if this was necessary to end the schism, he did his best to negotiate with *Benedict XIII; however, despite a general council held at Pisa in 1409 (which condemned both popes *in absentia*), the schism continued.

Alexander V (Pietro Philarghi [Peter of Candia], 1409–10) A Greek of humble origins from northern Crete and a Franciscan, he had studied in Oxford and Paris before becoming a successful bishop and archbishop. A skilled administrator and a scholar, he was prevented from achieving anything by his early death; there is some doubt about the legitimacy of his status.

John XXIII (Baldassare Costa, 1410–15) A former pirate from an impoverished family, he had great administrative talents and was a notorious womanizer. His appointment was said to be the result of simony and after a shaky period in office he fled, being brought back to deposition and imprisonment. This effectively ended the schism.

Martin V (Oddo Colonna, [1368] 1417–31) A hard and strong-minded Italian, he did much to restore Rome, then in a ruinous condition, and promote reform; he reorganized the papal state and began to restrict French influence. His diplomatic efforts did much to raise the prestige of the papacy; he was unusually moderate to the Jews. However, he was stubbornly against church councils and did all he could to prevent one being held in Basle. In the end public pressure proved too much, but he died before it met.

Clement VIII (Gil Sanchez Munoz, [1360] 1423 –29) A Spaniard, he was made pope by the three or the four cardinals loyal to *Benedict XIII and had a small court in Benedict's castle of Peñiscola. However, by now his following was insignificant. The fourth cardinal, absent from the election, decided that the appointment was invalid and nominated one Bernard Garnier from Rodez in France: *Benedict XIV* (1425–?). Nothing is known of him before or after his election.

Eugenius IV (Gabriele Condulmaro, [c.1383] 1431 –47) Of a wealthy Venetian family, he became a monk and later bishop of Siena. Though committed to carry on with the council at Basle reluctantly called by his predecessor, he tried to dismiss it when it convened. However, the council refused to dissolve itself, appealing to the theory that councils were superior to the pope. At the same time, his high-handed action in Rome, repossessing territory, led to a revolt in Rome. To complicate the situation further, the threat of a Turkish invasion led to urgent talks for union with the Eastern church. In furtherance of these the council was moved to Florence and then Ferrara. Temporary peace was made with the Greeks and by his astute move, Eugenius had restored the authority of the papacy over this attempt at church democracy. However, some members of the council refused to go to Florence, deposed him, and appointed an antipope,

Felix V (Amadeus, Duke of Savoy, [1383] 1439 –49) Born in Chambéry, he was a devout layman; however, after ordination and consecration he failed to gain recognition outside his own lands.

Nicholas V (Thomas Parentucelli, [1397], 1447– 55) A doctor's son, through tutoring the children of wealthy families in Florence he met leading figures in art and culture. He served as aide to the bishop of Bologna before joining the curia. A better and more patient politician than his predecessor, he did a good deal to achieve reconciliation in church and state. He rebuilt much of Rome, employing outstanding artists like Fra Angelico to beautify it; a great bookbuyer, he had a collection of manuscripts which formed the basis for the Vatican library and commissioned translations of Greek works into Latin. After the fall of Constantinople in 1453 he tried to encourage a crusade against the Turks.

Callistus III (Alfonso de Borgia, [1378] 1455–8) From Valencia, and a canon lawyer by training, he was appointed by his old age as a compromise candidate. Once pope, he devoted great energy to organizing a crusade against the Turks, but his efforts came to nothing because of the unsettled state of Europe, and the tithes he exacted to raise funds were deeply resented. This money-raising also put a stop to the rebuilding of Rome. He was responsible for reversing the verdict in the trial of Joan of Arc, but revived harsh legislation banning dealings between Jews and Christians. He instituted the feast of the Transfiguration of Christ on 6 August.

Pius II (Aeneas Silvius: Enea Silvio de' Piccolomini, 1458–64) Born of an impoverished noble family near Siena, he became a great humanist. He was secretary to *Felix V and wrote dialogues defending the view that councils were superior to the pope; he was also author of a famous love story, *Lucretia and Euryalas* (1444). Illness caused him to reform a dissolute life, and he rose to be bishop of Siena, also proving an able diplomat. He still found time to write a *History of the Emperor Frederick*. Once pope, he too worked hard for a crusade against the Turks which he planned to lead himself. However, he died before he could realize that ambition.

Paul II (Pietro Barbo, [1417] 1464–71) Born to a rich merchant of Venice, he exchanged business for the church when his uncle became pope and was a cardinal at twenty-three. A handsome man, he was fond of sports and carnivals, built a splendid palace and cultivated scholarly pursuits, though he took some surprisingly harsh measures against humanists. The ongoing war against the Turks was a drain on his financial resources. He died prematurely, of a stroke.

Sixtus IV (Francesco della Rovere, [1414] 1471– 84) Born of a poor family, he became a Franciscan, rising to be general of the order. However, as pope he proved unscrupulous with methods and money. He proclaimed yet another crusade against the Turks and set up the Spanish Inquisition, confirming the famous Torquemada as Grand Inquisitor. At home he sought to enrich his family and engaged in war to enlarge the papal territories. He founded the Sistine Choir and built the Sistine Chapel. He left the papacy much in debt when he died.

Innocent VIII (Giovanni Battista Cibo, [1432] 1484 –92) Son of a Roman senator, he was inexperienced, easy-going, loose-living and chronically ill. Under him the financial situation of the papacy grew yet worse, not least because of the way in which he held court. His lack of political expertise led to chaos in Rome and the papal states.

Alexander VI (Rodrigo Borja [Borgia], [1431] 1492 –1503) A Spaniard from near Valencia and nephew of Callistus III, he amassed a fortune through the favour of his uncle and lived a notably loose life. He was elected through bribery and his pontificate was determined by political and family considerations. He presided over the division of the New World between Spain and Portugal, the execution of Savonarola, and a crusade against the Moors.

Pius III (Francesco Todeschini, [1439] 1503) Born in Siena, and a nephew of *Pius II, he enjoyed favours from his uncle and became papal legate in Germany. Appointed as a neutral caretaker pope, he had a short reign because of ill health.

Julius II (Giuliano della Rovere, [1453] 1503–13) He came from an impoverished noble family, but his fortunes improved dramatically when his uncle became pope as *Sixtus IV. He fled to France under the papacy of *Alexander VI and was chosen as pope after promising a continuation of war against the Turks, which had lapsed, and the calling of a general council, promises which he did not keep. His policy consolidated papal power: at the same time he opposed simony and was a patron of Renaissance art, being a supporter of Raphael and Michelangelo. He was attacked by *Luther (over his indulgences for rebuilding St Peter's) and *Erasmus.

Leo X (Giovanni de' Medici, [1475] 1513–21) Born in Florence to a famous family, second son of Lorenzo the Magnificent, after a wandering life cultivating the arts he became pope at thirty-eight. Too easy-going, he was liberal with money and positions, and squandered the fortune left by his predecessor. He did not know what he was doing when he excommunicated *Luther.

Hadrian VI (Adrian Dedel, [1459] 1522–3) A carpenter's son from Utrecht, Holland, he became chancellor of Louvain university. He was appointed tutor to the future Charles V, as co-regent eventually becoming virtual ruler of Spain (and Inquisitor). Concerned to reform the Curia, bring reconciliation in Europe, fight Protestantism and deliver Europe from the Turks, he was killed by the effort.

Clement VII (Giulio de' Medici, [1479] 1523–34) Cousin of *Leo X, who made him bishop of Florence and cardinal, he proved a lax and irresolute pope, but was a patron of artists, including Cellini, Michelangelo and Raphael.

Paul III (Alessandro Farnese, [1468] 1534–49) A typical Renaissance figure, as cardinal he had three sons and a daughter by a mistress; he was a pleasure-lover and nepotist. He did much to encourage artists and writers, commissioning Michelangelo to complete the Last Judgment in the Sistine Chapel. At the same time, though, he was concerned for reform of the church and a general council (eventually opened at Trent in 1545) and he re-established the Inquisition. He excommunicated Henry VIII and put sanctions on England; however, they did not work.

Julius III (Giammaria Ciocchi del Monte, [1487] 1550–5) A lawyer by training, as papal legate he had presided over the opening of the Council of Trent. He was a compromise candidate. As pope he did much for the newly founded Jesuits and occasionally had bursts of reform work. Otherwise, however, he came to let pleasure dominate his life, causing open scandal.

Marcellus II (Marcello Cervini, [1501] 1555) Born in Siena, he became a scholar specializing in chronology; he was a conscientious bishop and was made pope as representative of the reform party. However, his health was bad and the strain of a hyperactive promotion of Rome killed him within three weeks of office. Palestrina wrote the *Misaa Papae Marcelli* in his honour.

Paul IV (Giampetra Carafo, [1476] 1555–9) The first of the Counter-Reformation popes, he came from a distinguished Naples family. Throughout his life he was a keen reformer; he was one of the founders of the Theatine order and reorganized the Inquisition. He was not elected pope until he was nearly eighty and then seemed preoccupied with exercising power, which made him unpopular. He was an implacable opponent of Protestantism.

Pius IV (Gian Angelo Medici, [1499] 1559–65) Not from the famous family, but son of a Milan notary, he had proved an efficient administrator but hardly a champion of reform. However, he succeeded in reconvening the Council of Trent and brought it to a successful conclusion, and then began to implement his decrees.

Pius V (Michele Ghisleri, [1504] 1566–72) Born of poor parents, a shepherd who became a Dominican, he was a zealous man, and became Inquisitor General. As pope he worked hard for the reform of the church. He forced home the decisions of the Council of Trent and reformed the breviary and missal; he himself led an ascetic life. His fight against the Reformation led him to excommunicate Elizabeth I of England.

Gregory XIII (Ugo Buoncompagni, [1502] 1572–85) Son of a Bologna merchant, he became a lawyer and judge. Though not as uncompromising as *Pius V, as pope he worked hard to implement the decrees of the Council of Trent, founded seminaries and colleges and encouraged missionary work. He instituted the Gregorian calendar, now in common use, which replaced the Julian calendar (devised by Julius Caesar). However, his widespread claim to papal ownership of land led to much eviction and consequent banditry, leading to a breakdown of law and order.

Sixtus V (Felice Peretti, [1520] 1585–90) Son of a farm worker, he became a famous preacher, inquisitor, and general of the Jesuit order. He was known as the 'iron pope'. He was a vigorous reformer in the church: much of his reorganization of its central administration, including a maximum of seventy cardinals and fifteen permanent congregations, lasted until Vatican II. He also introduced the rule that bishops should visit Rome regularly to report on their diocese. He imposed law and order ruthlessly on the papal states; he did much to make Rome a beautiful city, and built an aqueduct to provide a new supply of drinking water.

Urban VII (Giambattista Castagna, [1521] 1590) An able archbishop and papal administrator, from a noble family, he died of malaria the night after his election.

Gregory XIV (Niccolo Sfondrati, [1535] 1590–1) Born near Milan, a lawyer and friend of *Charles Borromeo who became a conscientious bishop of Cremona, he was inexperienced in papal politics. He was also a sick man. He did his best to further reform, but was hampered by his inexperience and the disastrous appointment of his self-seeking nephew as cardinal secretary of state.

Innocent IX (Giovanni Antonio Fachinetti, [1519] 1591) A lawyer by training, after a period as bishop he became a leading member of both the curia and the inquisition. Old and ill when he was appointed, he died after three months in office.

Clement VIII (Ippolito Aldobrandini, [1536] 1592–1605) Son of a controversial Florentine barrister, he too became a lawyer and distinguished himself in the papal service. As pope, he showed personal sanctity (he was a friend of *Philip Neri) and was an indefatigable reformer. His reforms included a revision of all the major service books, and he made the Inquisition more strict. However, ill health disrupted his life, and his indecisiveness meant that he was often ineffective.

Leo XI (Alessandro Ottaviano de' Medici, [1535] 1605) From the noble family, and a nephew of Leo X, he was the favourite disciple of *Philip Neri and rose to be archbishop of Florence. A deeply religious and conscientious man, he was old when appointed and died within a month.

Paul V (Camillo Borghese, [1552] 1605–21) Son of a famous Siena professor of law, he rose rapidly through the curia, becoming vicar of Rome and inquisitor. His now old-fashioned views on papal supremacy caused him political problems, and he clashed with James I of England in the aftermath of the Gunpowder Plot. He was actively concerned for mission and showed his concern for spirituality with many canonizations and beatifications. He was much devoted to Rome; he supervised the completion of St Peter's.

Gregory XV (Alessandro Ludovisi, [1554] 1621–3) Born in Bologna the son of a count, he was trained as a Jesuit and studied law. He became an important legal figure and diplomat, rising to be archbishop of Bologna. A popular figure, he was appointed by acclaim and because of his age relied much on his nephew Ludovico, whom he made a cardinal. Between them, they brought new life to reform: two lasting achievements were the establishment of what is virtually still the procedure for electing the pope, and the establishment of the Sacred Congregation for the Propagation of the Faith as the central authority for mission.

Urban VIII (Maffeo Barberini, [1568] 1623–44) From one of the oldest merchant families in Florence and a classical scholar, he was essentially a political pope and also a nepotist. He chose Castel Gandolfo as a papal summer residence and did much to beautify Rome. During his reign *Galileo, though a former friend, was condemned a second time and there were the first moves against *Jansenism.

Innocent X (Giambattista Pamfili, [1574] 1644–55) Born in Rome, he had a long legal career and was appointed pope as an old man. He broke with the influence of his predecessor's family, but fell under the thumb of a powerful sister-in-law who influenced his decisions. His protests against concessions to Protestantism at the end of the Thirty Years War went unheeded; he was personally involved in the unconditional condemnation of *Jansenism.

Alexander VII (Fabio Chigi, [1599] 1655–67) Born in Siena, he was a career diplomat who had distinguished himself as a nuncio in the negotiations leading to the peace of Westphalia at the end of the Thirty Years War. However, as pope he did not enjoy administration, and was happier with devotional practices and artistic pursuits. He became involved in a long political struggle with France and continued the attack on *Jansenism.

Clement IX (Giulio Rospigliosi, [1600] 1667–9) From a wealthy family of farming nobility, he had a Jesuit education in Rome and studied law at Pisa. He rose to be governor of Rome and secretary of State. As pope, he achieved better relations with the French and proved an able conciliator. However, his short term of office limited his achievements.

Clement X (Emilio Altieri, [1590] 1670–6) A not particularly distinguished and very elderly former judge and bishop, he was a compromise candidate. His papacy was not a happy one, marred by the activities of a cardinal Paluzzi whom he had appointed his assistant, and by great pressure from France.

Innocent XI (Benedetto Odescalchi, [1611] 1676–89) From a rich commercial family in Como, after a Jesuit education he worked in the family bank before reading law and entering papal service. For a while he was bishop but had to retire through ill-health. Much admired for his personal life-style and conscientious work, he attempted reform against current abuses, but with little success. Not unfavourable to *Jansenism, he was unhappy with current Jesuit moral teaching but could not escape their pressure to condemn *Molinos. His defence of the church's rights brought him into conflict with the French, despite the efforts of Louis XIV to secure his co-operation by treating the Huguenots harshly. He sought to ward off an increasing Turkish threat to Europe by forming a Holy League. He was regarded as the best of the seventeenth-century popes.

Alexander VIII (Piero Ottoboni, [1610] 1689–91) Born in Venice, he had a brilliant legal career in the papal service, becoming Grand Inquisitor under *Innocent XI. He managed to achieve a partial political reconciliation with France, but his concern for orthodoxy led him to condemn *Jansenism once again. In general, however, he had none of the rigour of his predecessor, and was a nepotist and *bon viveur*.

Innocent XII (Antonio Pignatelli [1615] 1691–1700) Born to a noble Neapolitan family, he had a Jesuit education and became a papal diplomat, rising to be archbishop of Naples. A devout man, he fought against nepotism and promoted reform. He achieved a reconciliation with France, but this led to strong pressure from Louis XIV for him to condemn *Fénelon and Madame *Guyon.

Clement XI (Giovanni Francesco Albani, [1649] 1700–21) Born to a noble family in Umbria, he had a career in the service of the curia, but was elected pope as someone who would be concerned with the church rather than politics. His problem was that his reign was dominated by political issues, over which he was ineffective. Yet again he condemned the persistent *Jansenist threat; though concerned with mission, he enforced conservative rules. He made the Feast of the Immaculate Conception of Mary obligatory in the church.

Innocent XIII (Fabrizio Paolucci, Michelangelo dei Conti, [1655] 1721–4) Son of a duke, with a career in the papal service, as pope he set out to counteract his predecessor's ineptitudes, with limited success. He was particularly hostile to the Jesuits.

Benedict XIII (Pietro Francesco Orsini, [1649] 1724–30) Another son of a duke, he became a Dominican. Despite high office awarded as a result of his connections, he lived the life of a simple monk. Unfortunately he was a weak figure, and was swayed by unscrupulous cardinals.

Clement XII (Lorenzo Corsini, [1652] 1730–40) From a wealthy Florentine family, he had a career in the service of the curia and was appointed as an old sick man, blind for his last eight years as pope. He made attempts to revive the papacy's declining financial fortunes, but his state inevitably lowered its reputation.

Benedict XIV (Prospero Lorenzo Lambertini,

[1675] 1740–58) Born to a noble family fallen on hard times, he had great talent and rose rapidly in the curia. As bishop he was a great success, and though he was appointed as a compromise candidate, he proved the right man in the right place. Enlightened and interested in science and learning, he was a model administrator and concerned to strengthen the moral influence of the papacy in politics. He wrote a classic treatise on beatification and canonization and an important work on diocesan synods.

Clement XIII (Carlo della Torre Rezzibuci, [1693] 1758–69) A Venetian lawyer with a Jesuit education, and descended from a rich family, he proved a model bishop of Padua. After being made pope he had to face attempts to abolish the Jesuits in Portugal, Spain and France, a development thought to have hastened his death. He was also confronted with the Febronianism prompted by von *Hontheim in Germany, which he could not counter because of the lack of support from local bishops. He was markedly hostile to the Enlightenment, and for reasons of modesty ordered the covering of nudities in Roman works of art.

Clement XIV (Giovanni Vincenzo Antonio Ganganelli, [1705] 1769–74) Son of a surgeon, he became a Franciscan and was appointed pope after a stormy conclave, since there was political pressure for someone whom would suppress the Jesuits. After diplomatic attempts to stem the political forces pressing for abolition, in the end he did have to suppress the Jesuits, though this did not gain him better international relations. His reign brought the papacy to the lowest level for ages.

Pius VI (Giovanni Angelico Breaschi, [1717] 1775–99) Of a noble family and trained by the Jesuits, he was never up to the demands of being pope. The Febronianism of von *Hontheim was an increasing threat, and during his reign the French Revolution broke out. In the last year of his life, French troops occupied Rome and took him prisoner; he died in captivity.

Pius VII (Luigi Barnaba Chiaramonti, [1740] 1800–23) From a noble family, he became a Benedictine and was a professor of theology and a bishop. A brave man, open to modern ideas, as pope he had to deal with church/state relations in France under Napoleon. Although initially successful, when war in Europe broke out again his position deteriorated, and when the French invaded Rome in 1808 he became a virtual prisoner and was deported to France, not returning to Rome until 1814, after Napoleon's fall. However, his personal qualities brought him through his trials with an enhanced reputation and his religious contribution enhanced the reputation of the papacy. He re-established the Jesuit order, and though attempting to modernize his role was an opponent of Protestantism and the Enlightenment.

Leo XII (Annibale Sermatei della Genga, [1760] 1823–9) Of a noble family, after ordination he became private secretary to *Pius VI, and was a papal diplomat under him and his successor. Supported by the conservatives, when he became pope he returned to earlier patterns. Reforms and laicization in church administration were stopped or even reversed, and support was offered to the more conservative political regimes in Europe. He worked for the emancipation of Roman Catholicism in Britain. However, this narrow clerical approach was too dated for the time, and Leo was highly unpopular.

Pius VIII (Francesco Saverio Castiglione, [1761] 1829–30) From a noble family, a canon lawyer by training and a bishop, he sought to return to the approach of *Pius VII. Though he was a traditionalist, his approach was not as rigorist as that of his predecessor. Ill-health meant that his reign was brief.

Gregory XVI (Bartolomeo Cappellari, [1765] 1831 –46) Son of an aristocratic lawyer, he became a Benedictine, rising to be procurator general of the order; he was also a professor of science and philosophy. In his mid-thirties he wrote a book promoting papal infallibility and the freedom of the papacy from all state control. He was also opposed to freedom of conscience and separation of church and state, and condemned *Lamennais. He also did much to promote mission and denounce slavery. Ascetical and opposed to developing modernism, he was faced with growing Italian nationalism, which led to rebellion in the papal states. This also led to financial crisis for the papacy.

Pius IX (Giovanni Maria Mastai-Ferretti, [1792] 1846–78) Son of a count, after ordination he took part in a papal mission to Chile in the 1820s and subsequently became archbishop of Spoleto and bishop of Imola. Elected pope as a champion of liberal ideas in reaction to his predecessor, he was caught up in events. On the one hand he found himself protesting against a steady loss of political power, ending with the seizure of Rome by Victor Emmanuel in 1870. On the other, he stressed the supreme authority of the pope in the church, promulgating on his own authority the doctrine of the immaculate conception of the Virgin Mary; in his *Syllabus Errorum* and an encyclical *Quanta Cura* (1864) he condemned virtually all modern intellectual movements. He convened the First Vatican Council (1869–70) which decreed papal infallibility, against a tradition of centuries; it was cut short by the Franco-Prussian War. His pontificate saw the establishment of new dioceses and the restoration of the hierarchy in England and Holland along with concordats with national governments; it also saw a breakaway Old Catholic Church and the persecution of Catholic in Germany (the Kulturkampf).

Leo XIII (Gioacchino Vincenzo Pecci, [1810] 1878 –1903) Born near Rome to an aristocratic family, he had a Jesuit training and studied in Rome. Missions to various European cities made him acquainted with modern social issues, and as pope he set out to reconcile the church with modern civilization, reversing the policy of his predecessor. He restored good relations with Germany, Belgium and Britain and developed links with America (though he censured Americanism), but failed with Italy and France. He stressed the compatibility of Catholic teaching with democracy, issued a famous encyclical on social questions and gave limited encouragement to historical and critical study. He was also concerned with church union, though the encyclical *Apostolicae Curae* rejected the validity of Anglican orders. Towards the end of his reign, his attitude significantly hardened, with an introduction of new means of censorship.

Pius X (Giuseppe Melchior Sarto, [1835] 1903–14) Born the son of a village postman, he became a country curate and parish priest. When consecrated bishop of Mantua he brought new life to the diocese and was equally effective as patriarch of Venice. He sought to be a religious rather than a political pope. However, he had to deal with the separation of church and state in France and Portugal; here he was a consistent supporter of the right wing against the left. He laid the foundations for what became Catholic Action, aimed at restoring Christ to society, by encouraging lay participation, but condemned Modernism, imposing an oath against it on the clergy. He embarked on a new codification of canon law and restored Gregorian chant to the liturgy. By commending daily communion he gave stimulus to the liturgical movement. Conservatively stubborn in his theology and paternalistic in his approach, he was nevertheless quite clearly a good and holy man, and he was venerated as a saint in his lifetime.

Benedict XV (Giacomo della Chiesa, [1854] 1914 –22) Born in Genoa to an aristocratic family, he became a papal diplomat, rising to be undersecretary of state before being made archbishop of Bologna. His election was not least influenced by the felt need for a diplomat in time of war, and during the First World War he played this role, seeking to keep the Holy See neutral, attempting to bring about peace, and protesting against inhuman methods of warfare. After the war he developed new international relations and sought conciliation between traditionalists and modernists in the church. He also worked for reunion between the Eastern and Western churches and for mission. Influenza cut short his activity.

Pius XI (Ambrogio Damiano Achille Ratti, [1857] 1922–39) Born near Milan the son of an industrial manager, he had a brilliant academic career as a linguist and palaeographer. After working at the Ambrosian Library in Milan he was put in charge of the Vatican Library. At the end of the First World War he went on a papal mission to Poland, and then became archbishop of Milan. Seeking to involve the church in society, he inaugurated Catholic Action and instituted a feast of Christ the King. His encyclicals were concerned with education and married life, while condemning contraception; the most famous, *Quadragesimo Anno*, was on social problems. He also worked actively to promote mission. He concluded the Lateran Treaty, which established Vatican City as a sovereign state, and wrote an encyclical against the rise of Nazism in Germany.

Pius XII (Eugenio Maria Giuseppe Giovanni Pacelli, [1876] 1939–58) Born in Rome to a family of lawyers, he entered the papal service and was much involved in the reformulation of canon law. A diplomat after the First World War, he was instrumental in concluding concordats with individual German states and then with Germany itself, which among other things gravely weakened Catholic opposition to Hitler. Whether he did enough to protest against the evils of Nazi Germany has been much debated. After the war he published an encyclical in 1950 against modernist tendencies in Roman Catholic theology (*Humani generis*), and defined the doctrine of the Assumption of the Virgin Mary.

John XXIII (Angelo Giuseppe Roncalli, [1881] 1958–63) Born to a poor farming family near Bergamo, after ordination he was secretary to the bishop of Bergamo. He served in the First World War and then became national director of the Congregation for the Propagation of Faith. Contact with the future *Pius XI through research at the Ambrosian library then led to a diplomatic career, first in Bulgaria, then in Turkey and Greece. During the Second World War he did important relief work under the German occupation, preventing deportations of Jews, and after it dealt effectively with the problem of former collaborationist bishops in France; there he encountered the worker-priest movement. In 1953 he became patriarch of Venice. Because of his age on election he was expected to be a 'caretaker' pope, but in fact he inaugurated a remarkable era of reform. He created the largest and most international body ever of cardinals and summoned the Second Vatican Council with the aim of bringing the teaching, discipline and organization of the church up to date. He died during its first session. He also set in motion the revision of canon law. His 1963 encyclical on peaceful co-existence, *Pacem in terris*, was a landmark.

Above all a pastor with a deep humanity, warmth and spirituality, he caught the imagination of the world.

Paul VI (Giovanni Battista Montini, [1897] 1963–78) Son of a wealthy landowner and newspaper editor, he worked for a long period in the papal secretariat and was much involved in papal relief work. He was given a prominent part in preparing Vatican II by *John XXIII, and on being made pope he continued the council, furthering his predecessor's concern for canon law revision and Christian union. Throughout his pontificate he travelled widely, and did much to achieve his aims, supervising the implementation of the decisions of Vatican II diplomatically against considerable opposition. However, his encyclical *Humanae vitae* (1968), condemning artificial birth control, indicated the deep conservatism within him; it proved a bitter blow to many in the Roman Catholic church and the other churches. The problems in church and world during his last years deeply oppressed him.

John-Paul I (Albino Luciani, [1912] 1978) Born to working-class parents, he became a seminary teacher and then a pastoral bishop, rising to be patriarch of Venice. His election as pope came as a surprise, but was hailed as the beginning of a new style of papacy. However, he died within three weeks of taking office, in controversial circumstances.

John-Paul II (Karol Wojtyla, [1920] 1978–   ) Brought up near Cracow largely by his father, a retired army officer, since his mother died young, he was a gifted sportsman and amateur actor. During a difficult life under German occupation in the Second World War he felt called to the priesthood, and after serving as a parish priest became a professor of ethics. In 1963 he became archbishop of Cracow, an office he held with great diplomacy. He also travelled as widely as circumstances would permit in the service of the church. Such journeys have since become the most distinctive mark of his papacy, and have made him internationally known as a symbol. As pope, however, he has been relentlessly conservative in theology, politics and ethics.

Index of Popes of Rome